Pension Policy and Governmentality in China

Manufacturing Public Compliance

Yan Wang

LSE Press

Published by
LSE Press
10 Portugal Street
London WC2A 2HD
press.lse.ac.uk

Text © Yan Wang 2022

First published 2022

This book is based on the author's doctoral thesis:
http://etheses.lse.ac.uk/4111/. The research was approved
by the LSE Research Ethics Committee (ref. 1264)

Cover design by Diana Jarvis
Cover photo: 'Three older women on bench from behind' by hanohikirf / Alamy

Print and digital versions typeset by Siliconchips Services Ltd.

ISBN (Paperback): 978-1-909890-88-6
ISBN (PDF): 978-1-909890-89-3
ISBN (EPUB): 978-1-909890-90-9
ISBN (Mobi): 978-1-909890-91-6

DOI: https://doi.org/10.31389/lsepress.ppc

The full text of this book has been peer-reviewed to ensure high academic standards. For full review policies, see http://press.lse.ac.uk.

Suggested citation:
Wang, Y. 2022. *Pension Policy and Governmentality in China: Manufacturing Public Compliance*. London: LSE Press.
DOI: https://doi.org/10.31389/lsepress.ppc. License: CC BY

To read the free, open access version of this book online, visit https://doi.org/10.31389/lsepress.ppc or scan this QR code with your mobile device:

To my beloved family and friends

About the author

Dr Yan Wang is a Research Fellow in the School of Public Policy at the London School of Economics and Political Science (LSE), and will join the Department of Sociology at Lancaster University as a Lecturer (Assistant Professor) in Digital Sociology in Jan 2023. Her research seeks to understand the issues of state legitimacy and social policy, public opinion, and political communication. She is especially interested in how actors' agency shapes authoritarian governmentality and the realisation of the public's social rights, and how and why public opinion changes during the state-society interactions. Dr Wang has won several research grants, including from the Research Infrastructure and Investment Fund (RIIF) at LSE, and a British Academy Small Grant. Her recent publications include articles in the *Journal of Chinese Political Science* and elsewhere. Dr Wang received a BS in Sociology (2013) and a MA in Management (2015), from the Tsinghua University, and a PhD in Sociology (2020), from the London School of Economics and Political Science.

Contents

Extended contents

List of figures and tables

Figures

Tables

Glossary

anti-corruption campaign: the large-scale anti-corruption campaign initiated after the 18th National Congress of the Communist Party of China in late 2012.

baoxian: insurance.

campaign against the 'four styles': campaign against formalism, bureaucracy, hedonism, and extravagance in bureaucrats. This was promoted along with the anti-corruption campaign.

CCP: Chinese Communist Party.

cishi: the '*CI SHI*' system, or 'feudal prefectural governor' system in China, which was originally established in the Qin and Han dynasty (around 202 BC) and continued to be used (with brief interruptions) until the Republic of China period in the early 1900s.

CNKI: China Knowledge Resource Integrated Database.

common sense: concept used by Gramsci, 'Every social stratum has its own "common sense" and its own "good sense", which are basically the most widespread conception of life and of man.' (Gramsci 1971, p. 326).

compliance: an umbrella concept of used in this book to cover many possible sources of legitimacy built up through individuals' expectations and judgement based on their experience and the information in existing studies. It covers both positive/active consent and the passive or even coerced acceptance against state authority of the population; capturing the 'willingness to defer to political authority regardless of the reasons', or 'with multiple motivations' (Grimes 2008; Levi 1997).

conduct of conduct: from Foucault's theory of state power. 'Perhaps the equivocal nature of the term conduct is one of the best aids for coming to terms with the specificity of power relations. For to "conduct" is at the same time to "lead" others (according to mechanisms of coercion which are, to varying degrees, strict) and a way of behaving within a more or less open field of possibilities. The exercise of power consists in guiding the possibility of conduct and putting in order the possible outcome. Basically power is less a confrontation between two adversaries or the linking of one to the other than a question of government.' (Foucault 1982, p. 789)

consent: concept used by Gramsci, who argued that 'consent' from the dominated population can be generated by the civil society. Specifically, '1. The "spontaneous" consent given by the great masses of the population to the general direction imposed on social life by the dominant fundamental group; this consent is "historically" caused by the prestige (and consequent confidence) which the dominant group enjoys because of its position and function in the world of production. 2. The apparatus of state coercive power which "legally" enforces discipline on those groups who do not "consent" either actively or passively.' (Gramsci 1971, p. 12)

corpus: the collection of text data.

danwei: work units.

daode: ethics.

DDD: the difference-in-difference-in-differences model, or triple difference model.

decommodification: key feature for modern social welfare policies which is among the main indices for social rights measurement. The idea is that social welfare policies provide the possibility that entail citizens to 'freely, and without potential loss of job, income, or general welfare, opt out of work when they themselves consider it necessary' (Esping-Andersen 1990, p. 23).

defined contributory (DC) pension scheme: occupational pension schemes where participant's own contributions and participant's employer's contributions are both invested and the proceeds used to buy a pension and/or other benefits at retirement. The value of the ultimate benefits payable from the DC scheme depends on the amount of contributions paid, the investment return achieved less any fees and charges, and the cost of buying the benefits. A DC scheme has a set contribution for the employee and a set contribution for the employer.

delicacy social management: an idea of social governance promoted in China, which intends to manage the society in a modern, scientific, and rational way.

DID: difference-in-differences model.

DMR: Dirichlet Multinomial Regression Topic Model.

dual system: description of the different schemes and return rates of pensions for government employees and enterprise employees.

DVs: dependent variables.

EE: enterprise employee.

falsification: a convenient word to describe the situation of people constructing their public images/attitudes/preferences, which may not be exactly the same as their private images/attitudes/preferences.

fazhan: development.

fully funding individual accounts: a pension reform conducted in early 2000s in China, to further clarify the division between the pooling of individual and social accounts, and to cover the deficit in individual accounts (State Council 2000).

governmentality: this is a concept from Foucault, an approach that deciphers the state power with a focus on its technologies, governance objects and calculation (Foucault, Davidson, and Burchell 2008). Foucault recognised three dimensions of meaning for governmentality as state rationality. Governmentality refers to the 'ensemble formed by institutions, procedures, analyses and reflections, calculations, and tactics that allow the exercise of state power … having the population as its target, political economy as its major form of knowledge, and the apparatuses of security as its essential technical instrument', 'the tendency, the line of force, that … has led to the development of a series of specific governmental apparatuses and the development of a series of knowledges', and 'the process, or rather, the result of the process by which the state of justice of the Middle Ages became the administrative state in the fifteenth and sixteenth centuries and was gradually governmentalized' (Foucault 2009, p. 109). Essentially it is about how the state – through information management, benefit distribution and coercion, among many other approaches – maintains its rule over the population, and its rationale of doing so.

Great Firewall: China's system of internet censorship.

hukou: a family registration programme in China that serves as a domestic passport, regulating population distribution and rural-to-urban migration.

hybrid pension: a hybrid pension scheme is one which is neither a full defined benefit scheme nor a full defined contribution scheme, but has some of the characteristics of each. In a defined contribution scheme, the member generally bears the full risk (of paying higher costs or receiving reduced benefits) if investment return or pension costs are not as good as expected. In a defined benefit scheme, the employer usually takes that risk and pays higher contributions in order to maintain the agreed level of benefits. In hybrid schemes, the risk can be shared between the employer and employees, and in some cases the government as well.

ILO: International Labour Organization.

involution: the notion of 'involution' is used in the book to capture the increasingly obvious trend in Chinese political attitudes. In a situation where the state is a central source of power, the state can construct the knowledge (political or social) in whatever form is most suited to maintaining its power. Individuals who have limited access to alternative explanations of social facts are less likely to interpret the environment in a different way. In the long term, even when citizens are provided with a new possibility, they are not capable of accepting a different version of the story, or reaching out on their own initiative (as shown in Y. Chen and Yang 2019). Social knowledge is still increasing in society; however, it increases without questioning past or current stories, and therefore is leading to an involution of the population's 'hard knowledge' (Kuran 1997).

iron rice bowl: a description of jobs in state-owned enterprises and public sectors before the 1980s. State-owned work units in urban China before 1978 were subsidised by the state so as to provide not only jobs to individuals, but also to generate from cradle to grave pensions, housing, education, and healthcare to employees and their dependents (Lu and Perry 1997).

jiuye: employment.

lagged time: time differences in pension burden across different enterprises, and in claiming pension benefits across different generations.

laid off: become unemployed. When the economic reform started in the 1980s, numbers of SOEs were re-structured and hundreds and thousands of employees were laid off (Gu 1999, 2001).

laodong: labour.

LDA: Latent Dirichlet Allocation.

legitimacy: the right and acceptance of an authority. The approach to conceptualising 'legitimacy' can be from the standpoint of legalism and normativity, as in issues of legality, or a particular normative definition of justice or procedure (e.g., Lord and Beetham 2001; Smoke 1994). It can also be analysed from the standpoint of belief, following Weberian notions (Weber 1978).

LI: can be interpreted as ethics, manners and rules.

LoR: locus of responsibility.

metadata: data of the text in addition to the content, such as publication date and author.

methodologically holistic and positive: focuses on the structure and involvement of the institution and interprets social facts in their historical context in order to understand the reasons for their emergence or change (Durkheim, Catlin, Mueller, and Solovay 1938).

methodological individualism: social phenomena must be explained by showing how they result from individual actions, which in turn must be explained through reference to the intentional states that motivate the individual actors (Weber 2017).

meticulous governance: similar term to **delicacy social management.**

multi-layered pension system: pension schemes proposed by the World Bank.

NDC: Notional Defined Contribution.

nine-nine-six (996): work schedule of from 9 am to 9 pm, six days a week.

OECD: Organisation for Economic Co-operation and Development.

old-age insurance: similar term to pension, but a more general term referring to pension insurance.

one study, one action: phrase meaning 'study Xi's thoughts, be a qualified youth league member'.

one-child policy: China's birth control policy which was introduced in 1979 and modified in the mid-1980s to relax regulations in rural areas (Scharping 2013).

opening up and reform: China's economic reform, launched in 1978.

others: otherness, 'others' may be other individuals, social groups, or certain institutions. This is crucial for identifying the formation of groups and group boundaries.

paradigm: a typical example or pattern of something; a pattern or model.

PAYG: pay-as-you-go pension system, referring to state pension systems that are funded by contributions from current workers (rather than by individual past contributions from current beneficiaries).

PAYG-DB: pay as you go-defined benefit.

PEE: pension plan for enterprise employees.

pension/social insurance: a pension that requires individual contributions.

People's Daily: the official newspaper (mouthpiece) of the Central Committee of the Communist Party of China and the biggest newspaper group in China.

PGE: pension plan for government employees.

PI: public institution.

pilot: referring to the regions that joined the experiment as a treated group in policy experimentations.

pluralistic ignorance: one possible mechanism of falsification in public opinion, such as when individuals may overestimate or underestimate the conditions of public opinion.

policy experiments: one type of policy instrument, where in many cases the central government led the promotion of a new policy for a certain population in some selected regions. Sometimes, local authorities would initiate policy experiments.

political status: referring to *hukou*, occupation, party membership and so on in China.

PoS: parts of speech.

PPIE: pension plan for public institution employees.

PRC: People's Republic of China

preference falsification: interchangeable in the book with 'falsified compliance', taken as the hidden discontent with and disdain for the authorities in people's voiced consent.

PRR: pension plan for rural residents.

PUR: pension plan for urban non-salaried residents.

QTA: the quantitative text analysis.

red-base: places such as Yan'an, Jing Gangshan, etc., where the CCP originated, or where some historical event has taken place.

renmin gongshe: people's communes, the highest administrative levels in rural areas of China.

retirement allowance: full state-funded pension.

retrenchment: a 'risk privatisation' process in welfare states, and the emergence of a hybrid welfare system in which individuals are given flexibility but increased responsibility for handling the various social risks related to their personal lives, such as 'unemployment, death of a spouse, retirement, disability, childbirth, [and] poverty' (Hacker 2002, p. 245).

RMB: official currency in PRC.

rongren: tolerance.

shengchan: production.

shouru: income.

social coordination: one approach to solving funding issues of pension contributions proposed by the Chinese government. For instance, the enterprises that performed better and had fewer retirements were encouraged (later on, required) to pay into a social pool, which would be used to relieve the enterprises that had got into difficulties.

Social Darwinism: the theory that human groups and races are subject to the same laws of natural selection as Charles Darwin perceived in plants and animals in nature.

social protection: a general type of social welfare, which consists of policies and programmes designed to reduce poverty and vulnerability by promoting efficient labour markets, diminishing people's exposure to risks, and enhancing their capacity to manage economic and social risks, such as unemployment, exclusion, sickness, disability, and old age.

social rights: proposed by Marshall, this is the idea that it is people's social right to receive the benefits brought by social protection, assistance, and insurance (Marshall 1964). It refers to rights to welfare and resources, such as the rights to health, education and a dignified level of social and economic wellbeing, regardless of economic standing (Plant and Jones 1991).

socialisation of social welfare: a process during the welfare reform in China, in which the state, the market, the sectors of society, and families share welfare responsibility and the work units no longer take on the welfare function; joint responsibility in the practical method of funding, service provision and social welfare regulation.

socialised self: self-regulated and self-motivated, a 'socialised individual' who can take care of him/herself while contributing to society and the general good.

SOE: state-owned enterprises.

State Council: the state council of PRC, this is the executive branch of the central government, executive body of the National People's Congress, and the highest organ of state administration.

statecraft: various tactics used by the state to generate public compliance.

STM: structural topic model.

stratification: a key measurement proposed in Esping-Anderson's model for classifying the type of welfare states, which takes in the social structure and the concern of redistribution (Esping-Andersen 1990). It describes the way in which social policy mediates and shapes societal inequalities.

Study (XI) Stronger Country: a Chinese app primarily designed to teach Xi Jinping Thought. It is strongly promoted by government institutions and party members are encouraged to download the app.

subjectivity: this philosophical term relates to ideas of consciousness, agency, personhood, philosophy of mind, reality, and truth.

supervised method: supervised machine learning, which infers a function from labelled training data consisting of a set of training examples.

three security lines: social security system with Chinese characteristics promoted by the government, including a basic guaranteed living system for those no longer working in an SOE, intended to safeguard basic living standards, pay social insurance contributions and encourage re-employment; second, an unemployment insurance system, which provides unemployment benefits and actively encourages re-employment; and third, guaranteed minimum living standards for all urban residents whose family income per capita is lower than the prescribed level (K. W. Chan and Buckingham 2008).

three-pillar system: pension model proposed by the World Bank in the 1990s.

trial and error: a commonly used description of policy experimentation, also, 'crossing the river by feeling the stones'.

two studies, one action: phrase meaning 'study the party regulations, study the leader's speech, be a qualified party member'.

typology: types, modes, classifications.

unit-based self: relying on the work unit and ultimately the state.

unsupervised method: unsupervised machine learning, automatically find interesting activity patterns in unlabelled data.

US-China trade war: trade war between US and China, which began in 2018 and intensified in 2019.

Wechat: a Whatsapp-like app used in China.

Weibo: a Twitter-like online social media platform.

WTO: World Trade Organization.

xiagang: laid off.

xiao: filial piety, caring for the elderly, not only caring for one's own parents but also showing love, respect and support for all older people.

xiaofei: consumption.

Yuan: unit of RMB.

zengzhang: increase.

zhigong: enterprise employee.

Zhongnanhai: current residence of the top leaders of the Party and central government (such as Central Politburo Standing Committee members).

zhongyong: middle course.

Introduction

Since the beginning of the 19th century Chinese society has been subject to a number of momentous transformations. It has experienced imperial aggrandisement, state collapse, imperial occupation, political revolutions, transformations in its class structure, and integration into global markets. Important as each of these has been in Chinese history and in determining the shape of contemporary society, their salience has been matched by the current effort of the authorities to engineer an unprecedented social and economic transformation since 1978. China's economic reform and opening up without loss of control raise fundamentally important issues for social scientists. The specific social and economic challenges during the transitional process – changes in economic endowment, ideological foundation, and social (re)distribution – provide a key opportunity for social scientists to re-examine theories of social change and regime domination. For instance, in Huntington's discussion of modernisation and political order, he argued that a mismatch between social modernisation and institutional modernisation tends to produce social frustration and political instability (Huntington 2006). China's 'reform and opening up' process strongly stimulated economic growth and social modernisation, and gave rise to an increasing demand for public participation. This transformation in the market, recalling Polanyi's description of 'great transformation' (Polanyi and MacIver 1944), incurred an accelerated commodification of human capital, natural resources and other non-market values, such as social practices, family functions, and so on.

However, the corresponding political institutions did not provide adequate channels for public participation. As shown in Figure I.1, the rapid development of the Chinese economy[1] is in sharp contrast to the generally static nature of its political institutions.[2] In addition to the gross increase in size of the economy, the economic structure has also changed; more diverse ownership of economic entities has emerged and contributes to the economic growth.

How to cite this book chapter:
Wang, Yan. 2022. *Pension Policy and Governmentality in China: Manufacturing Public Compliance.* London: LSE Press, pp. 1–8.
DOI: https://doi.org/10.31389/lsepress.ppc.a. License: CC BY

Figure I.1: Levels of economic development and the type of polity in China, 1950–2020

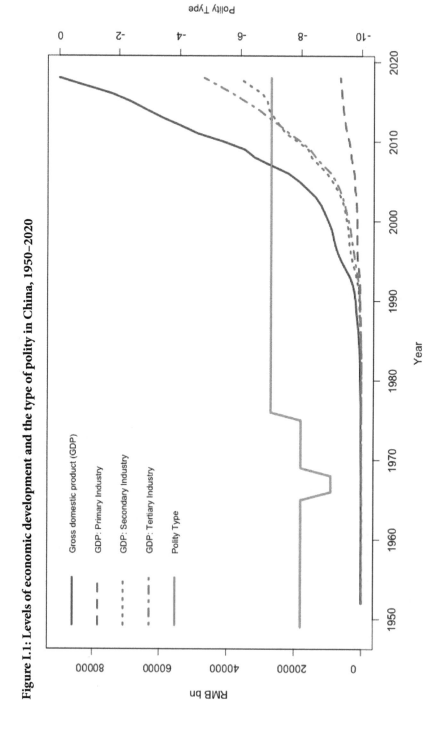

For instance, until 2015, civilian-run enterprises contributed more than 60% of GDP, provided around 80% of urban jobs, and attracted 70% (or more) of the rural migrant labour force (Bank 2017). Moreover, as indicated in Figure I.2 (and in more detail in Appendix Figure A.1), the modernisation of China's economy and society took place together and very rapidly, in a time-scale that had previously taken Western countries centuries to achieve. Its socio-economic modernisation can be judged not only from its rapid urbanisation process, involving large numbers of international and domestic migrant workers, but also its rising level of education and spread of literacy, which may have led to changes in public consciousness.

Thus, applying Huntington's formula to China's transition would predict identity erosion, inequality, and corruption, among other typical issues of socio-economic transformation, tending to disrupt society and lead to political instability. Barrington Moore's comparative study contains similar concerns drawn from the lessons of China's rural revolution. If 'something happens to threaten and destroy the daily routine' of most people, there may be a 'revolution from below' (Moore 1966, p. 204).

However, fundamental disruption has not occurred, even after the turbulence that occurred around 1989. More importantly, far from acting defensively to preserve the social relations and 'red' ideologies that originally gave it power, from the very beginning the Chinese Communist Party (CCP) has in fact led the social and economic transformation that could have been expected to directly challenge its authority. In other words, the central authority actively took the opportunity to secure the benefits of modernisation as brought by the social and economic reform, while also absorbing the risks brought by the trade-off between the opportunities and challenges of dramatic transformation. This study is inspired by the surprising degree of change in the Chinese social and economic transformation, and the fact that this drastic transformation has continued now for 40 years without rousing the radical challenges that might have subverted the authorities' rule. China's case brings up intriguing questions: how does the state maintain compliance from the governed in periods of rapid social and economic transformation? And how has the logic of its governmentality changed along with its priorities?

Building on the Weberian and Gramscian traditions of state theory that emphasise the importance of public consent, this book enriches the theoretical discussion by highlighting the role of the population in state governmentality, focusing on how the issue of 'dealing with the people' was handled so as to maintain authoritarian state rule. Empirically, I examine the case of the multi-wave reforms of pensions in China during its post-1978 period, deciphering a two-way story of statecraft in authoritarian regimes and the room that may be made for cognitional counter-conducts from the public.

My account differs from many books on the topic of social welfare in China, which either focus on the descriptive details of changes in policies,

Figure I.2: Education and urbanisation development in China, 1950–2020

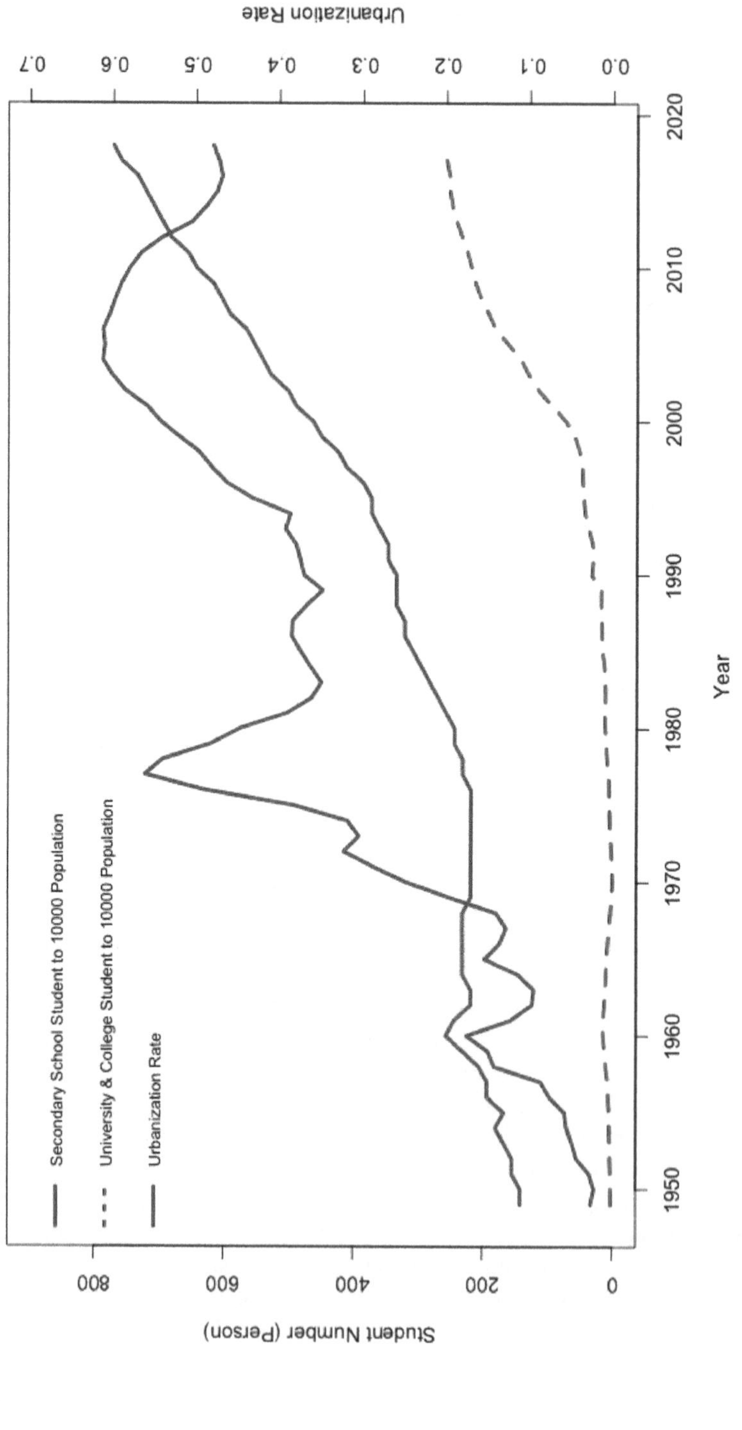

prioritising the institutional setting of the politics, or take a more simplistic approach by treating welfare policy as purely a 'tool of surveillance and repression' (e.g. Huang 2020; Meng 2018; Pan 2020). This book looks at the government's major social policy reforms in a more nuanced and dynamic way, and pays attention to the potential interaction between the state's policy designs and public reactions. Some other works on authoritarian resilience use China as the empirical case (e.g. Bernstein 2013; Gries 2004; Mattingly 2019; Nathan 2003; Yan 2017). I tend to treat China's statecraft as a comprehensive, sophisticated design rather than as a set of static and isolated skills. More importantly, by focusing on the interaction between state and individual as a typical power relation where the state needs to maintain its authority and expects compliance from the governed, my work highlights a two-way story between the state and individuals. I consider the ways that the state works to manufacture the public's compliance and the constraints these imply for the effectiveness of the state's governance and reproduction of legitimacy. I also explore the ways that individuals can find room for counter-movement and how the existence of possible counter-conduct in turn shapes the state's choices and the rationale of governmentality.

Chapter 1 begins the discussion with two questions. Theoretically, why does governmentality matter for tracing the question of legitimation and ruling of the modern state? And, practically, what conditions in China's case bring challenges to state governance and existing explanatory schemas? I also present a brief analytical paradigm of my project, which seeks to holistically integrate both consent-oriented statecraft and coercion-based statecraft. It highlights the strategic selection of strategies based on the state's particular character, objectives, and constraints.

The substantial logic of whom to govern and how to govern can be revealed by the design of governmental programmes, the specific ways in which social problems are defined and divisions or distinctions within the population are established. In Chapter 2 I identify the state governmentality revealed by the trajectory of the pension reforms in China, with its stress on differentiated benefit allocation. Segmented resource allocation within China's pension reform trend has favoured the core elites, while also distributing limited fiscal capacity to the pensions of social groups that cost least per person. The general strategy of differentiation was systematically based on the existing division on the lines of political status, while also taking advantage of changes in the bargaining power of different social groups during the social and economic reforms period.

Given that the pension reforms outlined in Chapter 2 show that a new differentiation system is being entrenched, how did the Chinese state frame and justify its pension policies and, through them, underpin and develop the wider legitimacy of the state itself? In other words, what kind of knowledge about pension benefits was produced and promoted by the state when it tried to persuade the public to accept the reform? Chapter 3 uses quantitative text analysis to show the persuasive strategies used in official discourse to try to shape public opinion and expectations. The state sought to reconstruct public knowledge and expectations of the redistribution of pension benefits, and the allocation of welfare responsibility between the state and individuals, by focusing chiefly on the reiteration of the principles of 'contribution and rewards' and 'rights and obligations'. Individuals' personal lives are now socialised and initiated within a broader pensions system with multiple components, rather than the previous reliance on unit-based and localised systems. The state sought to reconstruct subjectivity among persons who are directly or indirectly involved in the production process, who were encouraged to see themselves as self-motivated, self-regulated, and self-sufficient in building up pension provision.

If the state has the multiple capacities for manipulating policy design and promoting social policy reform as appears above, are these strategies effective in changing the public's attitudes? In Chapter 4 I use causal inference and investigate the effect of the government's strategies of combining experimentation and propaganda in a specific pension reform in China. The results demonstrate that in the short term the Chinese government's experimentation efforts can generate a significant change in people's attitudes and build a certain consensus that favours pension reform, while official newspapers' words of praise about the government's generosity and achievements increase people's political support. However, the disjunction of the policy content and propaganda content can actually backfire on levels of institutional trust in the long term. People are capable of identifying the potential inconsistency in how policy details work out and the propaganda. If the state (in a broad sense) is seen to 'go back on its word', this might lead to a loss of public confidence.

So, despite the Chinese state's well-designed statecraft in shaping public opinion and expectations, there are risks for the authorities of falsified public compliance from the people. Going beyond the pension reforms and moving back to the broader issue of legitimation and governmentality, Chapter 5 investigates the complexity of individuals' political attitudes in China. It uses a combination of participant observation and in-depth interviews to demonstrate the way that individuals disentangle their public behaviours from their private attitudes. The evidence shows that falsified compliance does exist among the Chinese population regarding the current authorities and certain public issues, but it is a mixture of intentional falsification and cognitive dissonance, rather than a simply coerced falsification. Moreover, individuals' political opinions present a smooth transformation between the public face and the private face. The interactions between people's personal experience and the existing cultural, historical, and educational factors that have socialised their ideas deeply shape the presentation of manufactured compliance.

My overall theoretical paradigm is constructed by integrating two important theoretical approaches in investigating state politics for dealing with the population – governmentality and public compliance. Using pension reforms in China as the empirical case, I demonstrate the interactive relationship of

governmentality being the means and population compliance being the outcome. The final chapter of the book revisits the key research questions that
built upon the two concepts, cross-referencing the evidence drawn from each
empirical chapter, and then integrating them moving beyond that to some comparative considerations. China's case is (almost) unique in many dimensions
(not least the state's population size), but it is also comparable to social welfare
reforms in many other countries. Despite having different political institutions
and state capacities, other governments in rapidly developing (if 'flawed') liberal democracies use some comparable reform rationale and tactics to try to
manage their population and manufacture compliance (within resource and
information constraints). I conclude with a brief discussion of pension provision and welfare reforms in some East Europe and Latin America countries,
and suggest how China's case helps in understanding their state–society rela-
tionships.

Notes

This book is based on the author's doctoral thesis: http://etheses.lse.ac.uk/4111/

1 Economic data source: CEIC data (https://www.ceicdata.com/en).
2 Polity data series: the 'Polity score' captures this regime authority spectrum on
   a 21-pont scale ranging from −10 (hereditary monarchy) to +10 (consolidated
   democracy). The Polity scores can also be converted into regime categories
   in a suggested three-part categorisation of 'autocracies' (−10 to −6), 'anocra-
   cies' (−5 to +5 plus three special values: −66, −77 and −88), and 'democracies'
   (+6 to +10) https://perma.cc/DGR9-P62Y.

References

Bank, C. M. (2017). *China Minsheng Bank Report*.
Bernstein, T. P. (2013). 'Resilience and collapse in China and the Soviet Union'.
   *Why Communism Did Not Collapse: Understanding Authoritarian Regime
   Resilience in Asia and Europe*, 40–63.
Gries, P. H. (2004). *China's New Nationalism: Pride, Politics, and Diplomacy*.
   University of California Press.
Huang, X. (2020). *Social Protection under Authoritarianism: Health Politics and
   Policy in China*. Oxford University Press. https://doi.org/10.1093%2Foso
   %2F9780190073640.001.0001
Huntington, S. P. (2006). *Political Order in Changing Societies*. Yale University
   Press.
Mattingly, Daniel C. (2019). *The Art of Political Control in China*. Cambridge
   University Press.

Meng, K. (2018). *China's Pension Reforms: Political Institutions, Skill Formation and Pension Policy in China*. Routledge. https://doi.org/10.4324%2F9781351061667

Moore, B. (1966). *Social Origins of Democracy and Dictatorship*. USA: Beacon.

Nathan, A. (2003). 'China's changing of the guard: Authoritarian resilience'. *Journal of Democracy*, vol. 14, issue 1, 6–17. https://doi.org/10.1353/jod.2003.0019

Pan, J. (2020). *Welfare for Autocrats: How Social Assistance in China Cares for Its Rulers*. USA: Oxford University Press. https://doi.org/10.1093%2Foso%2F9780190087425.001.0001

Polanyi, K.; and MacIver, R. M. (1944). *The Great Transformation*. USA: Beacon.

Yan, X. (2017). *How Is China Maintain Stable? Observation and Thoughts from Fieldwork [Zhongguo Heyi Wending: Laizi Tianye de Guancha yu Sikao]*. Hong Kong: Joint Publishing.

CHAPTER 1

Manufacturing compliance with 'rule by design'

Any power relation reveals the need of the dominant side to maintain its authority. The power relation between the state and the individual, which has been a fundamental topic in political sociology and political science, is a typical dominant–dominated power relationship. For a modern state, its survival requires order, stability, and effective governance – all demanding considerable cooperation from its population. While differing in content, several classical studies share the logic that the legitimation of the government must secure enough cooperation to maintain the system's capacity to withstand shock and failure (Giddens 1981; Lipset and Man 1960; Tilly 2017). From legitimacy, the subordinates in a power relationship can obtain moral grounds for cooperation and obedience, while the power- or authority-holder gets the right to expect their compliance. Under certain conditions the population renders to the authority cooperation and obedience – which provide enough stability for the authority to continue in being, withstanding some shocks and failures. At a point in their interactions with the state the public may change its compliance. People who have suffered during the interactions may choose to resist or withdraw compliance, for instance, because of the state's misbehaviour, or because they are dissatisfied with social policies.

Many political sociologists argue that the essential theme of state 'ruling' is the issue of *consent*. The Weberian tradition regards the legitimation of the government as an essential factor for sustaining people's compliance, since the state's rule fundamentally depends on consent, rather than any fear induced by coercion alone. States cannot do whatever they want and expect their citizens to acquiesce. Constant and crude coercion may cause a revolution from below and eventually state collapse. As Weber (1978) pointed out, consent from the public is necessarily rooted in people's belief. The consent

How to cite this book chapter:
Wang, Yan. 2022. *Pension Policy and Governmentality in China: Manufacturing Public Compliance.* London: LSE Press, pp. 9–26.
   DOI: https://doi.org/10.31389/lsepress.ppc.b. License: CC BY

that signals the people's active acceptance and compliance may take the form of ideological trust or spontaneous supportive actions.

However, beliefs are not arbitrary and can be manufactured by exogenous powers. Gramsci's hegemony theory (Gramsci, Hoare, and Nowell-Smith 1971) suggests that the interaction between the population and the state is never a simple, watertight match. People's seemingly 'spontaneous' attitudinal or behavioural consent results from some invisible and subtle ideological, cultural, or institutional infiltration from the state. In other words, in the state–society relationship the state can reconstruct and use people's knowledge, politics, and even daily lives in a way that favours the authority. The other side of the story is that resonating beliefs must be rooted in the experiences of individuals (Gramsci, Hoare, and Nowell-Smith 1971). Any inquiry into consent must grapple with both the expectations of citizens and the behaviour of states, and the fit of both with one another. Thus, although the state generally holds more institutional resources than individuals do, it is not all-powerful; its legitimacy can be earned or lost. A 'legitimacy crisis' ensues when the regime is finding it difficult to manage the equilibrium between state governance and the people's expectations.

The idea of 'governmentality' answers the questions of whom to govern and how to govern. As a form of state rationality, governmentality can be recognised as a power relation between 'man and things' (Foucault 2009, p. 97); state governance therefore involves governing 'a sort of complex of men [and women] and things' (Foucault 2009, p. 96). The objects of the governance include not only people and their complex relationship with things (such as resources) but also things' relationship with other things, such as customs, dependency, habits, and so on. The instruments that a government uses (such as statistics and biopolitics) to achieve a better well-being of the population (such as the population's wealth, longevity, and health) involve and act directly on the population itself. State governmentality can be identified as institutions, regulations, and procedures. It can also be identified as a tendency of changing forces which reveals the state's sophisticated understanding of the people, and thus the efforts that it makes to figure out proper ways of managing changes and consents, and the process of knowledge development (Foucault 2009, p. 109). Through the dynamic governmentality that has been designed and adjusted by the state, the boundary of the state, the boundary between being 'public' and being 'private', is revealed. A thorough investigation of governmentality will unpack not only the way that governmental activities unfold their effect but also how the individual's subjectification process is shaped by statecraft, and how the risks of resistance from the public affect statecraft in return. Unpacking governmentality, therefore, is important in addressing the legitimation and issue of ruling by the modern state.

In empirical investigations of governmentality, which indicators are appropriate in identifying the nature of the state's power over the people? Many concepts have been used to describe the ruling of authority over the people and could indicate the success of the state's governance. Commonly used terms include the ones mentioned above: 'legitimacy', 'consent', or other concepts such as 'political trust' and 'compliance'. The conceptual details of such notions are also debated by different scholars. For instance, the approach to conceptualising 'legitimacy' can be from the standpoint of legalism and normativity, as in issues of legality, or a particular normative definition of justice or procedure (e.g. Lord and Beetham 2001; Smoke 1994). It can also be analysed from the standpoint of belief, following Weberian notions (Weber 1978). As well as drawing on the Weberian and Gramscian tradition of understanding state rule and highlighting the individual's rationale of 'believing' and 'consent', my work also takes account of the Foucaudian 'governmentality' that the state uses to maintain its rule and investigates its underlying rationality. What then is the best way of integrating these approaches into one analytical model? Compliance, which covers both positive/active consent and the passive or even coerced acceptance of state authority by the population, seems to be a good indicator to measure the state's rule over its people in general. In this sense, the concept of compliance is more appropriate than consent in capturing the 'willingness to defer to political authority regardless of the reasons', or 'with multiple motivations' (Grimes 2008; Levi 1997). In the following section I further discuss the theoretical model constructed on the inclusive measurement of 'compliance'.

The statecraft used in different regimes consists of choices built from an authority's own political, social, and economic scenarios. Compared to their democratic counterparts, authoritarian states have more of a reputation for using oppression and violence in sustaining their authority. But no regime that relies only on oppression and violence can stabilise its governance and maintain its resilience in the long term (Gramsci, Hoare, and Nowell-Smith 1971). In his study, Dimitrov (2013) implied that, in a mature communist regime, the use of repression actually declines, and patronage is distributed to a wider segment of the population, citing the Soviet Union after the death of Stalin. If this is so, an authoritarian regime also needs to employ various strategies and skills to manufacture 'spontaneous' consent from the public. Moreover, such a regime in a prolonged transformational stage, like China over the past 40 years, requires significant public compliance to maintain overall stability.

1.1 Transitional scenarios in China and the state's 'rule by design'

China's transition is one form of the large-scale institutional changes in communist regimes that started in the late 20th century. The process of de-Stalinisation, liberation, and democratisation involved the deformation of central planning and a transition of state socialism. In these post-communist states, the newly emerged market has led to a change in the distributional principles and in the rate of return on financial, productive, and human capital, and has also altered the social structure. Meanwhile, the boundaries between state, market, and society have been redrawn and negotiated through interactions between different sectors. Challenges to the legitimacy of the Chinese government have followed one another since the economic reforms of 1978. Economic development has increased people's income, and also changed the public's expectation of the state–individual relationship. People's loyalty towards state authority has become more complicated. On the one hand, the benefits brought by economic development were able to help the state to buy public support; on the other, economic development brought people a keener consciousness and more demands for other rights, and therefore threatened the public's acceptance of the state's authority. Moreover, the transition process extended from the economy to society: 40 years of development in the economy has led to an expansion of social inequality along with the entrenchment of a social class system. The transitional scenarios brought by marketisation, privatisation, and institutional reform have led to some fundamental changes in distribution, redistribution, and social justice.

In addition to the large-scale economic-social reforms, the transition of socialist regimes features another key point, due to the special ideological foundation and historical legacy of China. As a communist government, the authorities rely heavily on the 'red ideology' in the political culture, which was also one of the main sources of the CCP's legitimacy during the civil war period and the early years after the founding of the People's Republic of China (PRC). With markets penetrating every aspect of social life, communist ideology has also been reformed in the post-Mao era, particularly in recent years to fit the new social and economic scenarios. For instance, the illusion of government omnipotence persists and coexists with mixed attitudes to liberal notions. Many people buy into the official story that individual merit is highly encouraged, while 'waiting, relying on, and demanding' (government help) is criticised (Gallagher 2011). The spirit of selfless devotion and equality from the revolutionary period has been undermined. In other words, the transitional process also shows a de facto shift away from the revolutionary communist legacy that originally gave power to the Party: a state-controlled planned economy, semi-universal welfare provision and a communist ideology.

Social welfare provision is one of the most important areas of change, partly because it can be directly perceived by the public. In this area there has been a noticeable trend, which has led to some degree of public discontent owing to the fear of loss of social benefits and an increased welfare burden on some social groups. Before the economic reforms of 1978, China was experiencing the 'creation of a socialist egalitarian society promising a relatively stable livelihood at the expense of economic development' (Leung and Xu 2015, p. 33). Work units (*danwei*) acted in urban areas as administrative social integration sections, as well as providers of public goods (Lu and Perry 1997). Urban work units provided not only jobs for life but also pensions, housing, education, and health care to employees and their dependants. More than 80% of the urban labour force was covered by the *danwei* system (Leung and Wong 1999). At the stage of state socialism the state's patriarchal role underwrote a collective welfare mechanism that collectively secured social rights (Xie 2016). Corresponding to the economic reform, the state promoted social reforms that helped to shift the state's welfare burden and boost efficiency. The ongoing reform in welfare provision threatens lifetime employment, pensions, health and the housing system in urban areas (Li and Zhong 2009; Wong and Ngok 2006). Very many employees of state-owned enterprises were laid off during the marketisation process. The newly established basic health insurance scheme also required contributions from individuals and employers. Furthermore, the hospitals started to employ market-competition principles in their operation. Individual workers found that their total welfare contribution accounted for quite a large proportion of their salary (Ringen and Ngok 2017). Many of these reform plans were understood to add up to a withdrawal of governmental responsibility and an emphasis instead on the roles of the market and the family. The schemes do not treat equally members of different age groups, occupation groups, and political identity groups; some enjoy more benefits than others.

Facing all the dramatic social and economic changes described above, the state needed to spend some time on generating public compliance to prevent a serious crisis of legitimacy and even regime change caused by bottom-up revolts against the transformation. Theoretically speaking, the skills in the state's governance toolkit include propaganda, repression, absorption, allocated benefits, and so on. In practice, what we can observe of the state's efforts to manufacture compliance is different 'strategies' that involve either one or several skills. For instance, in promoting certain policies, a state could combine economic benefits with propaganda (comparable to the 'social construction of target populations' (Schneider, Ingram, and DeLeon 2014)), while coercion and information censorship could also be used to attain its goal. The toolkit of maintaining compliance for an authority also changes depending on the various challenges in different periods. For example, in Mao's era, when the party class identified struggle as the main problem in China, an ideological campaign was the central approach to producing loyalty and consent. In the 'opening up and reform' period, many scholars have argued that the Chinese authorities has used performance-based legitimacy and maintains its rule by providing material security (Zhao 2001).

Some scholars have highlighted the institutional features and tricks in China's governance. For instance, Andrew Nathan used the term 'authoritarian resilience' to describe the situation whereby the Chinese government reconsolidated itself in the midst of the political instability and potential governance crises. He attributed the authority's resilience mostly to the 'institutionalisation' of the state, such as the normalisation of succession politics within the Communist Party leadership and the meritocratic promotion of bureaucrats (Nathan 2003). Scholars such as Yan (2017) have emphasised that the capacity of the state to absorb and assimilate is one of the main instruments that keeps the state and the party stable. Perry (2017) contended that, by strategically using symbolic resources such as the traditional culture, the state shapes the higher education institutions and wins the allegiance of social elites. Other descriptions in existing studies include 'a balancing act involving the supply of carrots and sticks' (Gallagher and Hanson 2009), a 'guerrilla policy style' (Perry and Heilmann 2011), 'nationalism ideological articulation' (Bernstein 2013; Gries 2004), and so on. One common issue in existing studies is that statecraft is treated as a set of static and isolated skills rather than as a comprehensive, sophisticated design. The role of 'the ruled' – the people or population – is also missing or under-emphasised in shaping the specific governmentality.

In this book I argue that the Chinese state uses a strategy that is hybrid, organic, and dynamic to respond to the potential crisis brought closer by social and economic transformation, and to generate public compliance even though it drifts away from the communist legacy. In particular, I emphasise that public compliance is not only acquired through buying off the public with governmental performance and transferred benefit but is also manufactured through an ideological foundation, such as nationalism, which has been rebuilt by the authority. China's authoritarian governance has been an active process of 'rule by design' that has constantly adapted to new social and economic situations, especially since the notorious repression in the late 1980s. On the one hand, the state monitors and captures public expectations and adjusts its own strategies to meet them; on the other, the state intentionally shapes the public's expectations and manufactures compliance to keep its reforms working. For instance, in the field of social welfare, where the process of privatisation might cause severe discontent, the authority has employed a mixture of retrenchment and generosity and designed diverse schemes for different social groups in order to effectively 'divide and govern'. Moreover, the state has carefully employed propaganda skills using traditional culture and the ideological legacy of the socialist period, in order to legitimise its choices and engender consent from the public. This research enriches the discussion of authoritarian resilience by highlighting the active consent role of the public and the constraints that it imposes on the effectiveness of the state's governance and production of legitimacy.

1.2 Manufacturing compliance in the state–individual interaction

States provide security, resources, solidarity, and identity through benefit allocation, propaganda, education, and many other approaches, in order to shape public expectations and justify their rule; while individuals can update their knowledge about the state from personal benefits, public policy, and current society (their peers) and decide whether to stay loyal or rebel. To better understand the logic of the state's rule and its choices of various forms of statecraft in dealing with its population, I first decipher the state's governmentality, moving from the Foucauldian theories to formal models and empirical analyses. The second subsection below explains the analytical logic of my work with a semi-modelled clarification. I adopt a holistic viewpoint, integrating across both consent-oriented statecraft and coercion-based statecraft, and highlighting the state's strategic selection of statecraft based on its objectives and constraints. Thus, the analytical paradigm of my research uses an interactive model with two actors' strategies and behaviours involved: the state authority and the population.[1]

Coercion or consent: why coercion alone cannot do the work

Gramsci argued that the state is an entire complex of practical and theoretical activities with which the ruling class not only justifies and maintains its dominance but manages to win the active consent of those over whomever it rules (Gramsci, Hoare, and Nowell-Smith 1971). The state is a combination of dictatorship and hegemony in which the state power relies on both *political society* (force) and *civil society* (consent), and these choices match up with using either force and coercion against its population, exercising dictatorship; or using consensus building, cultural hegemony, and maintaining moral and intellectual leadership (Kohli, Shue, and Migdal 1994). A coercion-based approach is very efficient in maintaining short-term stability and long-term fear. However, consent-based governance enables the state to enjoy more compliance and the 'expression of these subaltern classes who want to educate themselves in the art of government' (Gramsci, Hoare, and Nowell-Smith 1971, p. 126). In the spectrum of coerced compliance and voluntary compliance, authoritarian states have the reputation of using oppression and violence to sustain their rule. Therefore, in the context of an authoritarian regime, an inevitable question arises: why would the state need to manufacture consent if it can instead just use coercion or force to stay in power? The questions 'why can't coercion alone do the work' and 'why is manufacturing active compliance from the population important for rulers in authoritarian regimes?' have been studied in many empirical and theoretical works.

Empirically, we do see some authoritarian regimes, or regimes at an authoritarian stage, showing significant use of coercion and force in their rule. For instance, mass terror, repression and indoctrination were frequently used in totalitarian periods by Stalin, Mao, Pol Pot, and military regimes such as Franco's Spain and Pinochet's Chile. Compliance generated by fear was common in these regimes. But any regime that relies only on oppression and violence cannot stabilise its governance and maintain its resilience in the long term. The integrated global economy and the development of the internet have also made mass killing costly and less attractive for autocrats. In recent years, we have observed more non-democratic regimes using sophisticated statecraft to hold on to power. For instance, some imitate the format of democracy and hold elections to obtain normative legitimacy, while their election processes exhibit wholesale bribery, illegal competition, and information manipulation. Wedeen's case of Asad's cult in Syria argued that rhetoric and symbolic display reduces the need to rely on sheer repression as a mechanism of control (Wedeen 1999).

Some studies have also employed formal models to demonstrate the unsustainability of using violence in non-democratic regimes and justify an authority's choice of hybrid statecraft to maintain compliance. By combining the manufacture of consent with coercive tools, the state can maintain a stable hegemonic position vis-à-vis the population. Repression/violence are among the most extreme ways to crush protest/revolution and alter public opinion through physical coercion (Gregory, Schröder, and Sonin 2006). However, repression is not a once-and-for-all solution. In Kricheli, Livne, and Magaloni's (2011) working paper, they presented a formal model of protest under authoritarianism. Their two-period signalling model showed that, although regimes which are more repressive in the first period can better deter civil opposition, they are more likely in the second period to experience a cascade of power since protests' information-revealing potential is maximised in these regimes. In addition, the work of Acemoglu, Ticchi, and Vindigni (2010), Svolik (2012), and Egorov and Sonin (2011) showed that the authority may experience a greater threat from its military allies once the period of acute repression is over.

Thus, in most cases, the authority tends to consider integrating different tactics in preventing revolution and gaining compliance after rational assessment by the governed. Scholars citing theoretical and empirical evidence have identified many specific combinations. Wintrobe (1990; 2007) modelled two instruments – repression and loyalty – that dictators used to stay in power, dividing such regimes into four categories – tinpots, tyrants, totalitarians, and timocrats – according to their different objectives and correspondingly invested instruments. For instance, totalitarians always aim to maximise their power; therefore, they combine high repression with a capacity to generate loyalty, while tinpot dictators prefer to maximise their own benefits under the constraint of minimum power, so their investment is low on both counts. Although theoretically feasible and easily achieved, eliciting compliance through a redistribution of benefits – irrespective of whether the distribution is to the ruling alliance or to the remaining population – needs credible commitment from the authority (e.g. Boix and Svolik 2013; Gehlbach and Keefer 2011; Myerson 2008). In non-democratic regimes such commitment is often fragile without relevant institutional guarantees. When the state can make only fragile commitments, those who benefit from distributions will discount the effectiveness of its effort to allocate benefits to ensure compliance.

In addition to buying compliance through material means, a more sophisticated way of generating voluntary compliance is to wisely use information and manipulate through censorship, guidance by propaganda, or knowledge construction. For instance, a state authority may allow free social media so as to obtain the information about the population that the state needs, even though the information may also be used by society to coordinate its protest (Egorov, Guriev, and Sonin 2009). To avoid a potential backfire from the free media, the authorities may also actively send out biased signals through their own propaganda to mislead the public in evaluating the state's capacity (Edmond 2013). Chen and Xu's work (2017) presented a new view: that allowing people's information communication in society actually helps the authorities to obtain material and prevent coordinated revolt from the public.

To return to the main question of this subsection, how useful are these sophisticated tactics compared to simple violence? Guriev and Treisman's work in 2015 proposed a comprehensive argument about the different ways in which modern dictators could help themselves survive. In a game of political leaders trying to convince citizens (some of whom are informed elites) of their competence, a 'dictator can invest in making convincing state propaganda, censoring independent media, co-opting the elite, or equipping police to repress attempted uprisings' (Guriev and Treisman 2015, p. 4). The authors showed that the portfolios of states' techniques differ with the competence of the leader and result in multiple equilibria while:

> violence either is a last resort when all else has failed, or is used sparingly when it is possible to conceal it, since competent dictators do not need to use repressions, and reverting to repressions immediately reveals the dictator's incompetence to the public and ultimately results in his [or her] downfall. (Guriev and Treisman 2015, p. 33).

To summarise, violence alone cannot do the work of maintaining governance for an authority which wants to rule in the long term. The modern state enjoys considerable choices of statecraft that enable it to stay in power without much challenge from the population.

Generating compliance: a two-actors model and the state's options

The ultimate goal for the state is to remain in power, in other words to ensure that the population is compliant. Putting the population's reaction on a continuous scale, the state would prefer sincere support (active consent) to forced obedience, while the public's collective non-compliance is more dangerous for the state than a single individual's public non-compliance. There are cases where an individual's private non-compliance goes unnoticed or is tolerated by the authority as long as it does not turn into public non-compliance or, worse still, public collective non-compliance. The state as ruler enjoys resources (such as economic or organisational resources) that could be used to achieve its objectives, but it may not master every detail of the population or its views.

Figure 1.1: Thought map of compliance typology and respective statecraft

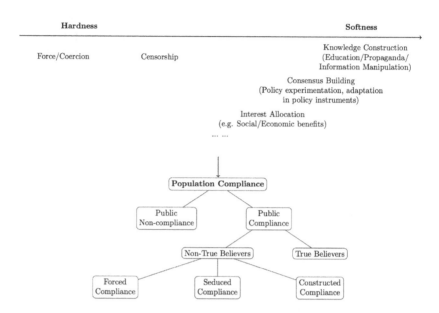

In the model, the objective of the population is to optimise its own living conditions, economically, socially, and politically, though the ranking of importance of these different aspects of living standards differs for different social groups. A population ruled by an authority may express compliance, non-compliance, or collective non-compliance such as coordinated rebellion and revolution. The engine of this interactive model's operation in my work is not simply the objective economic situation, as in Wintrobe's pioneering model, but the general design of the ruler, which is constantly updated according to its understanding of the current situation, the public, and its own objectives, or simply as 'governmentality'.

Although overall named 'compliance', the population's acceptance of the authority's rule differs in degree. In Figure 1.1, I present a thought map of the means and outcome of statecraft of modern state. The upper panel displays the various possible statecrafts the state could use in a continuum of hard–soft approaches. In the bottom panel, I demonstrate that, in the scale of outcome of statecraft, public reaction could vary, from sincere believers who present their full consent, to forced compliance for which the population would choose alternative options rather than the incumbent authority if they are given the chance, and to collective non-compliance, which could be dangerous to the state's rule. The typologies in Figure 1.1 do not exhaust all the possibilities, but they act as a guidance about the interactive relation between the state's actions and the potential outcome from the public.

A population has true believers who are sincere loyal to the incumbent ruler. It has supporters who accept the governance, while not necessarily holding the beliefs that the true believers hold. It should be noted that these two categories of 'supporters' may not be easily identifiable from their daily behaviour, but they may choose altogether differently when presented with alternative options of governance. The population's obedience may also be generated by interest exchange, or coercion, as commonly identified in existing studies. The compliance categories are not mutually exclusive – they may be generated simultaneously in response to either a single item or a package of statecraft. As presented in the following table, the state can either construct social knowledge through propaganda, education, or manipulated information, building consensus through policy experiments, or use interest exchanges to buy the population off. It may also use coercive approaches such as censorship and force to maintain public compliance. Again, these tactics can be used by the state either alone or as a package and (if necessary) they can also be tailored for different social groups.

Constructing social knowledge is among the most sophisticated but commonly used tactics for generating compliance. Education is a traditional approach that can impose specific knowledge when an individual is in a formative stage, being socialised and forming his/her value system. Even individuals who have established a relatively stable value system can have their existing knowledge reshaped by a strong input of information from outside. Modern techniques allow the state more possibilities for promoting its ideology and shaping public opinion. Online platforms have become more and more popular in the propaganda toolkit, in addition to conventional media such as newspapers, TV, radio broadcasts, books, and journals. The mouthpieces of the state can publicise well-constructed information about policy, social facts, and excuses for the state's latest moves. The state may also employ internet trolls or hire real people – such as the '50 Cent Party' in China's case (Han 2015; Simon 2014) – to lead the online public opinion and diffuse pro-government arguments. These seemingly 'soft' tactics can in fact signal the repressive capacity of the state. As H. Huang (2015) showed in his work, the capacity to broadcast propaganda and the capacity to repress rebellion are positively correlated.

Consensus building through policy experimentation differs from other compliance generating processes in its way of highlighting the adaptations of state governance and the dynamic process of governmentality. It is especially useful in cases where the population is divided, the regional features are distinctive, and the policy that the state wants to promote is somehow controversial. In China, policy experiments are among the most commonly used strategies; the central government takes a moderate approach to policy changes and allows enough space for it to practise 'trial and error'. Referred to as 'crossing the river by feeling the stones', policy experiments are of great importance in avoiding radical changes in national policy.

Policy experimentation is frequently used in social welfare reforms due to the geographical variation and social and economic diversity between provinces. The reform of a social welfare scheme can be very costly for the central government if it wants to collect comprehensive information about the population. Moreover, since most of the current social welfare schemes in China are fragmented and specific to certain social groups, it is impossible to push any comprehensive social reforms. Therefore, the central government regularly uses policy experimentation when it implements new policies. For instance, in health care, about 60 cities from 1994 onwards participated in the reform in basic urban social health insurance. In education, a pilot policy of abolishing fees for rural compulsory education was initiated in 2006 and expanded to other non-pilot areas in the two years afterwards.

Benefits allocation is another commonly used strategy in exchange for people's compliance with the state, and may cover material rewards, such as incomes, bonuses, tax reduction and so on. They can also be welfare benefits, such as access to certain subsidised programmes. In some cases, it can be political incentives, for instance permission to join a party (membership) or being promoted within the bureaucratic system. The governed decide on their consent and support after reviewing the social and economic benefits received from the authority. Constructed on the social and economic outcome of governmental behaviours, some scholars refer to the population compliance generated by benefits allocation as a specific source of state legitimacy – performance legitimacy.

Censorship is not as direct as pure violence, nor as sophisticated as the knowledge construction approach, but it still can achieve the goal of generating compliance because of its value in increasing the information asymmetry between the individual and the state (Bennett and Naim 2015; McMillan and Zoido 2004). By blocking publication, filtering the internet, bribing the owners and journalists in the 'independent' media, and even threatening these content producers with jail, the authority can prevent the spreading of unfavourable information. Not only can the capacity of the state be shown in the process but, more importantly, it discourages any prospect of coordinated protests and aggravates the pluralistic ignorance in society. The strategic use of censorship that adjusts to different levels of social tension can bring the state more benefit than the use of free media (Lorentzen 2014).

Constraints, choices, and state–individual interaction in transitional situations

In ruling the population, the state faces two constraints. One is the state's own resources for dealing with popular revolt/revolution. The resource constraint is closely related to the state's economic capacity, organisational capacity, and military capacity. Available fiscal resources can be used to fund such means of knowledge construction as education and propaganda, or they can be used for economic/social/political benefits that can buy off compliance. Resources can also be used to censor unwanted information or fund the state apparatus (such as the police, the military, and prisons). All these investments will help the state remain in power and keep the population compliant, while collective non-compliance and regime change are kept at bay.

In an interactive power relation, the second constraint that the state faces is the information asymmetry regarding people's desire to be non-compliant, both individually and collectively. In its power relationship with the state, the story from the population's side is that they would expect to (feasibly) optimise their living situation. In theory, if the living conditions enjoyed by individuals meet their expectations, they will repay the state with compliance. In this sense, individuals' objectives can be understood as the price of their compliance with the state (it should be noted that, although the state might prefer sincere loyalty, this does not necessarily entail a higher price). If their expectations are not met, individuals may choose non-compliance or revolt, which will also carry certain costs to themselves. But the people's intention to rise up and their doing so are not crystal clear to the state. The possibility of the people's collective non-compliance is a function of their capacity, motivation, and coordination, which are supported by traditional social movement theories about the resources, grievances, political opportunities, and social networks of the activists (Le Bon 1897; McCarthy and Zald 1977; Meyer and Staggenborg 1996). The state, therefore, needs to tackle all these aspects in order to reduce the collective non-compliance of the public.

Under the two constraints above, the state chooses a hybrid solution from its toolkit that includes both tolerant approaches – such as consent construction and benefit allocation – and intolerant approaches – such as censorship and force – to maximise the compliance from the governed. Each of these tactics has its distinctive effect on the public. The state's intolerant statecraft may be useful in whittling down the capacity as well as the coordination of the population's rebels. However, it may also cause non-cooperation/non-compliance in the long term and increase people's motivation for further revolt/revolution. Tolerant strategies such as propaganda, education, and benefit allocation may not be as efficient as force, but they can be useful for undermining the motivation of the prospective rebels. The knowledge construction approach tends to gain more stable compliance than strategies based on benefit exchange do. However, radical loyalty could turn into radical opposition if ever the believers' expectations of the authority are disappointed. The tolerant and intolerant approaches are strategic substitutes limited by a specific capacity at a certain time, while they become strategic complements when obtaining information from the population. When the state's resources are given at a certain time, the state can increase its investment either in strategies of force or strategies that could manufacture public consent. When seeking certain information from the population, a state must complement any increase of force by efforts to create consent in order to avoid further challenge from the governed.

As I have suggested above, the state's rationale and its implementation of statecraft face the risk that its tactics to maintain state legitimacy will backfire in the population: all these techniques, no matter how sophisticated or powerful, must make sense, meshing with individuals' experience and resonating with their 'common sense'. If a backfire does result, this can be dangerous for tolerant strategies that are designed to shape people's ideology. For instance, in a situation where people's personal knowledge and public knowledge mismatch, the state's efforts to construct knowledge in a certain way may result in discontent rather than advocacy. The state may add force to supplement its governance and ensure that its intentions are executed, for example by pushing reforms while censoring opposed opinions. However, when individuals cannot say what they think, they may falsify their reported/public consent and the accumulated falsification of political attitudes may produce 'cascades' (Kuran 1991). In this case, any initial small-scale protest, if it can ever be formed, will act as an important signal for the whole society to update its belief with regard to the state (Kuran 1991; Lohmann 1993; Lohmann 1994). The possibility of room for people's counter-conduct therefore leads to further implications about the state's action and forces the state to include the estimated population reaction in its decision-making process.

A state's conduct, or governmentality, in dealing with its people is not just a static design. It is a dynamic process of governing and using the best possible portfolio of statecraft practices in response to changing conditions. This feature is especially easy to identify when dramatic social/economic changes occur. For instance, an individual's expectations of redistribution, as well as their estimation of the general expectations of society as a whole, will change when a reformed distribution is under way. In this case, the government's demand for information regarding the public's expectations and the distribution of public opinion can be especially strong. The increased demand for information then needs a decent amount of tolerance in the authority's approach to minimise the cost ascribed to the information asymmetry. Meanwhile, following economic development, a shift of the capacity curve will permit an increase in both the investment in force and the manufacture of consent. In this case, the equilibrium point of various forms of statecraft shifts, and the specific direction of the shift, or the portion of each strategy, depends on the slope of each constraint line.

Conclusions

This paradigm elaborated in this chapter clarifies the way in which the two-way story of state–individual interaction in modern society works and how a rapidly changing social and economic scenario may prompt a state to adjust its governmentality. The analytical paradigm is designed to be as comprehensive as possible to capture all the possible options in the state–individual interaction and can be formally developed in the future. In the chapters that follow I take the first step in illustrating the theoretical schema with empirical evidence. A key step here forms the focus of the next chapter, looking at the ways in which state policy demarcates subpopulations where different governmentalities may be applied.

Notes

1 Since this book deals with the state–society/individual relationship, I do not include bureaucrats in the model, as many studies using a similar approach do.

References

Acemoglu, D.; Ticchi, D.; and Vindigni, A. (2010). 'A theory of military dictatorships'. *American Economic Journal: Macroeconomics*, vol. 2, issue 1, 1–42. https://doi.org/10.1257/mac.2.1.1.

Bennett, P.; and Naim, M. (2015). '21st century censorship: Governments around the world are using stealthy strategies to manipulate the media'. *Columbia Journal Review*. https://archives.cjr.org/cover_story/21st_century_censorship.php

Bernstein, T. P. (2013). 'Resilience and collapse in China and the Soviet Union'. *Why Communism Did Not Collapse: Understanding Authoritarian Regime Resilience in Asia and Europe*, 40–63.

Boix, C.; and Svolik, M. W. (2013). 'The foundations of limited authoritarian government: Institutions, commitment, and power-sharing in dictatorships'. *The Journal of Politics*, vol. 75, issue 2, 300–316. https://doi.org/10.1017/s0022381613000029

Chen, J.; and Xu, Y. (2017). Why do authoritarian regimes allow citizens to voice opinions publicly? *The Journal of Politics*, vol. 79, issue 3, 792–803. https://doi.org/10.1086/690303. OA: https://ssrn.com/abstract=2318051

Dimitrov, M. K. (2013). 'Understanding communist collapse and resilience'. *Why Communism Did Not Collapse: Understanding Authoritarian Regime Resilience in Asia and Europe*, 3–39. https://doi.org/10.1017%2Fcbo9781139565028.002

Edmond, C. (2013). 'Information manipulation, coordination, and regime change'. *Review of Economic Studies*, vol. 80, issue 4, 1422–1458. https://doi.org/10.1093/restud/rdt020

Egorov, G.; and Sonin, K. (2011). 'Dictators and their viziers: Endogenizing the loyalty–competence trade-off'. *Journal of the European Economic Association*, vol. 9, issue 5, 903–930. https://doi.org/10.1111/j.1542-4774.2011.01033.x

Egorov, G.; Guriev, S.; and Sonin, K. (2009). 'Why resource-poor dictators allow freer media: A theory and evidence from panel data'. *American Political Science Review*, vol. 103, issue 4, 645–668. https://doi.org/10.1017/s0003055409990219. OA: https://ssrn.com/abstract=898888

Foucault, M. (2009). *Security, Territory, Population: Lectures at the Collège de France, 1977–78* (M. Senellart ed.). Palgrave Macmillan.

Gallagher, M. E. (2011). *Contagious Capitalism: Globalization and the Politics of Labor in China*. Princeton University Press.

Gallagher, M.; and Hanson, J. K. (2009). 'Coalitions, carrots, and sticks: economic inequality and authoritarian states'. *PS: Political Science & Politics*, vol. 42, issue 4, 667–672. https://doi.org/10.1017/s1049096509990096

Gehlbach, S.; and Keefer, P. (2011). 'Investment without democracy: Ruling-party institutionalization and credible commitment in autocracies'. *Journal of Comparative Economics*, vol. 39, issue 2, 123–139. https://doi.org/10.1016/j.jce.2011.04.002

Giddens, A. (1981). *A Contemporary Critique of Historical Materialism: The Nation-State and Violence*. University of California Press.

Gramsci, A.; Hoare, Q.; and Nowell-Smith, G. (1971). *Selections from the Prison Notebooks of Antonio Gramsci*. Lawrence and Wishart Limited.

Gregory, P. R.; Schröder, P. J.; and Sonin, K. (2006). 'Dictators, repression and the median citizen: An "eliminations model" of Stalin's Terror' (Data from the NKVD Archives). https://doi.org/10.2139/ssrn.948667

Gries, P. H. (2004). *China's New Nationalism: Pride, Politics, and Diplomacy*. University of California Press.

Grimes, M. (2008). 'Consent, political trust and compliance: Rejoinder to Kaina's remarks on "Organizing consent"'. *European Journal of Political Research*, vol. 47, issue 4, 522–535. https://doi.org/10.1111/j.1475-6765.2008.00774.x

Guriev, S.; and Treisman, D. (2015). *How Modern Dictators Survive: An Informational Theory of the New Authoritarianism*. Retrieved from https://doi.org/10.3386%2Fw21136

Han, R. (2015). 'Defending the authoritarian regime online: China's "voluntary fifty-cent army"'. *The China Quarterly*, vol. 224, 1006–1025. https://doi.org/10.1017/s0305741015001216

Huang, H. (2015). 'Propaganda as signaling'. *Comparative Politics*, vol. 47, issue 4, 419–444. https://doi.org/10.5129/001041515816103220

Kohli, A.; Shue, V.; and Migdal, J. S. (1994). *State Power and Social Forces: Domination and Transformation in the Third World*. UK: Cambridge University Press.

Kricheli, R.; Livne, Y.; and Magaloni, B. (2011). *Taking to the Streets: Theory and Evidence on Protests under Authoritarianism*. Paper presented at the APSA 2010 Annual Meeting Paper.

Kuran, T. (1991). 'Now out of never: The element of surprise in the East European revolution of 1989'. *World Politics*, vol. 44, issue 1, 7–48. https://doi.org/10.2307/2010422

Le Bon, G. (1897). *The Crowd: A Study of the Popular Mind*. Fischer.

Leung, J. C.; and Wong, H. S. (1999). 'The emergence of a community-based social assistance programme in urban China'. *Social Policy & Administration*, vol. 33, issue 1, 39–54. https://doi.org/10.1111/1467-9515.00130

Leung, J. C.; and Xu, Y. (2015). *China's Social Welfare: The Third Turning Point*. John Wiley & Sons.

Levi, M. (1997). *Consent, Dissent, and Patriotism*. Cambridge University Press.

Li, B.; and Zhong, Y. (2009). 'How did China's transitions impact people's welfare benefits in the reform era?' *Journal of Contemporary China*, vol. 18, issue 62, 813–829. https://doi.org/10.1080/10670560903174606

Lipset, S. M.; and Man, P. (1960). *The Social Bases of Politics*. USA: Johns Hopkins University Press.

Lohmann, S. (1993). 'A signaling model of informative and manipulative political action'. *American Political Science Review*, vol. 87, issue 2, 319–333. https://doi.org/10.2307/2939043

Lohmann, S. (1994). 'The dynamics of informational cascades: The Monday demonstrations in Leipzig, East Germany, 1989–91'. *World Politics*, vol. 47, issue 1, 42–101. https://doi.org/10.2307/2950679

Lord, C.; and Beetham, D. (2001). 'Legitimizing the EU: Is there a post-parliamentary basis for its legitimation?' *JCMS: Journal of Common Market Studies*, vol. 39, issue 3, 443–462. https://doi.org/10.1111/1468-5965 .00298

Lorentzen, P. (2014). 'China's strategic censorship'. *American Journal of Political Science*, vol. 58, issue 2, 402–414. https://doi.org/10.1111/ajps.12065

Lu, X.; and Perry, E. J. (1997). *Danwei: The Changing Chinese Workplace in Historical and Comparative Perspective*. Me Sharpe.

McCarthy, J. D.; and Zald, M. N. (1977). 'Resource mobilization and social movements: A partial theory'. *American Journal of Sociology*, vol. 82, issue 6, 1212–1241. https://doi.org/10.1086/226464

McMillan, J.; and Zoido, P. (2004). 'How to subvert democracy: Montesinos in Peru'. *Journal of Economic Perspectives*, vol. 18, issue 4, 69–92. https://doi .org/10.1257/0895330042632690

Meyer, D. S.; and Staggenborg, S. (1996). 'Movements, countermovements, and the structure of political opportunity'. *American Journal of Sociology*, vol. 101, issue 6, 1628–1660. https://doi.org/10.1086/230869

Myerson, R. B. (2008). 'The autocrat's credibility problem and foundations of the constitutional state'. *American Political Science Review*, vol. 102, issue 1, 125–139. https://doi.org/10.1017/s0003055408080076

Nathan, A. (2003). 'China's changing of the guard: Authoritarian resilience'. *Journal of Democracy*, vol. 14, issue 1, 6–17. https://doi.org/10.1353/jod .2003.0019

Perry, E. J. (2017). 'Higher education and authoritarian resilience: The case of China, past and present'. Harvard-Yenching Institute Working Paper Series. OA: https://dash.harvard.edu/handle/1/30822717

Perry, E. J.; and Heilmann, S. (2011). 'Embracing uncertainty: Guerrilla policy style and adaptive governance in China'. *Mao's Invisible Hand: The Political Foundations of Adaptive Governance in China.*

Ringen, S.; and Ngok, K. (2017). 'What kind of welfare state is emerging in China?' *Towards Universal Health Care in Emerging Economies*, 213–237. Springer. https://doi.org/10.1057%2F978-1-137-53377-7_8

Schneider, A. L.; Ingram, H.; and DeLeon, P. (2014). 'Democratic policy design: Social construction of target populations'. In P. Sabatier and C. Weible (eds), *Theories of the Policy Process*, 3rd edn, 105–149.

Simon, J. (2014). *The New Censorship: Inside the Global Battle for Media Freedom.* Columbia University Press. https://doi.org/10.7312%2Fcolumbia%2F9780231160643.001.0001

Smoke, R. (1994). 'On the importance of policy legitimacy'. *Political Psychology*, 97–110. https://doi.org/10.2307/3791441

Svolik, M. W. (2012). *The Politics of Authoritarian Rule.* Cambridge University Press. https://doi.org/10.1017/CBO9781139176040

Tilly, C. (2017). 'Coercion, capital, and European states, AD 990–1990'. *Collective Violence, Contentious Politics, and Social Change*, 140–154. Routledge. https://doi.org/10.1080/714005469

Weber, M. (1978). *Economy and Society: An Outline of Interpretive Sociology*, vol. 1. University of California Press.

Wedeen, L. (1999). *Ambiguities of Domination: Politics, Rhetoric, and Symbols in Contemporary Syria.* University of Chicago Press. https://doi.org/10.7208%2Fchicago%2F9780226345536.001.0001

Wintrobe, R. (1990). 'The tinpot and the totalitarian: An economic theory of dictatorship'. *American Political Science Review*, vol. 84, issue 3, 849–872. https://doi.org/10.2307/1962769

Wintrobe, R. (2007). 'Dictatorship: analytical approaches', *The Oxford Handbook of Comparative Politics*. UK: Oxford University Press. https://doi.org/10.1093%2Foxfordhb%2F9780199566020.003.0016

Wong, L.; and Ngok, K. (2006). 'Social policy between plan and market: Xiagang (off-duty employment) and the policy of the re-employment service centres in China'. *Social Policy & Administration*, vol. 40, issue 2, 158–173. https://doi.org/10.1111/j.1467-9515.2006.00482.x

Xie, Y. (2016). 'Understanding inequality in China'. *Chinese Journal of Sociology*, vol. 2, issue 3, 327–347. https://doi.org/10.1177/2057150x16654059. OA: https://europepmc.org/article/MED/29854420

Yan, X. (2017). *How Is China Maintain Stable? Observation and Thoughts from Fieldwork [Zhongguo Heyi Wending: Laizi Tianye de Guancha yu Sikao].* Hong Kong: Joint Publishing.

Zhao, D. (2001). 'China's prolonged stability and political future: Same political system, different policies and methods'. *Journal of Contemporary China*, vol. 10, issue 28, 427–444. https://doi.org/10.1080/10670560120067126

CHAPTER 2

Who gets what and how: governance based on subpopulations

Looking at observable public policies in order to capture the tactics used by the state in maintaining its legitimacy is complicated, especially as regards social policies that change frequently and differ across various social groups. However, the governmentality logic underlying whom to govern and how to govern is shown in the design of governmental programmes, in the way that social problems are defined and divisions/distinctions are established, and in the different kinds of knowledge produced to shape people's ideologies. Here and in the next chapter, I probe into the different designs of policy experiments and schemes, examine the techniques intentionally used by the Chinese government to shape the public's expectations and manufacture public consent, and discuss the rationale behind these practices.

In China's current, massive transition, social welfare provision is one of the most important areas that can be directly perceived by the public. It is also an arena in which we can vividly see a close interaction between the state and the public. For instance, there may be a 'trade-off' between the opportunities and challenges of promoting a welfare reform in pensions or health care. Going ahead affects how the state manages its budget, whether it can increase economic efficiency through privatisation and so on. At the same time, it also brings challenges due to the fact that some sectors will disappear during the process, and the allocation of social benefits will face a possible major reshuffle. To best capture the details from a specific area of social policy, my empirical work in this chapter focuses on the case of major pension policy changes during the social welfare reform conducted by the Chinese government after the 'reform and opening up' in 1978. I look intensively at social policies relating to welfare for the elderly (such as old-age insurance, pensions, and so on) because this area is one that can reveal the state's purposeful design in modifying the distribution of public goods and balancing the role of the government and

How to cite this book chapter:
Wang, Yan. 2022. *Pension Policy and Governmentality in China: Manufacturing Public Compliance*. London: LSE Press, pp. 27–48.
DOI: https://doi.org/10.31389/lsepress.ppc.c. License: CC BY

the public in welfare provision. The existence of multiple programmes – such as basic social security, old-age insurance, and pension plans – also suggests that social policies relating to old-age benefits are in an area where many negotiations are possible. People are less likely to give up their existing benefits; thus, the state needs to devote greater effort to the changes that it plans.

The key questions I answer in this chapter are 'How is access to welfare resources distributed among different social groups, and how does the distribution change along with the reforms?' In the reformed welfare system of China, the social rights to income and social security are now more frequently defined on an individual basis than they were in the previous system. They used to be defined collectively through work units (*danwei*, a place of employment) and people's communes (*renmin gongshe*, the highest administrative levels in rural areas). Unlike the old system, in the new system, the issue of who gets what and how they get it has gradually become connected to individuals' endowments, such as their social status, political status, social capital, and so on. From the late 1990s, the government promoted various pension scheme reforms, under which people with different occupations have their own distinctive accessibility to various welfare benefits. For instance, the reform of basic pension scheme for enterprise employees distinguishes the individual contribution rate levied on different age groups, a scheme that was not applied to employees from other sectors such as public institutions before the 2010s. Identifying how and why the state distributes certain benefits but not others, and to some groups/regions but not others, may help to answer the questions regarding the state's overview of population-based governance and its tactics of resource differentiation.

To address the question of resource differentiation, I trace the social schemes related to old-age benefits in China from the early 1950s (with a focus on the period after 1978's 'reform and opening up') and sort out comparisons among the different policy schemes that were available to people of different political status (different urban/rural areas or *hukous*,[1] occupations, party membership, and so on). In the 2010s there were several parallel pension plans, because distinct schemes were devised to cover people of different status. There are pension plans tailored for government employees, for employees of public institutions, employees of enterprises, urban non-salaried residents, and rural residents. The political status that combines residential and occupational difference is crucial for Chinese people seeking access to these differentiated welfare benefits.

2.1 How do entitlements differ: differentiation in benefit entitlement

Welfare benefits, as a type of scarce resource (or public good), can be used by the state in exchange for loyalty, forming coalitions and breaking down a population's capacity to coordinate any critical collective action. In theory, the distribution of welfare benefits can be the result of the authority's intentional manipulation, negotiations between interest groups, and the influence of socio-historical factors – for instance, demographic and geographical features that may respectively lead to the varied distribution of health issues, and change the distribution of certain health care benefits. Therefore, it is difficult to image a welfare regime in which everyone enjoys exactly the same social benefits – we are more likely to see various welfare schemes and programmes tailored for different social groups and regions, some enjoying more social benefits than others (Frazier 2010). In his book *The Divided Welfare State: The Battle over Public and Private Social Benefits in the United States* (2002), Hacker described the coexistence of public and private social benefits that are unequally distributed to different populations in the USA. Some programmes are fully funded by public expenditure, and some programmes benefit the recipients through tax breaks and credit subsidies. There are also programmes that are promoted and regulated by the government while they are completely funded by private contributions – normally from higher earners. So China is not unusual in having multiple welfare schemes and programmes.

However, the mechanism that leads to the coexistence of multiple programmes may not be the same for regimes with distinctive political institutions and paths. In the USA, Hacker identified the timing and sequence of policy development during which the public–private social benefits were constructed through political debates. Business interests played a central role in shaping the landscape of welfare distribution. In an authoritarian regime such as China, the central government has enjoyed far more power in the process of policy-making and resource allocation. Even in a typical policy experiment, which is assumed to be more flexible and open-ended than policies announced as one-off decisions, the central government would set the direction and guidance. Provincial and local governments would enjoy only a conditional and limited autonomy in localising and reinterpreting the details of the policies. So in China multiple social programmes coexisting is more a consequence of centralised policymaking.

So, if the central government operates under constraint from a limited budget, how has it designed the differentiation of social rights and what were its main criteria? In the existing studies of China's society, one important standard that was identified in the differing accessibility of resources was political status (Bray 2005; Lu and Perry 1997; Q. Zheng 2015). The difference of political status mainly resulted from the *hukou* system (Cheng and Selden 1994). People in China were born with the political status of being either rural or urban residents of their local area and were not supposed to move freely across regions. The rural/urban status, or *hukou*, was 'political' in the sense that it largely determined an individual's access to initial public resources such as education (since schools are mostly localised resources), and local elections occurred at the village and district level. Thus it was constructed on residential variation. When individuals got a job, they entered into an occupation-based status, joining the staff of the government, staff of a public institution, staff of an enterprise, working as a peasant, and so on (M.-k. Lee 2000; Xie, Lai, and Wu 2009). These status categories determined certain other public resources that an individual could access, such as pension plans and health care plans (Wang and Chai 2009). To give an example, as the economic reform proceeded, many rural residents left the countryside to search for temporary jobs in cities. However, even though they worked in the cities, their *hukou* status was still that of rural residents and they were ineligible for public goods such as education, housing, and pension benefits in the cities where they lived and worked (Y. Song 2014). In other words, people with different endowments did not enjoy the same public resources in China. Moreover, the unevenness of benefit allocations across different types of public resource schemes was distinctive. For instance, Cai and his colleagues (2018) identified the differentiation and polarised pension benefit allocation in China, using public transfer data. They showed that the public transfer in pension benefits was more concentrated in the top quartile of earners than was the case for those in education and health care. Those from the top quartile aged 75 received an annual pension of RMB 12,029 on average, and from the second quartile received around RMB 3,460 per person, while the elderly from the bottom quartile received less than RMB 189 a year (Cai, Feng, and Shen 2018).

The variation of welfare benefits in China's case did not merely apply to differentiation in one policy scheme; rather, it was systematically designed to provide different social groups with different programmes in order to maintain a balance of loyalty as well as avoid the risk of any hostile coalition. The formation process of such segregation entailed less political conflict than occurs in representative political systems, and showed more sense of 'overview' or 'seeing the bigger picture' from the ruler's standpoint. It would seem quite in order if certain groups were privileged or sacrificed to improve 'the general good' or to reduce 'the general cost'. The question that then arises is 'who is to be sacrificed and who is to be kept safe in the era of transformations, and what tactics will the state use if public discontent is stirred up over the inequality?'

2.2 Pension reforms in China: a de-synchronised story

The allocation of welfare benefits is recognised as a useful tool for showing the generosity of the authority and buying loyalty from the public (Haggard and Kaufman 2008; Karshenas and Moghadam 2006; Rimlinger 1971). If budget constraints occur in a given period, one reasonable assumption regarding the allocation of welfare benefits is that the government will distribute the limited fiscal capacity to the social group that costs least per unit (that is, per person, or per group of people), and can maximise the gains for the state. But how to decide which group to favour and which to give up? There are two common assumptions about the objectives of the state: to maintain broad social stability, and to maintain active compliance, such as support or consent. The former is more basic, while the latter is more desirable, but they are in general not mutually exclusive. If the priority/objective for the government is 'political stability', then the resource will be allocated to those who enjoy the greatest negotiation and bargaining power. For maintaining compliance objective, the public's consent is fundamental to the state's legitimacy; it relies heavily on people's perceptions that social justice and equality are being considered (at least shown superficially by state attempts to redistribute benefits) and the belief that the authority will meet the public's expectations. Hence the central authority does its best to meet (or seem to meet) the public's needs in order to get loyalty in return when the authority senses pressure or risks over legitimation. Under the assumption of consent manufacture and maintaining compliance, the state is more likely to redistribute public resources to social groups who are relatively disadvantaged.

I develop my hypothesis about the government's choice in welfare allocation on the basis of careful consideration regarding these two assumptions, and take into account the nature of authoritarian authority – which has an instinct to share power and benefits within its inner power circle. A strategic resource differentiation, therefore, is a reasonable hypothesis: the state will uphold favouritism towards core elites, but wield the weapon of redistributive equality when necessary, and only to a certain extent. Meanwhile, the government employs other tactics such as persuasion by propaganda, and gradual experiments to keep the general public opinion under control. To support this argument I draw evidence from institutional analysis and statistical comparison of China's pension reforms. The institutional analysis focuses on variations in timing, direction, and content of reforms, so as to collectively present a whole image of strategic differentiation in welfare benefit allocation by the government. To precisely identify the different entitlements to benefit across pension schemes, I collected statistical data from the China Labour Statistical Yearbooks, Local Fiscal Statistical Yearbooks, National Statistical Bureau Dataset and other datasets (such as G. Zheng 2016),[2] and compared variations including the eligible population, participating population, coverage rate, pension benefit (per person per year), incremental rate of pension benefit, and so on.

In the 2010s there were five parallel pension plans,[3] each tailored for one group of people – government employees, public institute employees, employees of enterprises, urban non-salaried residents, and rural residents. The fragmented pension scheme was compatible with the categories of political status, which originated from the socialist planning economy that locked the whole populace into a registered permanent category of residence (rural or urban) and a work unit (in an SOE, government post, or elsewhere) (Whyte 2012). From Table 2.1, we can identify the differences in accessing the public resources between the distinctive social groups. In the present pension system, only government employees enjoyed a full fiscal-funded retirement payment (Pozen 2013). Before the 2000s and 2010s reforms of the scheme, public institution employees used to enjoy a similar political status and comparable welfare

Table 2.1: Comparison between different pension schemes in China (in 2015)

Scheme recipients	Scheme name	Nature	Funding source
Government employees	Pension Plan for Government Employees (PGE)	Government-funded pension	Government
Public institution employees	Pension Plan for Public Institution Employees (PPIE)	Government-funded pension→social insurance	Government→ government and individual shared
Enterprise employees	Pension Plan for Enterprise Employees (PEE)	Enterprise-funded pension→social insurance	Enterprise (government takes ultimate accountability) → government, enterprise, and individual shared
Urban non-salaried residents	Pension Plan for Urban Non-salaried Residents (PUR)	Social insurance	Government and individual shared
Rural residents	Pension Plan for Rural Residents (PRR)	Social insurance	Government and individual shared

Source: author.

Note: Arrows in the table indicate reforms of the pension schemes.

benefits to those of government employees. Afterwards they were now confined to a hybrid pension system in which individuals shared the responsibility for making pension contributions. Enterprise employees before the economic reform had their workplace unit and the government as accountable welfare providers. Nowadays, however, the pension plan for enterprise employees shares this responsibility between government, the enterprise, and the individual themselves. The pension plans for urban non-salaried residents and rural residents were similar; both became defined contribution pension insurance schemes that enjoyed a certain (slim) subsidy from the government compared to other types of employee (Wang, Béland, and Zhang 2014). Still, before the late 2000s, these groups had no systematic pension plan at all.

As the main embodiment of state authority, government officials with formal contracts enjoy the most generous payments after they retire. There is solid evidence from previous studies that have demonstrated the welfare privileges of government-related work units compared to the enterprise units and urban residents compared to migrant workers and rural residents (Chan and Buckingham 2008; Chan and Zhang 1999; Selden and You 1997). Right after the foundation of the PRC, in 1955, a non-contributory pension scheme was issued for government officials. The employees were not required to contribute to the pension pool since the whole fund was subsidised by the state budget. The income replacement rate for retired government employees could reach 90% or 100%, according to the 'Tentative Retirement Regulation for Government Employees' issued by the State Council in 1956. The 'Notice of Salary Reform for Government and Public Institution Employees' issued in 1993 specified that the in-service salary for a government worker would consist of four parts: the duty wage, rank wage, basic wage, and seniority wage. A retired government employee could enjoy their full previous basic wage plus the seniority wage. The retiree also received some subsidy from the government in line with the duty wage and rank wage based on their working years: the longer the employee worked, the higher replacement rate that they got after retirement. Starting from 2006, when the 'Civil Service Law' was issued, the salary system for government employees changed to a two-tier structure: duty wage and rank wage, plus the corresponding allowances. Since the reform, a retired government employee can still enjoy a replacement rate above 80% of their previous income.

Public institution (PI for convenience in the following discussions) employees, such as schoolteachers, doctors in public hospitals, employees of radio or TV stations, and so on, are also generally thought to be people who enjoy an 'iron rice bowl'. The pension plan for PI employees was exactly the same as that for government employees before the 2006 salary reform: officially, the PI employees were subsidised by the state budget in full or in part (depending on the nature of the work units). The 2006 salary reform specified that the retirees of public institution no longer enjoyed the allowance and performance wage, though the pension was still much better than that of people in other occupations such as enterprise employees. The generous pension plan for government and public institution employees has caused great discontent in other social groups[4] for quite a long time. Under huge pressure from society, the government claimed to have changed the dual track of one pension plan for government public institution employees and another for the remaining social groups in early 2008. The reform plan launched in 2008 (as a policy experiment) turned out to be a proposal that differentiated the pension benefits of PI employees from those of government employees: the old non-contributory pension scheme was changed into a defined contributory pension insurance scheme. Started in 2008 as a pilot policy, it was then implemented across the nation in 2014; all PI employees from then on had to add their own contribution to their future retirement fund.[5] In Figure 2.1, I show the chronological changes in the pension scheme reforms for government employees and public institution employees.

Before the economic reform in the 1980s, only state-owned enterprises (SOEs) were allowed to exist in the PRC. During that time their employees enjoyed high social and economic status, and had an enterprise-funded,

Figure 2.1: The timeline of segmented pension plan reforms, 1955–2011

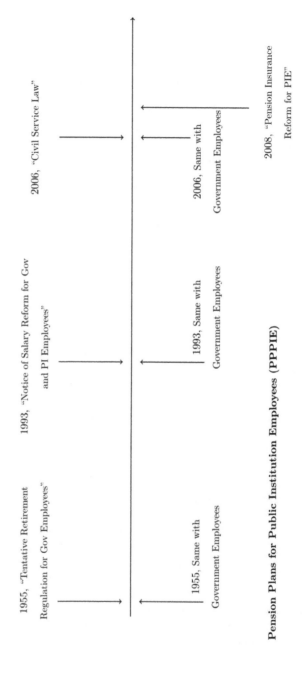

Pension Plans for Government Employees (PPGE)

1955, "Tentative Retirement Regulation for Gov Employees"

1993, "Notice of Salary Reform for Gov and PI Employees"

2006, "Civil Service Law"

1955, Same with Government Employees

1993, Same with Government Employees

2006, Same with Government Employees

2008, "Pension Insurance Reform for PIE"

Pension Plans for Public Institution Employees (PPPIE)

Figure 2.1: The timeline of segmented pension plan reforms, 1955–2011 (continued)

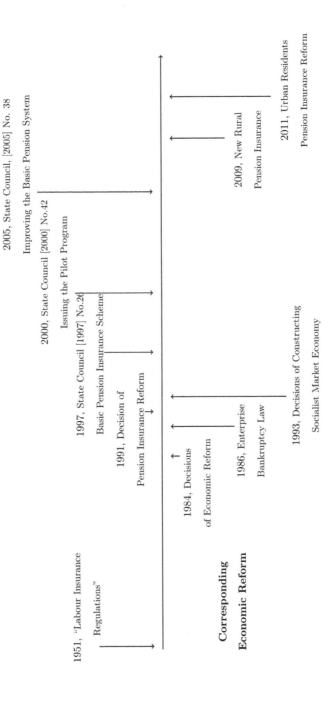

Pension Plans for Enterprise Employees (PPEE)

1951, "Labour Insurance Regulations"

1991, Decision of Pension Insurance Reform

1997, State Council [1997] No.26 Basic Pension Insurance Scheme

2000, State Council [2000] No.42 Issuing the Pilot Program

2005, State Council, [2005] No. 38 Improving the Basic Pension System

2009, New Rural Pension Insurance

2011, Urban Residents Pension Insurance Reform

Corresponding Economic Reform

1984, Decisions of Economic Reform

1986, Enterprise Bankruptcy Law

1993, Decisions of Constructing Socialist Market Economy

government-accounted form of social insurance (as had all the enterprises owned by the state) that included education, health care, pensions, and many other benefits. However, when the economic reform started in the 1980s, numbers of SOEs were restructured and hundreds of thousands of employees were laid off (Gu 1999; Gu 2001). The remaining SOE employees suffered from the retrenchment of pension benefits,[6] while the new pension scheme was designed to fit the economic reform of marketisation, cut fiscal expense, and relieve the work units and the government of their burden. Today, enterprise employees are the main component of the labour force, and are a key group for the government. In work they form what is seen as the core engine for economic development. But when they retire they are bad assets – the ruler is impatient to shake off the burden of their welfare provision.

In more detail, the key changes started from the late 1980s and early 1990s, when the dilapidated old pension system for enterprise employees was redesigned as a multilayered pension system. The State Council issued the 'Decision on a Pension Insurance Reform for Enterprise Employees' in 1991, calling for a division of pension responsibility between state, enterprises, and individuals. The pension system pictured by this 'Decision' included a basic retirement programme managed by the state, supplementary retirement programmes funded by the enterprises, and individual savings in the form of a retirement account chosen by each employee (Chao and Dickson 2003). But this announcement was more like a proposal and proved difficult to set in motion due to the lack of funding. People were still expecting the government to admit fiscal accountability and the enterprises were unable to fund the pension pool on their own.

A more official-looking reform started in 1997 when the State Council issued Document no. 26, named *Decision on Establishing a Unified System of Basic Pension Insurance for Enterprise Employees* (State Council 1997). Again, this 'Decision' promoted the idea that the responsibility for raising funds for this new pension system should be shared between enterprises, employees, and government, although, de facto, it was still not compulsory. However, the 1977 'Decision' did have a clear plan for the size of contributions: individual accounts should be kept at 11% of the employee's salary and individuals had to contribute 8% of their salary (starting with 4%). The employer should make up the shortfall in individual accounts, namely 3% of the individual's salary, while separately contributing no more than 17% to the social coordination account (the total contribution of an enterprise should not exceed 20% of an individual's total wages).

To further clarify the divisions between individual and social pooling accounts, as well as to make up for the deficit in individual accounts, the central government issued Document no. 42 in 2000 (State Council 2000) and no. 38 in 2005 to promote the new policy experiment of 'fully funding individual accounts'[7] (State Council 2005). These documents clearly spelt out how to construct a workable three-dimensional hybrid pension reform for urban enterprise employees. First, at the individual level, contributions to individual accounts were to be borne solely by employees paying in at a rate set at 8% of their wage. Meanwhile, the separate contributions from the enterprise per employee should not be partially diverted to individual accounts but paid in full into an account under the social coordination plan. This definition of the contributory pension scheme clarified the private nature of individual pension accounts and implied that individuals should play a larger role in the funding of their pensions. In addition, the reform emphasised that the longer the employees contributed, the more they would receive when they retired, thus strengthening the connection between an individual's working history and their entitlement to the related welfare. The reform also expanded the coverage of the pension system to wage earners in other categories, such as the employees of small private businesses, in addition to the employees of state-owned or collective-owned enterprises. This was to pluralise the sources of the funding, as well as the enterprise annuities, encouraged by the government as a way of supplementing the basic pension insurance. In the meantime, the reform recommended that individuals explore the possibilities of registering with commercial pension schemes. Until they did so, however, a multi-sourced, defined contributory pension plan was established for all enterprise employees.

Unlike the salaried urban citizens, rural residents and urban non-salaried residents had no clear pension plan at all until the late 2000s. Although some scattered pilot policies to pay pensions to rural residents were implemented at county level in 1992 (also called the 'Old Rural Pension Plan'), these initiatives were mostly unsuccessful and none of them was turned into a national policy. In 2009, the State Council issued 'Guidance on Establishing a New Rural Pension Scheme (Pilot)', also called the 'New Rural Pension Plan'. The nationwide policy started in 2011 and thereafter rural residents were able to register with a pension plan where they could contribute a certain amount of money (the original plan in 2009 included five contributory rates – of RMB 100, RMB 200, RMB 300, RMB 400, and RMB 500 per calendar year. The scales would be adjusted every year according to the annual net per capita income of rural residents as a national average and they would enjoy accordingly a subsidy from the government's fiscal budget. The pension plan for urban non-salaried residents was issued in 2011, and was similar to the rural residents' pension plan. They are both defined contributory pension schemes funded jointly by individuals and the state.

The reforms for different social groups were conducted at various times and went in various directions. As shown in Table 2.1 and Figure 2.1, the pension policy reform process was a multi-track segregation in the fulfilment of social rights. State employees enjoyed the most generous pension benefit and the government budget took full responsibility for their lives after retirement. Facing the big wave of economic reform and pressure on the fiscal capacity, it was the enterprise employees (of state-owned enterprises in particular) that suffered from the large-scale lay-offs and were encouraged to take charge of their own social risks. Later on, when popular discontent about the dual track heated up, the central authority was happy to reduce its responsibilities and shift the burden onto public institution employees in order to appease the widespread sense of grievance. A follow-up tactic to replenish the political support pool for the government was to launch the pension plan for rural residents and urban non-salaried residents in order to buy off the seemingly least costly population. I give more details below of the state's efforts to carry out a 'loyalty buyoff' with rural residents in the section on the generosity of the pension scheme.

2.3 Generosity and coverage: segmented resource allocation

How generous were the detailed benefit differences between the schemes? The size of benefits received per person and the extent of the schemes' coverage are commonly used indices for identifying the details of welfare programmes (X. Huang 2014; Ratigan 2017; Riedmüller 2008). Accordingly, I collected statistical data from multiple sources of datasets and considered the variations across schemes, including their eligible population, participating population, coverage rate, pension benefit (per person per year), incremental rate of the pension benefit or welfare provision, and other statistics showing how they compare.[8]

The pension plans for government employees (PGE) and public institution employees (PPIE)

Since the government data are constantly kept confidential and vague, I used two approaches in my calculation to estimate the high replacement rate of the pension plan for government employees and public institution employees – the most privileged groups. I also show that they have a higher coverage rate than the enterprise employees and rural residents. Both calculation approaches listed below endorse this argument.

Calculation method 1: according to the pension policy content. First, we can address the generous pension benefit for government employees and PI employees directly from the policy content. The following calculations for pension benefit come from the 'Civil Service Law' issued in 2006. In this reform, the salary structure for government employees was split into two levels: duty wage and rank wage, plus the due allowance. The replacement rate of pension benefits is quite high. As shown in the calculation, pension benefit (b) is related to the pre-retirement salary (s_{r-1}) and an employee's working years (n):

If n<10, $b=0.5s_{r-1}$;

10≤n<20, $b=0.7s_{r-1}$;

20≤n<30, $b=0.8s_{r-1}$;

30≤n<35, $b=0.85s_{r-1}$;

35≤n, $b=0.9s_{r-1}$;

Here note that s_{r-1} was calculated differently according to the different stages of the reform of the pension plan. Employees with less than 10 years' service when they retired enjoyed only a replacement rate of 50%. But someone who had worked for more than 20 years would enjoy a replacement of above 80% of their previous salary (it could even reach 90% if they had worked for 35 years before retirement). The pension plan for public institution employees was quite similar.

Calculation method 2: published statistical data. We can also check the generosity of the pension benefit for government and public institution employees from the published statistical data. Columns 2 to 7 in Table 2.2 come from the China Labour Statistical Yearbook, while the total data on employee numbers and salaries come from the Local Fiscal Statistical Yearbook. The other columns are self-calculated statistics based on the fiscal statistical yearbook data and the number of total employees (for instance, in column 9, I weight the average salary of all government and PI employees according to size). Due to the grouping method in the original data, I can display only a number for all government and public institution employees combined here, rather than separate numbers for the two groups for the purpose of comparison. Pension benefits are calculated in Yuan per person per year.

From 1999 to 2015, the rate of retirees' compensation compared to the workers in post increased from 18.6% to 37%. The burden of pension funding also increased greatly; in other words, the state budget investment also increased. Although the data seem less than 100% precise, we can still see a typical pattern of the high replacement rate of pension benefit for government and public institution employees (above 80% in the late 1990s and early 2000s), especially when compared to the situation for enterprise employees (about 50% in the 2000s, shown in Figure 2.2). The low coverage rate may result from the calculation problem in the original data, since the statistical bureau of the government published only the numbers of participants in the pension insurance schemes that needed self-contribution, while most government employees did not need to contribute anything and had access to full repayment from the public pension budget fund. Thus, the coverage rate in Table 2.2 can probably be better calculated by the number participants in public institution employee schemes *divided by* the number of public institution employees and government employees combined. Either way, it is clear that the pension benefit for government and public institution employees is generous and is largely covered by the state budget.

The pension plan for enterprise employees (PEE)

Enterprise employees experienced the most frequent modifications of their pensions during the whole reform period, and Table 2.3 presents the changes

Table 2.2: Pension benefit for government employees and public institution employees

Panel a. Data from statistical yearbooks					
	Persons participated at the year end (millions)			Revenue and expenses of pension fund (100 million Yuan)		
	Total	Workers	Retiree	Revenue	Expense	Balance
1999	7.62	6.42	1.19	93.2	61.8	89.3
2000	11.31	9.77	1.53	189.8	145.4	186.1
2001	12.78	10.68	2.09	253	204.4	233.2
2002	14.58	11.99	2.58	387.8	340.1	364.5
2003	16.25	13.22	3.03	470.6	405.9	441.7
2004	16.74	13.46	3.27	529.9	470.9	475.7
2005	17.72	14.09	3.62	601.6	545	534.3
2006	19.09	15.12	3.96	677.2	609.4	619.8
2007	19.02	14.92	4.09	823.6	811.3	633.2
2008	19.39	15.04	4.35	940.1	882	690
2009	19.83	15.24	4.59	1,070.3	1,007.8	751.8
2010	20.72	15.79	4.93	1,201.1	1,145	818.1
2011	21.08	15.95	5.13	1,409.9	1,339.3	888.5
2012	21.54	16.20	5.34	1,638	1,553.3	973.3
2013	21.68	16.12	5.56	1,831.7	1,729	1,076.9
2014	21.78	15.98	5.79	2,004.2	1,907.4	1,173.7
2015	22.37	16.32	6.05	2,727.7	2,671.8	1,229.6

Source: China Labour Statistical Yearbook (2016).

Table 2.2: (Continued)

Panel b. Self-complied data of pension benefits

	Total employees (millions)	Salary p/y (weighted)	Benefit p/y (Yuan)	Increase rate	Coverage rate	Replacement rate
1999	38.60		5,150		20%	
2000	38.52	8,738	9,481	84%	29%	109%
2001	38.31	9,886	9,766	3%	33%	99%
2002	37.77	11,670	13,152	35%	39%	113%
2003	37.95	13,459	13,382	2%	43%	99%
2004	38.38	14,897	14,374	7%	44%	97%
2005	38.89	16,884	15,042	5%	46%	89%
2006	39.45	19,317	15,357	2%	48%	80%
2007	40.04	21,854	19,802	29%	48%	91%
2008	40.71	26,645	20,247	2%	48%	76%
2009	41.13	30,932	21,957	8%	48%	71%
2010		34,248	23,210	6%		68%
2011			26,106	13%		
2012			29,049	11%		
2013			31,085	7%		
2014			32,897	6%		
2015			44,125	34%		

Sources: Local Fiscal Statistical Yearbooks; Author.

Note: The data shown in the table are all rounded up, therefore may have slight differences with the read numbers.

in their pension benefit and rate of increase. It shows the combined statistical data of pension benefits for employees of SOEs and other types of employment (such as self-employed persons) from the China Labour Statistical Yearbook. In addition, Figure 2.2 shows the enterprise employees' pension coverage rate, benefit per person per year, and replacement rate data from the report by Zheng (2016). Compared to government employees and public institution employees, enterprise employees enjoyed far lower pension benefits, considered both in terms of their raw benefit per person per year and the rate of increase. The average benefit per person per year for government employees and public institution employees in 2015 was above 44,000 yuan, while for average enterprise employees it was around 27,000 yuan (or 28,236, in Zheng's calculations) even

Table 2.3: Pension benefit for enterprise employees and others

| | Persons participating at the year end (millions) | | | Revenue and expenses of pension fund (100 million Yuan) | | | | |
	Total	Workers	Retiree	Revenue	Expense	Balance	Benefit p/y (Yuan)	Increase rate
1989	57.10	48.16	8.93	146.7	118.8	68	1,330.1	
1990	61.66	52.00	9.65	178.8	149.3	97.9	1,547	16%
1991	67.40	56.53	10.86	215.7	173.1	144.1	1,592.8	3%
1992	94.56	77.74	16.81	365.8	321.9	220.6	1,914.4	20%
1993	98.47	80.08	18.39	503.5	470.6	258.6	2,558.6	34%
1994	105.73	84.94	20.79	707.4	661.1	304.8	3,179.2	24%
1995	109.79	87.37	22.41	950.1	847.6	429.8	3,781.9	19%
1996	111.16	87.58	23.58	1,171.8	1,031.9	578.6	4,375.5	16%
1997	112.03	86.70	25.33	1,337.9	1,251.3	682.8	4,940.1	13%
1998	112.03	84.75	27.27	1,459	1,511.6	587.8	5,542.6	12%
1999	117.22	88.59	28.63	1,871.9	1,863.1	644.2	6,505.9	17%
2000	124.86	94.69	30.16	2,088.3	1,970	761	6,530.9	0%
2001	129.04	97.33	31.71	2,235.1	2,116.5	818.6	6,674	2%
2002	132.78	99.29	33.49	2,783.6	2,502.8	1,243.5	7,472.8	12%
2003	138.81	103.24	35.56	3,209.4	2,716.2	1,764.8	7,636.4	2%
2004	146.78	109.03	37.75	3,728.5	3,031.2	2,499.3	8,029.7	5%
2005	157.15	117.10	40.05	4,491.7	3,495.3	3,506.7	8,726.9	9%
2006	168.56	126.18	42.38	5,632.5	4,287.3	4,869.1	10,114.9	16%
2007	182.34	136.90	45.44	7,010.6	5,153.6	6,758.2	11,341.5	12%
2008	199.51	150.83	48.68	8,800.1	6,507.6	9,241	13,368.1	18%
2009	215.67	162.19	53.48	10,420.6	7,886.6	11,774.3	14,746.8	10%
2010	236.34	178.22	58.11	12,218.4	9,409.9	14,547.2	16,191.6	10%
2011	262.84	199.70	63.14	15,484.8	11,425.7	18,608.1	18,095.8	12%
2012	282.71	213.60	69.10	18,363	14,008.5	22,968	20,270.1	12%
2013	300.49	225.64	74.84	20,848.7	16,741.5	27,192.3	22,367.3	10%
2014	319.45	239.32	80.13	23,305.4	19,847.2	30,626.3	24,766.9	11%
2015	331.23	245.86	85.36	26,613.2	23,140.9	34,115.2	27,108.2	10%

Data sources: China Labour Statistical Yearbooks; Author.

Figure 2.2: Pension benefit for enterprise employees (averaged), 1995–2015

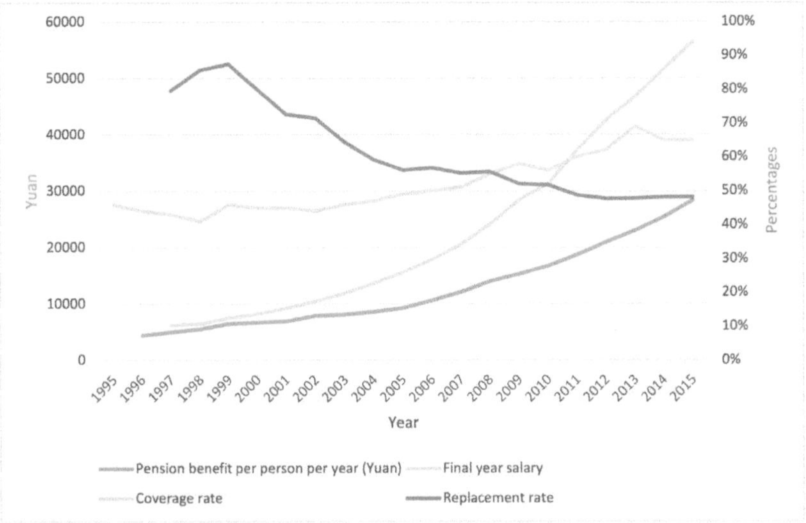

Data source: Zheng (2016).

though their on-duty salary was around 56,000 yuan before retirement. In other words, enterprise employees would have experienced a steeper drop in living standards after retirement. Moreover, although the coverage rate increased after 1997, the replacement rate went in the opposite direction: it dropped from 80% in the late 1990s to 50% in the late 2000s, as Figure 2.2 shows.

The pension plan for urban non-salaried residents (PUR) and rural residents (PRR)

These two pension plans both started quite late on, and involved very limited payments. Table 2.4 shows the pension benefit change for rural residents from Zheng's report in 2016, and demonstrates that their pension scheme had a far lower coverage rate and a low replacement rate. The average (mean) pension benefit per person per year for rural residents was about 1,000 yuan, which is far less than their urban counterparts received (e.g. enterprise employees got 20,270 yuan in 2012 on average). In terms of the value of benefits, the replacement rate in the rural residents' pension scheme was around 13% in 2015, while urban enterprise employees enjoyed a replacement rate of 50% (2015) and government/public institution employees enjoyed 67% (2010, weighted).

To better understand the strategic aspects of benefits differentiation in China, Table 2.5 shows the changing population numbers of the different social groups from 1987 to 2009.[9] Though one cannot point to solid evidence

Table 2.4: Pension benefit for rural residents

	Expense (100 million Yuan)	Recipients (millions)	Benefit p/y (Yuan)	Income per year (Yuan)	Replacement rate
2011	598	87.60	683	6,977.3	9.8%
2012	1,150	130.75	880	7,916.6	11.1%
2013	1,348	137.68	979	8,895.9	11%
2014	1,571	143.13	1,098	9,892	11.1%
2015	2,117	148	1,430	10,772	13.3%

Data source: Zheng (2016).

supporting the hypothesis, a reasonable strategy for a government wanting to reduce its burdens would be to push the largest working population – enterprise employees – towards the open market. And, when a government needs to show generosity and appease discontent over inequality, it could give a modicum of 'alms' to a large but less advantaged population – rural residents – in exchange for more loyalty at relatively low cost. According to my preliminary interviews in summer 2016, many rural residents, especially the older ones, were very content with receiving any subsidy from the government. This was mainly because they had enjoyed few benefits from the state budget beforehand and most of the old people were being cared for by people from their families or the local community. Any cash subsidy from the government seemed like a bonus to them, especially in view of their relatively low income compared to urban employees.

Conclusions

The empirical evidence suggests that the strategy of differentiation in the government's welfare allocation has been to sacrifice the social benefits for employees of state-owned enterprises (SOEs) first, and later on the employees of public institutions, so as to reduce the state's fiscal burden. At the same time, modest or slender welfare benefits were provided for social groups that could be bought off with minimal benefits. During the process, government officials (including the core elites of governance power) consistently enjoyed the most generous social benefits. The various policy shifts of different pension schemes strongly support these propositions, especially the retrenchment policy reform for SOE employees; the expanded coverage for rural residents and migrant workers from rural areas; and the reform of the contribution ratio reform in the pension scheme for public institution employees. The segmented resource allocation in China's social welfare reform has favoured the core elites, while it distributed limited fiscal capacity to the social groups that cost least per person.

Table 2.5: Raw population numbers by type of pension scheme recipient

	Government employees (millions)	Public institution employees (millions)	Enterprise employees (millions)	Permanent rural residents (billions)
1987	8.05	20.32	103.76	8.16
1988	8.43	21.01	106.62	8.23
1989	8.85	21.75	105.64	8.41
1990	9.13	23.01	106.97	8.41
1991				8.46
1992				8.49
1993	9.86	24.26	114.36	8.53
1994	10.43	26.53	115.60	8.56
1995	10.22	27.36	115.42	8.59
1996	10.50	28.23	113.47	8.50
1997	10.62	29.05	110.68	8.41
1998				8.31
1999	10.68	27.92	82.69	8.20
2000	10.73	27.78	77.59	8.08
2001	10.70	27.60	73.34	7.95
2002	10.54	27.23	72.07	7.82
2003	10.71	27.24	71.72	7.68
2004	10.92	27.46	72.60	7.57
2005	10.96	27.93	75.14	7.45
2006	11.11	28.33	77.68	7.31
2007	11.30	28.74	80.19	7.14
2008	11.56	29.14	81.20	7.03
2009	11.83	29.29	84.12	6.89

Data sources: China Labour Statistical Yearbooks; National Statistical Bureau; and author.

Notes

[1] China's 'hukou' system is a family registration programme that serves as a domestic passport, regulating population distribution and rural-to-urban migration. For decades it was a tool for social and geographic control,

enforcing an apartheid structure that denied farmers the rights and benefits that were enjoyed by urban residents.

[2]   A more detailed discussion of the codebook is available in the appendix.

[3]   In China's case, the full state-funded pension is literally called the 'retirement allowance', and a pension that requires individual contributions is called a 'pension/social insurance'.

[4]   *People's Daily Report*, 2012, 'Unfair dual track of old-age care: [dramatically] different treatment for people with different status'.

[5]   *China News*, 2014, 'Track convergence of pension scheme: 30 million public institution employees will start paying into social insurance from July 1st'. https://perma.cc/2MCS-FJ4L [accessed 2018-11-12].

[6]   This pension plan was later applied to employees of all enterprises, regardless of ownership.

[7]   More information on this policy experimentation is available in Chapter 4.

[8]   Owing to a highly scattered and incomplete condition of welfare yearbooks, I tried my best to collect all available data from various sources. There are certain places where the data do not match very well since the statistical bureau stopped publishing many indexes (such as the population and pension benefit for government employees after 2009) and often changed the grouping methods. Thus, I appended notes to each table to clarify the sources and calculations. More information on the codebook is available in the appendix.

[9]   The government stopped publishing the employee number and related conditions of government units and public institution units from 2009.

References

Bray, D. (2005). *Social Space and Governance in Urban China: The Danwei System from Origins to Reform*. Stanford University Press.

Cai, Y.; Feng, W.; and Shen, K. (2018). 'Fiscal implications of population aging and social sector expenditure in China'. *Population and Development Review*, vol. 44, issue 4, 811–831. https://doi.org/10.1111/padr.12206

Chan, K. W.; and Buckingham, W. (2008). 'Is China abolishing the hukou system?' *The China Quarterly*, vol. 195, 582–606. https://doi.org/10.1017/s0305741008000787

Chan, K. W.; and Zhang, L. (1999). 'The hukou system and rural-urban migration in China: Processes and changes'. *The China Quarterly*, vol. 160, 818–855. https://doi.org/10.1017/s0305741000001351

Chao, C.-m.; and Dickson, B. (2003). *Remaking the Chinese State: Strategies, Society, and Security*. Routledge.

Cheng, T.; and Selden, M. (1994). 'The origins and social consequences of China's hukou system'. *The China Quarterly*, vol. 139, 644–668. https://doi.org/10.1017/s0305741000043083

Frazier, M. W. (2010). *Socialist Insecurity: Pensions and the Politics of Uneven Development in China*. USA: Cornell University Press.

Gu, E. X. (1999). 'From permanent employment to massive lay-offs: the political economy of "transitional unemployment" in urban China (1993–8)'. *Economy and Society*, vol. 28, issue 2, 281–299. https://doi.org /10.1080/03085149900000006

Gu, E. X. (2001). 'Dismantling the Chinese mini-welfare state?: Marketization and the politics of institutional transformation, 1979–1999'. *Communist and Post-Communist Studies*, vol. 34, issue 1, 91–111. https://doi.org/10.1016 /s0967-067x(00)00025-8

Hacker, J. S. (2002). *The Divided Welfare State: The Battle over Public and Private Social Benefits in the United States*. Cambridge University Press. https:// doi.org/10.1017%2Fcbo9780511817298

Haggard, S.; and Kaufman, R. R. (2008). *Development, Democracy, and Welfare States: Latin America, East Asia, and Eastern Europe*. Princeton University Press.

Huang, X. (2014). *Social Protection under Authoritarianism: Politics and Policy of Social Health Insurance in China*. Columbia University.

Karshenas, M.; and Moghadam, V. M. (2006). *Social Policy in the Middle East: Economic, Political and Gender Dynamics*. UK: Palgrave Macmillan.

Lee, M.-k. (2000). *Chinese Occupational Welfare in Market Transition*. Springer. https://doi.org/10.1057/9780333982549

Lu, X.; and Perry, E. J. (1997). *Danwei: The Changing Chinese Workplace in Historical and Comparative Perspective*. Me Sharpe.

Pozen, R. C. (2013). *Tackling the Chinese Pension System*. USA: Paulson Institute.

Ratigan, K. (2017). 'Disaggregating the developing welfare state: Provincial social policy regimes in China'. *World Development*, vol. 98, 467–484. https://doi.org/10.1016/j.worlddev.2017.05.010

Riedmüller, B. (2008). *Private Pensions Versus Social Inclusion?: Non-state Provision for Citizens at Risk in Europe*. Edward Elgar Publishing.

Rimlinger, G. V. (1971). *Welfare Policy and Industrialization in Europe, America and Russia*. USA: Wiley.

Selden, M.; and You, L. (1997). 'The reform of social welfare in China'. *World Development*, vol. 25, issue 10, 1657–1668. https://doi.org/10.1016/s0305-750x (97)00055-7

Song, Y. (2014). 'What should economists know about the current Chinese hukou system?' *China Economic Review*, vol. 29, 200–212. https://doi.org /10.1016/j.chieco.2014.04.012

State Council. (1997). *Decision on Establishing a Unified System of Basic Pension Insurance for Enterprise Employees (State Council [1997] No.26)*. Retrieved from http://www.gov.cn/ztzl/nmg/content_412509.htm.

State Council. (2000b). *The Notice of Issuing the Pilot Program of Urban Social Security System (State Council [2000] No.42)*. Retrieved from http://www .gov.cn/xxgk/pub/govpublic/mrlm/201011/t20101112_62507.html.

State Council. (2005). *Decision on Perfecting Basic System of Pension Insurance for Enterprise Employees (State Council [2005] No.38)*. Retrieved from http://www.gov.cn/zwgk/2005-12/14/content_127311.htm.

State Council. (2009). *New Rural Old-age Social Insurance Plan (State Council [2009] No. 32)* Retrieved from http://www.gov.cn/zwgk/2009-09/04/content_1409216.htm.

Wang, D.; and Chai, Y. (2009). 'The jobs–housing relationship and commuting in Beijing, China: the legacy of danwei'. *Journal of Transport Geography*, vol. 17, issue 1, 30–38. https://doi.org/10.1016/j.jtrangeo.2008.04.005

Wang, L.; Béland, D.; and Zhang, S. (2014). 'Pension fairness in China'. *China Economic Review*, vol. 28, 25–36. https://doi.org/10.1016/j.chieco .2013.11.003

Whyte, M. K. (2012). 'China's post-socialist inequality'. *Current History*, vol. 111, issue 746, 229–234. https://doi.org/10.1525/curh.2012.111.746.229. OA: https://online.ucpress.edu/currenthistory/article-pdf/111/746/229/392449 /curh_111_746_229.pdf

Xie, Y.; Lai, Q.; and Wu, X. (2009). 'Danwei and social inequality in contemporary urban China'. *Research in the Sociology of Work*, vol. 19, 283. https://dx .doi.org/10.1108%2FS0277-2833(2009)0000019013. OA: https://www.ncbi .nlm.nih.gov/pmc/articles/PMC2828673

Zheng, G. (2016). *Evaluation of China's Social Protection Policies*. Retrieved from https://www.euchinasprp.eu/images/documents/Component1Cn/2017 -assessment-eport/EvalSSCn.pdf

Zheng, Q. (2015). *Identity Acceptance and Production Politics: Research on Labour Relations in Changes of State-Owned Enterprises*. China: Beijing Book Co.

CHAPTER 3

Who deserves benefits and why – constructing fairness, pension expectations, and subjectivity

What kind of truth and knowledge about pension benefits is produced and promoted by the Chinese state when it tries to persuade the public about the many policy experiments and reforms of recent times? The question is complicated by an underlying epistemological assumption here, that what we know about society is never entirely consistent between individuals or uniform over time. Sociologists have long discussed the process of 'socialisation' during which every individual gradually internalises norms and ideologies about society. The state is among the major powers that provide inputs for the socialisation process. It is equipped with various tools to intervene in political socialisation, such as education, the public media, and legal systems (Glasberg and Shannon 2010). Using them the state can produce certain truths and knowledge that shape the way that people understand their society and where they can expect to fit within the social 'blueprint'.

While accomplishing considerable socio-economic transitions, the state cannot simply cut benefits to a certain group of people in order to minimise the budget or ease its burden. The government needs to keep a minimal degree of public consent for its own survival and stability, employing additional tactics to help promote major institutional changes that hurt someone's existing interests (as almost all pension reforms will do, and certainly in China). Institutionalism generally supposes that the state has a sophisticated understanding of its subordinate population (though it is not necessarily 100% correct), and uses this knowledge to try to figure out the optimal or proper ways to manage changes in public compliance. The state, therefore, can decide to manipulate people's emotions through shaping, sculpting, and mobilising the options, expectations, and daily lives of individuals. Government and governance not only signal the

---

How to cite this book chapter:
Wang, Yan. 2022. *Pension Policy and Governmentality in China: Manufacturing Public Compliance*. London: LSE Press, pp. 49–90.
DOI: https://doi.org/10.31389/lsepress.ppc.d. License: CC BY

power relationship but also provide versions of 'selves' and identities to its population (Dean 2010). The process and the rationale of designing/shaping people's ideas and behaviour can be drawn from the *conduct of conduct* in Foucault's theory of state power (Foucault, Davidson, and Burchell 2008). Hence, an analysis of the various tactics used by the state to shape public cognition can dig deeper by asking such questions as 'what does the state want the public to expect?' and 'what identities and roles have been established for the governed and the governors?' In practice, there are many objects that the authority can borrow in its framing or discourse: for instance, ideologies of materialism and rationalism, doctrines from traditional culture or religion, experiences from comparable countries, and so on. The follow-up question that is worth asking is 'when are these elements being employed and what kind of "structures of incentives" are being promoted in these narratives?'

In *The Political Sociology of the Welfare State* (2007), Stefan Svallfors argues that one aspect of the welfare state is to embody and create norms about what is fair and just, and to form citizens' expectations and demands. More importantly, his discussion stresses that the interaction between the state and its subordinates is dynamic, which pushes the governance into a reflective and experimental process. On the one hand, the correspondence between institutions, rules, and policies provides a stable imagination of the state–individual relationship in the delivery of welfare. On the other hand, however, if the imagination of individuals about what to expect and what to demand is deep-rooted, any changes to the value and policies promoted by the state may cause a legitimation problem. The state therefore needs to make a new effort to try to rebalance the relationship and reproduce the corresponding knowledge.

To explore these large themes empirically and in methodologically reliable ways I turn to the powerful tools provided by quantitative text analysis, which are introduced in the next section. The second section shows in detail how pension reforms were an instrument for the state's achieving its wider socio-economic reforms. Section 3.3 looks at how the state also sought to construct and reshape concepts of fairness and deservingness in the redistribution of pension benefits. The chapter concludes by examining 'the socialised self', which was used to renew how the state's relation to individuals was now to be understood.

3.1 Text analysis of state discourses

Through an examination of official discourse about the desired rules, norms, and social values, it is possible to capture the state authority's changing governmentality. The implications of the theoretical discussions in Chapters 1 and 2 for a detailed exploration of China's case is to be aware of the hidden design of the policies that are issued, and to be sensitive to the changes in the discourse. Accordingly, I collected text data from thousands of relevant articles in official newspapers to figure out the ways that the state legitimised and promoted its social policies. The rich text in these collections provides vivid evidence of the government's strategic employment of language, concepts, and sentiments. By classifying topics and estimating category percentages with quantitative text analysis (QTA) (Grimmer and Stewart 2013), I was able to identify the kind of messages being sent out through the descriptions of the policies. For instance, are collectivist discourses more frequently used in promoting a policy that expands the coverage of pension benefits? Are more individualist discourses used when issuing a retrenchment-oriented policy? In addition, to better understand the techniques of persuasion, I identified what is 'praised' and 'denounced' in the policies promoted by the state, analysing how sentiment in the official discourses tends to one polar position or another.

To capture the details in the official discourse in a precisely measured way (and constrained by the availability of other data in China), my analysis focuses mainly on two sets of pension reforms. The first set concerns enterprise employees in the late 1990s and early 2000s. There were several waves of pension experiments for enterprise employees, all closely connected with the economic reform of the state-owned enterprises and reallocation of state–individual responsibility for care in old age. The state had to persuade the enterprise employees that there was good reason to take care of pensions themselves, and tell them what they should expect from the state. The second set of pension reforms centred on rural residents in the early 1990s (as pilot projects in local regions) and was mainly used to help promote the one-child policy, while the other nationwide reform in the late 2000s was part of the process of rapid urbanisation. For these reforms, the state needed to show the public why rural residents deserved to receive expanded pension benefits.

The text data analysed include official news data mostly from the *People's Daily* dataset, where the original text is in Chinese (and hence all the translations and quotes later in the chapter are mine). I also used supplementary data from the China Knowledge Resource Integrated Database (CNKI database) and the Wisenews dataset. The *People's Daily* is the official newspaper and mouthpiece of the Central Committee of the Communist Party of China and the biggest newspaper group in China, with a circulation of 3 million. It functions as the weathercock of current Chinese political, social, and economic trends, delivering information to the public from the central government. It publishes the Party's main policies, the leader's activities, and journalistic reports, and (in addition) editorial comments, readers' mail, scholars' theoretical discussions, and so on. It differs from the rigid contents of the official policy statements issued, because the media can elaborate more on the policy design, targets, and details in various styles, whereas the policies themselves are mostly published or issued in a particular restrictive format. Analysing the text in the *People's Daily* is one of the best ways of decoding the policy direction and 'top-level design' in China. Since the original *People's Daily* dataset contains only the articles published from 1946 to 2003, I supplemented the original dataset with news data from the CNKI and Wisenews datasets. The consolidated dataset of

People's Daily articles covers the time period from 1946 to 2008. To fit the plan of analysing the two sets of pension reforms, I generated the analytical data by searching with the keywords 'old-age insurance' and 'pension' while confining the time period to 1978–2008, resulting in 3,390 articles with these keywords in the context. Full descriptive statistics for the corpus and more discussions about the potential restrictions on topic analysis posed by the specific sample pool can be found in section A3 of Appendix A.

Analysing text content with computer assistance has been popular among researchers in the past few years, especially when automated text analysis is used in text mining (Grimmer and Stewart 2013; Hopkins and King 2010; Lucas et al. 2015). Unlike traditional hand coding and dictionary methods, which are mainly based on the frequencies of selected keywords, supervised and unsupervised automated text analysis extracts richer information from the content. Moreover, some new methods can provide more choices for researchers who want to validate the categorisation of text and integrate information with documents' metadata, such as dates, column types, authors, and even the length of documents.

I used a combination of inductive and deductive approach in addressing the topics, key classifications, and elements of knowledge construction in the documents. An unsupervised method helps with the identification of topics discussed in the articles, as well as the relationship within topics, without imposing too much by way of pre-assumptions. The descriptive information from the topic identification process yields rich data on the priorities of government's efforts on policy promotion in various periods and circumstances during the pension reforms. It also reveals the latent structure of knowledge that has been employed in state news outputs. Using supervised methods takes advantage of the current literature and my understanding of the text to classify the documents into various key categories. Combined with the metadata for the articles, it provides further information on the elements used by the government to construct people's knowledge about the reforms in specific stages. In the analysis part, I integrated the topics with the categories to make further investigations about the features of official discourse.

Unsupervised text mining allows researchers to explore the topics in the whole meta-text data without much *ex ante* classification. The structural topic model (STM) uses mixed-membership topic models and is able to incorporate contextual covariates (i.e. document-specific metadata) in the prior distribution. This is suitable for long texts: each document is assumed to present a mixture of topics, each topic is represented by many words, and each word therefore has a certain probability of belonging to certain topics. With STM, metadata such as dates and sentiments can be included in the topic model through either topical prevalence or topical content. The former approach allows us to identify the way that the metadata affect the frequency with which a topic is discussed, while the latter allows the observed metadata to affect the rate of word use within a given topic – that is, how a particular topic is discussed (Roberts, Stewart, and Tingley 2014).

For their part, supervised learning methods require researchers to read and code some training documents in advance, and then use certain algorithms to accomplish the categorisation of the remaining documents. This approach is useful for analysing the text more precisely with the classifiers designed by the researcher to address particular research interests. In this section, I used results from the support vector machines classifier, as well as the human coded results from the sampled corpus to support my analysis. The original training and test set was generated by randomly selected a sample of 400 documents. Then the documents were manually categorised into the categories of 'locus of responsibility', 'praise', 'denounce', 'national conditions', and 'international experience'. The 'locus of responsibility' included five responsibility allocations regarding care for the elderly (covering pension payments, daily social care, and so on), which are: 'no clear direction of locus', 'state/party', 'individual/family', 'enterprise', and 'social coordination'. (A flowchart of coding rule for category 'locus of responsibility' is provided in Appendix A, Section A3.) 'Praise' and 'denounce' refer to the tone of the document. Then 'national conditions' and 'international experiences' refer to the main highlights in the document – whether the whole document emphasised the local situation in China and Chinese characteristics, or experiences from other countries. With the hand-coded data, the classifiers followed up and classified the remaining documents with specific rules. A complete comparison of the performance metrics of various classifiers is available in Appendix A, and the original code can be found in the replication files (available upon request).

To prepare the data, I used SegwordCN in the 'tmcn' package (J. Li 2019) (and validated the text pre-processing with the 'JiebaR' package) to carry out the word segmentation. I then turned the words into a word corpus after cleaning the punctuation, stop words, and blank spaces. For details of the dictionaries used, see Appendix A3. The first step in inspecting the data is to figure out the themes in the metadata using the unsupervised text mining method. The topic model presents the probability distribution of terms in the corpus, and can assess the similarity of documents; it is therefore suitable for describing a text collection. Since all the documents are connected to cover pension benefits in one way or another, I used a mixed-membership model in order to include as much information as possible from the corpus. In this case, the documents were not assumed to belong to single topics, but simultaneously to form part of several topics, with the distribution varying across documents.

As with all mixed-membership topic models, the estimation of topics and correlations depends on the starting values of the parameters, such as the distribution of words for a particular topic. In the following analysis, I employ spectral initialisation which uses a spectral decomposition (non-negative matrix factorisation) of the word co-occurrence matrix, and is deterministic and globally consistent under reasonable conditions (Roberts, Stewart, and Tingley 2016).

With the help of the STM package (in which Latent Dirichlet Allocation is also the default option), I generated topics setting the topic number K=30 and

60, respectively (validation of the optimal K number can be found in Appendix A3). I also used the 'topicmodel' package (Grün, Hornik, and Grün 2018) to validate the generated topic; the main identified topics are similar, as further validated in the appendix. I estimated with spectral initialisation and topical prevalence the parameter 'year_month' (time when the article was published). Topical prevalence captures how much each topic contributes to a document (Roberts, Stewart, and Tingley 2014) and this prevalence varies with the metadata. The results present the highest-probability words, FREX (frequent and exclusive) words, lift weighted words, and score words. Weighted words are identified by their overall frequency and how exclusive they are to the topic. Lift weighted words are generated by dividing the frequency of the words in other topics, thus giving greater weight to words that appear less frequently in other topics. Score words come from dividing the log frequency of the word in the topic by the log frequency of the word in other topics (Roberts, Stewart, and Tingley 2014).

Most of the topics are meaningful and easy to interpret, such as those related to economic development, including such core words as development (发展), increase/growth (增长), income (收入), consumptions (消费), production (生产); and those related to the reform of state-owned enterprises and laid-off workers, including core words such as employment (就业), labour (劳动), enterprise employees (职工), work unit (单位), insurance (保险), lay-off (下岗), etc. There are some junk topics that are meaningless or have no relationship with pension reform. Their bias is tolerable in my analysis since 1) it would only increase the probability of identified topics if there are no junk topics; 2) my analysis is built on my own thorough reading of the full corpus, which allows me to identify the same meaningful topics as human coders. Moreover, I provide a full list of topics from the unsupervised models in Appendix A, with validations of the different word segmentation and preprocessing processes and of K settings. The selection of topics in Table 3.1 is mainly the most meaningful topics that relate to pension reform and old-age care setting K=30. In labelling them, I focus on the main issues addressed from the topic descriptions, and label them use the most intuitive and informative words.

To better understand the relations of these topics, in Figure 3.1 I present the topic correlations (with K=30 in order to have a manageable graph) using a force-directed layout algorithm. Positive correlation suggests that both topics are likely to be discussed within a given document. The distance (or position in the graph) does not mean a high or low degree of topic connection, nor does the size of the circle. From the correlation graph, we can identify a cluster of Topics 4 (SOE Reform), 20 (Economic Reform), and 23 (Institution Reform. Topic 4 refers to the reform of state-owned enterprises, while Topics 20 and 23 concern economic reform, marketisation, and redistribution). Another clear cluster involves Topics 9 (Laid-Off Workers), 19 (Enterprise Employee or EE Pension Plan), and 29 (Retired/Pension Fee). Topics 9 and 19 relate respectively to the theme of enterprise employees' layoff and their pension plan, while

Table 3.1: Selected topics with keywords explanations

Topic 4 'SOE Reform' top words:	Topic 9 'Laid-Off Workers' top words:
Highest probability: enterprise, reform, state-owned, market, economy, operation, management FREX: state-owned, amalgamation, shares, transfer, bankrupt, enterprise, assets Lift: final fight, bad debt, strategy Score: enterprise, state-owned, reform, market, operation, assets, amalgamation	Highest probability: employment, employee, laid off, enterprise, labour, insurance, staff FREX: laid off, employment, unemployment, Liaoning, assure, positions, difficult Lift: apathetic, bureaus, bring Score: employment, laid off, employee, unemployment, state-owned, enterprise, insurance (protection)
Topic 20 'Economic Reform' top words: Highest probability: economy, development, reform, market, society (social), job, state FREX: macro, control, current, price, rectify Lift: international market demand, victory, soft landing, signs, Keqiang, braveness, nothingness Score: economy, macro, reform, currency, finance, development, market	**Topic 19 'EE Pension Plan' top words:** Highest probability: insurance, elder-care (social security), social (society), enterprise, protection, employees, fees FREX: elder-care (social security), pay, insurance, trust, participate, social coordination, account Lift: rest of the life, transgression, account division, current, employed Score: insurance, elder-care (social security), pay, employee, society (social), protection, enterprise
Topic 23 'Institution Reform' top words: Highest probability: society (social), development, protection, institution(system), economy, reform, construction FREX: harmony, distribution, public, society (social), institution (system), ideology, fairness Lift: missing parts, variables, overstep, should Score: society (social), protection, institution(system), reform, economy, ideology, market, harmony	**Topic 29 'Retired/Pension Fee' top words:** Highest probability: retire, employee, yuan, fees, salary, enterprise FREX: factory director, factory, own, working years, surrender insurance, retire Lift: rumours Score: retirement, factory, employee, yuan, salary, fee, pension
Topic 16 'Birth Control' top words: Highest probability: reproduction, plan, population, giving birth, work, women, development FREX: reproduction, women, plan, female, population, couple Lift: still, early marriage, boys, contraception, pregnancy, as low as Score: reproduction, population, women, plan, contraception, couple, giving birth	**Topic 5 'Old-age Care' top words:** Highest probability: old, old people, society (social), disabled, elderly care, age, service FREX: old people, disabled, old age, care, recover Lift: few children Score: old people, old age, disabled, age, old, home-based, care

(Continued)

Table 3.1: (Continued)

Topic 25 'Rural Migrants' top words:	Topic 2 'Commercial Insurance' top words:
Highest probability: peasant, rural area, worker, urban-rural, agriculture, city	Highest probability: insurance, company, invest, bank, market, China
FREX: peasant, lose land, urban-rural, land, migrant, city	FREX: client, life, annuity, life insurance, company, business
Lift: Dujiangyan, deep water, whole scale, Pujiang, Xinyang	Lift: be clever, actuary, collusion
Score: peasant, rural area, urban-rural, lose land, agriculture, worker, rural	Score: insurance, life insurance, company, life, annuity, client, bank

Notes: Some Chinese words have several meanings or act as several parts of speech (PoS); I include word extensions inside brackets. 'Dujiangyan', 'Pujiang', and 'Xinyang' are all the names of places.

Topic 29 mainly addresses pension fees. There are some other clusters or topics that do not seem directly related to the pension reform. For instance, Topic 30 (Letter/Visits) addresses the theme of appeals, issues and the government. Topic 15 (State Budget) discusses fiscal problems, the budget, and expenditure. Topic 7 (Community Care) covers key words such as people, difficulty, life, disability, warm, street-level administration, and so on.

To give specific examples of relevant discourse (all of which I have translated), I selected some excerpts that best describe the feature of certain topics, based on my understanding of the full corpus (with a full reading of the whole sample text) and the instruction of the key topics (with unsupervised models). The isolated Commercial Insurance (Topic 2) in the figure addresses the promotion of purchased rights to cover social risks. In relevant documents here the social risks for each individual are treated as capital, are calculable, and are avoidable once complete preparations have been made. A selected letter to the newspaper editor from a former worker read:

> Dear Editor: Both my partner and I have retained our posts in our original work unit while [our] salary payment has been suspended. We have started a small private business since our 'iron rice bowl' has disappeared. Therefore, we have quite a strong sense of (potential) risks and want to invest in some basic insurance to avoid future problems. I know there are several insurance companies and many kinds of insurance. Can you tell me what I should pay attention to when choosing insurance? ('What we should pay attention to when choosing personal insurance', Reader's letter, 1997-05-28)

The editor replied with a long discussion of the difference between various types of commercial insurance, addressed from the angle that people who make plans for their own and care about preparing for risks in life (especially those who have been laid off due to the SOE reform) should be warmly

Figure 3.1: Correlations of topics

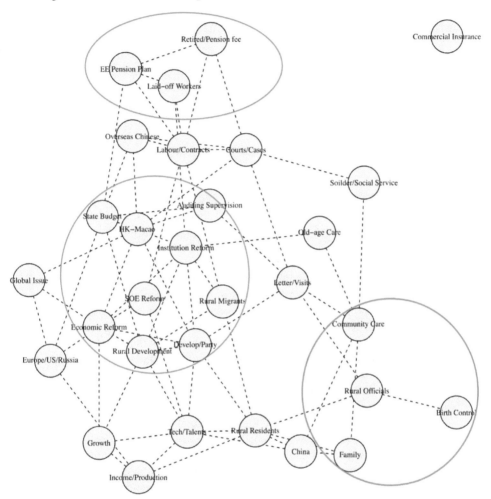

Notes: Each topic in the figure is labelled with one or two key words for easier
identification, but note that each topic contains far more complicated information than these labels.

encouraged. In another document, 'commercial insurance' is identified as the
stabiliser of society:

> The social attributes of commercial insurance make it capable of adding
> up to and supplementing the government's social insurance scheme. (Its
> existence) is good for reducing people's anxieties and it functions as 'the
> stabilizer of the society'. ('Bring out the role of commercial insurance as
> "the stabilizer of society"', Zeng Yujin, 2004-09-18)

Another special topic not directly related to either cluster 4–20–23 or cluster 9–19–29 but worth highlighting here is Topic 16 (Birth Control). This refers to the 'one-child policy' and birth control, correlating with Topic 8, which covers the keywords rural officials, village, and towns. It also correlates distantly with Topic 5 (Old-Age Care), which addresses the social group of elderly people through Topic 7 (Community Care). To see why these topics show up here, I move on in the next section to discuss how social welfare policies were used as instruments of other contemporary major reforms.

3.2 Pension reforms as instruments of broader socio-economic reforms

Policies and their promotions are never isolated or arbitrary; they are proposed and framed in a way that is consistent with their socio-economic conditions. In particular, welfare policy is not just concerned with the allocation of social benefits but also extends to employment policy, tax policy, and demographic policy. After sorting out the content and correlations of the core topics, it is important to connect the topics and their longitudinal variations with the major socio-economic reforms initiated by the government. The interaction or dialogue between welfare policies and other policies at the same time shows the comprehensive and sophisticated design of governance being used. It also shows how the details of a welfare policy are shaped by their social and economic circumstances, looking at eligibility standards and subsidy methods. My chief objects in the text analysis are urban enterprise employees (especially SOE employees), and rural residents, key groups for reasons set out in Section 3.1. Thus, in this section I explore the way that pension reforms interact with the other reforms imposed on these two social groups.

To situate the text analysis, it is worth recapping a little on Figure 2.1 (showing the chronological schedule of pension reforms). The 'Decisions on Economic Reform' were issued in 1984 and the 'Enterprise Bankruptcy Law' was promulgated in 1986. In 1993, the 'Decisions on Constructing [a] Socialist Market Economy' accelerated the process of economic reform following Deng's visit to southern China. SOEs formed the backbone of China's economy during the central planning era, so their transformation was the most prominent of the changes in China's enterprise system made in tandem with other institutional and policy reforms (Garnaut, Song, and Fang 2018). The marketisation of the SOEs was followed by the laying-off of millions of workers. The official total of redundancies increased from 3 million in 1993 to 17.24 million in 1998 (Cai 2002; Jefferson and Rawski 1994). The numbers of laid-off workers brought challenges to social stability and pressure towards pension reform. According to the OECD's report, the unemployment rate in urban areas increased from 7.6% to 12.7% between 1995 and 2001 (OECD 2005). Thus, the government needed to persuade people of the need for the reform and tell them what the employees of enterprises (SOEs in particular) should expect in future in social benefits from the government.

In addition to the reforms of the state-owned enterprises, the emergence and exponential growth of private enterprises following the economic reform also brought challenges to the existing pension system for enterprise employees. In 2003, private firms (about 3 million domestic private enterprises and 24 million sole proprietorships) comprised 59% of the economy (OECD 2005). Their employees were not covered in the traditional socialist pension system, and the central government was unlikely to provide 'cradle to grave' social protection, as in the old system. Therefore, the authority needed to push for the acceptance of a new welfare system for employees of enterprises (whatever their ownership), one where individuals shared the responsibility for pensions.

Figure 3.2 presents the change of expected topic proportions in the text analysis for the themes of economic reform (Topic 20), SOE reform (Topic 4), pension reform (Topic 19), and laid-off workers (Topic 9). I also highlight the critical events during the reform. The green dashed vertical lines here show the dates of critical events for the economic reforms – specifically, 'Decisions on Economic Reform' (1984), 'Enterprise Bankruptcy Law' (1986), and 'Decisions on Constructing [a] Socialist Market Economy' (1993). The blue dashed vertical lines show the dates of critical events for the pension reforms of enterprise employees – namely, 'Decision on Pension Insurance Reform' (1991), 'Basic Pension Insurance Scheme' (1997), the pilot programme of fully funded individual accounts for the reform of pensions for enterprise employees (issued in 2000), and 'Improving the Basic Pension System' (2005).

The first chart in Figure 3.2 shows the changing trend of topics to do with both the SOE reform, marketisation and the reform of pensions for enterprise employees. The incidence increased in the 1980s and reached a high point in the early 1990s. By contrast, the topic of macro economy growth (shown in the second chart) did not show strong fluctuations in its topic proportions. A reasonable understanding is that the documents are mainly about pensions, and the issues of macro economy growth have relatively weak presence here. The topic of institutional change in enterprise pension reform (shown in the third chart) has a similar pattern of responding to the key events of pension reforms. In sharp contrast, the issue of laid-off workers (shown in the fourth chart of Figure 3.2) was not highlighted until 1997, when the lines on the chart shot up, at a late stage of the marketisation and the pension reform for enterprise employees after 1993. How does the content of these topics dialogue with and echo each other? In the following section, I consider some typical examples of each topic, then discuss the governance logic behind the discourse usage.

The economic reform itself was described by the state as a desired future for everyone in Chinese society. Topic 20 (Economic Reform) refers to the macro of economic growth and emphasised the urgency of the 'overall situation' in

Figure 3.2: Topic proportions by year: economic reform and pension reform for enterprise employees

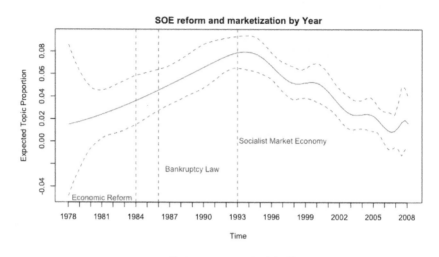

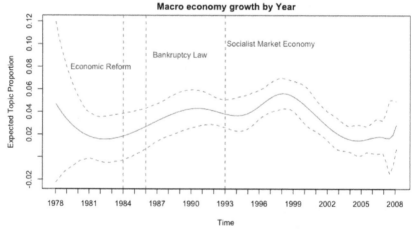

Figure 3.2: (Continued)

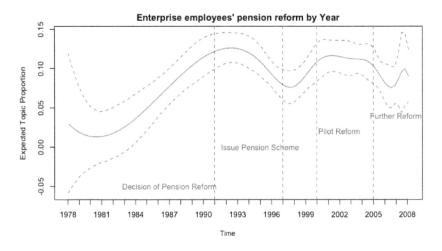

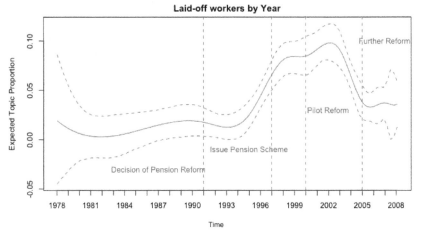

current society in terms of development, social stability, and long-term vision. For instance, a 2003 article argued:

> Dealing with the relations between reform, development, and stability correctly, and resolving the important issues during the process, are crucial for the progress of socialism with Chinese characteristics, in order to attain the goal of building a society prosperous in every sense, for the long-term advancement of all kinds of socio-economic affairs. ('Making the effort to resolve the crucial questions of the overall situation', Shi Zhongxin, 2003-09-04)

As a main component of economic reform, the reform of the SOEs was described as the most efficient and effective way of achieving a 'prosperous society'. From the texts within Topic 4 (SOE Reform and Marketisation), the main points of promoting the efficiency of the reformed SOEs was tied up with economic performance and statistics. For instance, in a passage of the text introducing an example model of SOE reform, the discourse read:

> When we liberate the small SOEs we cannot use a unified mode of 'one size fits all', or just leave them on their own. Here is a summary of the Xinle city's practices for liberating small SOEs. The reform started in the second half of 1992, when the debt-asset ratio of eight branches of SOEs (including industry, light industry, and retailing, etc.) was close to 100%, and the scale of loss was about 63%. The nation's fiscal capacity was almost exhausted. Three years after the liberalisation of the small SOEs, the profits and taxes from the SOEs had increased dramatically. [This precedes a long statistical justification] ('Using multiple strategies, coordinating the government and enterprises, Xinle's reform for small SOEs is alive and stable', Wang Qingxian, 1996-07-18)

Along with the SOE reform, an important task of the pension reform was to help the state and enterprises ease the burden of funding employees' pensions. As the state started to reform for enterprise employees in the early 1990s, official discourse warmly commended the necessity and importance of this reform:

> The decision from the State Council pointed out that the reform of the enterprise employees' pension insurance system was an important move protecting the lives of retirees and maintaining social stability. It's also very important for reducing the burden on the state and on enterprises, advancing the reform of the economic system, and guiding domestic consumption in a rational way. This work [of reform] is highly policy-centred and will affect many aspects of socio-political life. All levels of government need to enforce leadership, follow the spirit of this decision, design concrete implementation plans based on the local situation and promote the reform in positive and steady ways. ('The State Council

made the decision to reform the pension insurance system for enterprise employees; [we will] gradually construct a system which combines basic pension insurance, enterprise-supplemented insurance and employees' personal savings', 1991-10-10)

And, in a summary text about welfare reform, the difference between the desired new hybrid welfare system (with shared responsibilities) and the unwanted old system (social protection based on the work unit) was stated as a welcome change that fitted the overall trend of the social and economic reforms:

> The old system, unit-based, fully covered, exclusive and inefficient, in which the state takes full responsibility, has been replaced with a new multilayered system of shared responsibility, socialised basic protection and inclusive schemes. A new welfare system which fits the requirements of a socialist market economy is now built. ('The new opportunity for deepening the social welfare reform brought about by the advent of WTO membership', Zhang Yitian, 2002-03-23)

The SOE reform left many employees either experiencing being laid off or facing the risk of becoming unemployed. High levels of unemployment can pose many risks to social stability. In response, the central government proposed a 'social security system with Chinese characteristics' based on 'three security lines' (2002):

- a basic guaranteed living system for those no longer working in an SOE, intended to safeguard basic living standards, pay social insurance contributions, and encourage re-employment;
- an unemployment insurance system, which provides unemployment benefits and actively encourages re-employment; and
- guaranteed minimum living standards for all urban residents whose family income per capita is lower than the prescribed level (Chan and Buckingham 2008).

In the official discourse addressed to laid-off workers, the government drew attention not only to the importance and correctness of the reform but also to the point that the government would never abandon this group of people, but still encouraged them to make a new life, if they could.

> [In a visit to Liaoning] Zhu Rongji [then premier] pointed out that the policies of 'encouraging amalgamation, regulating bankruptcy, redirecting laid-off workers, cutting jobs and boosting efficiency, [and] implementing a re-employment scheme', and of constructing basic protection for the SOEs' laid-off workers, pension insurance and unemployment insurance, secure minimum living standards, and so on, have shown themselves to be absolutely correct. These policies play an important

part in deepening the reform of the SOEs, advancing the adjustment of the institutions, and maintaining social stability. Hence, they should be carried out comprehensively. The path of pension reform in Liaoning is absolutely correct and we should persevere unwaveringly. ('Zhu Rongji emphasised during his visit to Liaoning, that [we] need to pursue to the end the path of pension reform and use our best efforts to improve the state of employment and re-employment', Liu Siyang, Meng Huan, 2002-07-25)

All these discourses refer either to economic efficiency, the national interest, and well-being for everyone, or simply to the competence of the government, serving the intention of carrying out economic reform while preserving social stability.

Another good example of social policy as an instrument of reform is the changes made in the rural pension plan, which was not as well designed or widely implemented as the pension reform for employees of urban enterprises. As the discussion of differentiation in Chapter 2 showed, this plan started as a policy piloted in scattered local regions in the late 1980s and early 1990s, initiated and promoted by local governments. The central government at this stage only acted as cheerleader. The text analysis identified that Topic 16 (Birth Control) was related to the rural pension scheme. To see why this was, consider a typical example of the text promoting the rural pension policy but connected to the one-child policy:

The priority of controlling birth is in rural areas, which is also one of the most difficult work [in one-child policy implementation]. But Zhejiang's practice tells us that the difficulties can be overcome. Recently we investigated 100 households in 50 villages from 10 counties in the company of officials from the Zhejiang Birth Control Association. Our experience made us feel that their work here has made renewed progress ... The way that this progress was made benefited from several skills. First of all, they promoted the birth control policy in every household. The association members paid many visits to households, bringing educational materials specifically designed to combat the difficulties in each of them, combining reasons of different kinds and clarifying misunderstandings with detailed information. For instance, the chair of the birth control association from Hengdu village, Anji County, visited all the villagers and helped them to calculate possible future expenses like this: parents who already have a girl must, if they have a second child who is a boy, pay at least 150,000 yuan when he marries and at least 200,000 yuan for his education. But if the household participates in the pension insurance programme they need to pay less than 30,000 yuan in order to receive a pension of 800 yuan when they get old [60 for males, 55 for females]. This calculation totally persuaded the villagers. Many couples of childbearing age said that, even if their first child was a girl, they wouldn't try to have a second child. ('Birth control birth while enjoying a pension is a good idea', Zhao Xiangru, 1988-12-17)

Thus, pension benefits are being presented here as an exchange for the willingness of rural residents to practise birth control. Another example reads as follows:

> Currently more than 800 counties have started to pilot the pension insurance system, and about 7 million [people] are participating. Peasants are thrilled and praise the pension insurance scheme, saying 'The party and the government have given us a dutiful son', '[it] is a nursing home without fences'. ('Our social welfare is going ahead vigorously', Chen Hong, 1992-10-06)

The one-child policy was introduced in 1979, modified in the mid-1980s to relax regulations in rural areas (Scharping 2013), and finally replaced by a 'second child' policy that encouraged couples to have more children at the end of 2015. In order to promote the policy, the government from the 1980s allocated five yuan per month to families with only one child (the amount gradually increasing in step with the economic development). It also gave these households a 'one-child glory certificate', with which the parents could enjoy longer maternity leave, subsidised social insurance, and so on. The one-child limit was most strictly enforced in densely populated urban areas, where the government found it easier to grant benefits and impose punishments (such as heavy fines or mandatory contraception) through the citizens' work units.

The situation in rural areas was more difficult to manage. For rural residents, one extra child meant a bigger labour force on a smallholding or farm, and the government had no way of enforcing punishment on all who 'deserved' it. Thus, rural residents were now allowed to have two children, especially those whose first child was a girl (so long as they waited for some years after her birth). Since it was difficult to enforce birth control among rural citizens, the government had to use other means such as subsidies and praise. Social policy hereby was effectively used to encourage birth control and safeguard gender balance. (China has a long-term problem in families preferring to have boys rather than girls, causing significantly more men than women in the population.) Figure 3.3 presents the chronological changes in the expected topic proportions for Topic 16 (Birth Control), which was high from the early 1980s, dropped in the mid-1980s and increased again in the early 1990s. However, since the 1990s the overall trend has declined.

The interactions between pension reforms and their parallel social and economic policies, and the ways in which the pension reforms were used as instruments for other reforms, demonstrate that the state authority's governance in China is dynamic, reflective, and experimental. The increased proportion of references to pension reform for enterprise employees when the policy was being introduced, plus the later steep rise in attention to the laid-off workers,

Figure 3.3: Topic proportions by year: birth control

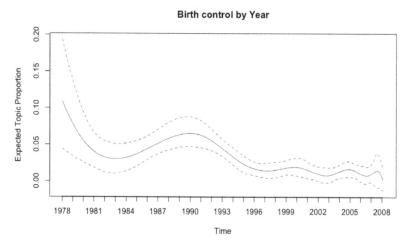

clearly shows the government's anticipation of potential problems from the economic reforms and the SOE reform. The promotion of birth control, and the pension plan (albeit in a scattered pilot form) for rural residents (especially parents who already had a daughter) also functioned effectively to buy greater willingness by households to comply with demographic controls.

3.3 Reconstructing fairness and deservingness in welfare redistribution

Given the topics discussed in the pension-related news articles, what are the elements being employed and notions been promoted by the state in its official discourse relating to the key topics? An important function of social welfare is to redistribute social benefits so that the state can reward some social groups with more social benefits than other social groups. The reforms for both enterprise employees and rural residents reallocated some social benefits, such as subsidies from the government, or access to certain welfare programmes. What we can learn from the official discourse is how the state construed fairness: 'why someone deserves social benefits and who should pay for them (or contribute to them)'. In this section I also investigate how government redistribution embodied existing norms about what is fair and just, or sought to create new norms.

Redistribution among different social groups

Several difficult dimensions of 'inequality' had to be addressed by the government during the whole reform of pensions and social insurance for elderly people. The first 'inequality' problem for the SOEs' employees' reform was the different performances of the enterprises. A second aspect was the rural–urban difference when the coverage of social insurance scheme was expanded. The third related to the rural migrants who worked in cities. Owing to the dual welfare system opposing urban to rural status, rural residents who moved into urban areas could not (and in most cases still cannot) enjoy urban social benefits. So as the urbanisation process in China involved millions of migrant workers from rural areas, their lack of social protection became a crucial issue. For all these situations, the government had to explain why the differences existed, why the government was transferring social benefits (out of the public budget) to a certain social group, and (to some extent) whose interests needed to be 'sacrificed' for this redistribution and why.

Before the early 1990s reforms, the burden of paying for the pensions of the retired SOE employees was considerable. In addition, to help promote their modernisation, a policy of early or 'internal' retirement was adopted by many SOEs as a means of shedding older or less skilled workers who had not actually reached retirement age (normally about 40 to 50 years) and were thus not formally eligible for a pension. Because many enterprises were uneasy about paying for the laid-off workers, retired workers, and early retirements, the solution imposed by the government was to redistribute the burden (of paying the benefits) to the SOEs through *social coordination*. In other words, enterprises that performed better and had fewer retirements were encouraged (later on, required) to pay into a social pool, which would be used to relieve the enterprises that had got into difficulties. In defending the redistribution of the obligation to pay benefits, the government used several types of discourse. One theme stressed that sharing the burden of retirement followed the general design of the country's economic reform, and helped to change the current distributional system into something better and fairer. For example:

> The State Council announced the 'Decision on reforming the Basic Pension Insurance for Enterprise Employees' in 1991. The 'Decision' clearly addressed the proposal that 'following the economic development, [we should] gradually build a system that combines the basic old-age insurance, enterprise pension insurance and the individual's personal savings as insurance' … The principle of the basic pension insurance reform is [to combine] 'fairness and efficiency', 'rights and obligations' and 'sharing social benefits brought by the economic development'. ('The reform brings benefits for enterprise retirees', Li Boyong, 1993-04-29)

In addition to the abstract description of 'rights and obligations', giving more details of how the better-performing enterprises could actually benefit from contributing into the social pool sounded more attractive to the audience. Here is one example elaborating on the reason why the pension fund needed to be socially coordinated:

For a long time, the enterprise employee's pension in our country was paid by the extra revenue of each unit. However, the number of retirees for each enterprise varies dramatically different from one to another, making the burden of pension payment, unequal. According to census data from the Labour Bureau of Zigong City, Sichuan Province in 1983, the pension expenditure for some new enterprises is only about 2% of their total payroll, while in some old enterprises, the proportion is as high as 60%. Such differences threaten the progress of reform in our distributional system. One of the basic elements of the reform of this system is to connect the total payroll directly with the economic revenue of each enterprise. The current method of pension payment hinders the evaluation of enterprises' economic performance. For some old enterprises, although they may run well and are properly managed, the heavy pension cost leads to less tax revenue than less burdened enterprises must pay ... In such cases, the taxes and profits cannot reveal the real economic performance of the enterprise, and its connection with the total payroll cannot hit the target of reforming the distributional system.

[The older pension payment method] also violates the principle of fair distribution. From the very beginning, the new enterprises were able to develop by using the profits of the old enterprises. For instance, the total handed-in tax and benefits from Zigong's salt industry is around 2.3 billion yuan. This is why the newly emerged enterprises should share the increasing cost of paying the retirees from the old enterprises. If the employees of the new enterprises enjoy a higher income from exploiting such unfair advantages, it will cause disputes between the two sets of employees. Thus, we need to reform the distribution of responsibility for pensions. We should make an overall arrangement and collect pension funding from all kinds of enterprises according to certain proportions and coordinate the money to the retired employees under a central body. In the long term, as the number of retirements increases naturally, the new enterprises will not be taken advantage of; by then their retirees will enjoy pension benefits from the socially coordinated pool. Most importantly, the overall arrangement of the pension fund can direct a smooth reform of the distributional system. ('The pension fund should be (socially) coordinated', Tang Liang, 1985-06-09)

Shown in numbers and comparisons, these arguments seem to have been quite useful in demonstrating the government's rational and careful design in solving the problems.

Another way in which the government described the benefits brought by sharing the pensions responsibility argued that it was beneficial for all enterprises to prepare for the 'lagged risks' and uncertainties brought by a steadily ageing population. For example:

Participating in the social coordination of pensions would generally have two results: either enterprises that had a lighter burden of retirements would need to contribute, or those which already had numbers of retirees would seem to benefit from the coordination process. For instance, one nitrogen fertiliser factory in Changde, Hunan province, had 829 employees at work and only 92 retirees. After the social coordination of pension contributions, the factory needed to contribute 40,000 yuan more to the social insurance office, so it counted as a contributing unit. Another catering company in the same city had a pension burden of 498,300 yuan each year to pay for its retirees, who occupied 78% of its payroll. Since the company could afford only 56% of the pension total, after social coordination, the social insurance office had to refund the company 220,000 yuan every year. This categorised the company as a benefiting unit.

Does contributing mean losing and does benefiting mean gaining? The chief of Changde's Labour Bureau told us that the employees from the fertiliser factory initially thought so: they were upset about 'losing' 40,000 yuan to other enterprises. But the officials of the Labour Bureau went on to explain to them that their money was just temporarily being used to support other enterprises. When the retirees from this factory increase in the future, other enterprises with fewer retirees will come and support them. The money they contributed to others will ultimately become their own pension in return. ('An investigation of pension coordination', Gong Jinxing, 1991-10-08)

This text's core message was that it is ethical and moral for enterprises that are running well to make contributions to the social pool.

Combinations of such moral arguments with rational arguments (such as forestalling lagged risks in the future) were used to ease the anxieties of many enterprises that felt others were taking advantage of them. For instance, another commentator argued:

The Baoding No. 1 Cotton Mill does not find paying more social insurance fee to be a sign of exploitation. This spirit is valuable. It's valuable in that the workers' strong sense of social responsibility [means] they care not only about the mill's own employees, but also about social obligations. It's also valuable in showing that they have a strong 'sense of risk': even when their factory is performing quite well and salaries are steadily rising, they choose without hesitation to contribute to the pension pool and actively participate in the social coordination. Such action shows their boldness regarding reforms and their long-term vision of the future.

Accelerating social welfare reform is one of the most important tasks for this year's reform. The core element of welfare reform is to achieve the social coordination of enterprise employees' pension contributions, and extend the coverage to different types of enterprise. In doing so, we intend to increase the social capacity to confront risks and create a better environment for SOE reform. The nature of the pensions' social coordination is actually a redistribution of benefits imposed by the state on enterprises. Thus, enterprises that perform better economically and have fewer retirees will support others that are less efficient and have more retirees.

If we base our conclusions only on temporary contributions and cry that 'We are being taken advantage of', we will have a short-sighted view. The reform needs to be understood and recognised by its long-term benefits and the changing situations of market risks. The economic performance, employees' age structure and the expected welfare burden will never reach their optimum [for individual enterprises], because these change so much. 'I help you today and tomorrow someone else will help me'. In other words, the social coordination of pensions is the 'shock absorber' [of risk] for enterprises. They should open their eyes and make full use of the shock absorber! ('Make full use of the shock absorber', Mo Cun, 1995-04-13)

In the case of promoting rural pension reform, the fairness of redistribution was also useful in showing why rural residents were eligible to enjoy the expansion of social benefits without waiting, and urban areas might have to share the responsibility of paying for it. In the 2000s, when the government was planning to establish a new rural pension scheme for rural residents, an emphasis could be observed in news articles on the 'unfair' rural–urban differences, the threat of social instability, and the importance of the 'common interest'. This well-argued document demonstrates how the issue was discussed:

How huge is the urban–rural inequality? Here are some informative statistics from 2003. The disposable income per capita for urban residents was 8,472 yuan, and 2,622 yuan for rural residents; the participants in [the urban] basic pension insurance numbered 155.06 million, while the participants in the rural pension insurance numbered 54.28 million; across the country there were 22.35 million urban residents who were covered by the Minimum Living Standard Security programme while only 4 million rural residents were covered. The imbalance of rural–urban growth has created a bottleneck that obstructs all social and economic development.

Yuyao City in Zhejiang province, where the GDP per capita already exceeds 3000 dollars, coordinates the rural–urban development in order to share the fruits of development [with everyone] ... The repayment to rural residents in Yuyao benefits from several innovative principles. First of all, [Yuyao City] persists in unifying the contributors and beneficiaries. Rural residents were the main forces in the opening up and reform; they are the constructors of our socialist career, they are the creators of our social goods ... most importantly, the rural residents have the right to enjoy the fruits of social progress just like urban residents. Second, [the city government] holds the principle of considering 'the fundamental interests of the majority'. The traditional social welfare system favours the urban enterprise employees. The frequent occasions of illness-led poverty, [and] natural disaster-led poverty in rural areas relate, to some extent, to the absence of a social welfare system for rural residents. 60% of the population in our country live in rural areas, but we cannot let the peasants lose out, we cannot betray the ultimate goal of common prosperity. Third, it perseveres in taking people into accounts. As a relatively advanced region on the eastern coast, Yuyao has the political and fiscal ability to tear down the fence between rural and urban areas. Subsidising the peasants won't be in vain; rather, it's a 'grand vision' of development, and is beneficial to social stability and long-term growth. ('Sharing the fruits of development with the peasants', Wang Binlai, 2004-07-25)

A common description of sharing the responsibility for rural development with urban areas was 'promoting agriculture with industries, and powering the rural areas with the efforts from urban areas'. By highlighting the fact that the countryside and agriculture had contributed to urban and industrial development – a similar argument to the one concerning the contribution of old enterprises – those who had benefited from them should now pay back their debt for the sacrifices made. Here an example of a text that integrates the moral argument with the fairness argument to do with rural–urban inequality:

The special industrialisation stage, the complexity of developments in agriculture and rural areas determine that we have arrived at the phase of 'promoting agriculture with industries, and powering the rural areas by the efforts made by urban areas' ... Industry repaying agriculture sums up the changed urban–rural, industry–agriculture relationship when industrialisation reaches a certain point ... Generally speaking, at the early stages of industrialisation, agriculture acts as the main strength in the national economy. In order to create more material wealth and increase the level of development and living standards, we need to rely on the accumulation of agricultural production. When industrialisation reaches the point when industry becomes the main engine, we need to coordinate the industry–agriculture relationship by having the state increase its support and protection of agriculture in addition to the (existing) market intervention, so we can convert from the model of agriculture-feeding-industry to that of industry-repaying-agriculture.

Experience from other countries shows that when the process of industrialisation and urbanisation accelerates, the whole economy attains the phase of industry-repaying-agriculture. If we strengthen and repay agriculture, the national economy will achieve industrialisation and modernisation in a healthy way. Otherwise, if we still exploit and ignore the agriculture, it will lead to agriculture lagging behind, growing inequality and a wider urban–rural gap. Moreover, it will sharpen social conflict and lead to social instability and retrogression. ('Industry repays agriculture and the urban supports the rural: how to support the rural areas and agriculture in the new scenario', Han Jun, 2005-11-18)

When rural migrants flooded into the cities on a large scale in the urbanisation process, the question of pensions for them and, more generally, social welfare for them, became a knotty problem. Owing to the existence of the *hukou* system, rural residents had only restricted or even no use of schools, hospitals, and other public facilities in urban areas – with many depending on private payment solutions instead. In the 1990s and 2000s, when the number of migrant workers surged, the absence of a proper welfare scheme for them led to many social unrests. However, if the migrant workers had been allowed to enjoy the same welfare system as the urban residents, the competition for resources would have been fierce and that would have caused discontent from urban residents. Thus, the government tried to persuade society, mainly the urban residents, that there were good reasons for these migrant workers to receive some more social benefits and fiscal support. As we might expect, one of the most obvious and frequently used reasons was that the migrant workers contributed to the construction of the cities:

Among the manufacturing, construction, mining and service industries (such as domestic service, catering and so on), rural migrants constitute more than half of the employees. As one important part of the labour force, they deserve fair treatment. This is not only a necessary action defending the migrant worker's legitimate rights, but also directly relates to a defence of social justice and fairness ... Compared to urban workers, rural migrant workers receive low wages (which sometimes can't even be paid on time) and take on dirty and dangerous jobs, while enjoying none of the social welfare benefits [of urban workers]. They contribute to the growth of cities, yet they enjoy none of the convenience enjoyed by urban employees in their daily lives and suffer greatly in such areas

Figure 3.4: Topic proportions by year: social justice and rural migrants

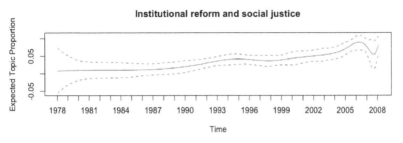

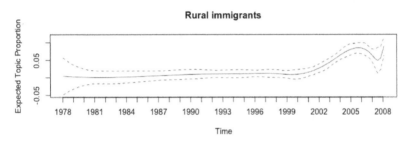

as children's education ... Treating them fairly requires the government to serve them faithfully, consider their troubles, improve their employment situation, and protect their legal rights with efficient rules. Urban employees have quite different situations from rural migrants; thus some existing policies may not be appropriate for them. The government therefore should be aware of the extreme mobility of rural migrant workers and design policies that fit their needs. Luckily, the central government is already working on the issue of migrant workers. Early this year the 'State Council's guidance on solving migrant workers' issues' was examined and passed by the State Council. ('Treat rural migrant workers with fairness and justice', Bai Tianliang, 2006-03-27)

In addition to such text examples, Figure 3.4 shows that the text analysis data identify the increasing proportions concerning the fairness and social justice topic (Topic 23). Comparing the patterns over time for Topic 23 with references to the rural migrants shows a resemblance. References to social justice rose gradually up to the late 1990s, while references to rural migration remained stable. From 1999 on, references to rural migration increased sharply and the Topic 23 proportion also soared a little more slowly (with both showing a marked dip and recovery in 2007–8). The emphasis on social justice and fairness thus increased with the increased visibility of rural migrants, as well as its connection to certain social problems (such as rural migrants) from the topic model. As noted above, Topic 23 refers to the fair distribution and redistribution in the macro issue of institutional reform.

Redistribution between different generations

The nature of social insurance also brings up the problem of redistribution between different generations, especially for pensions. For trust in the pension system to work, the government needed to raise funding from current employees, particularly because the state was trying to transform China's previous 'pay-as-you-go' system into a mixed two-tier system comprising both social and individual accounts. The cost of the social transition had to be met by someone. What kinds of reason were provided by the government to justify the redistribution of social benefits between different generations? The first and most convenient tool was highlighting traditional Chinese culture. Filial piety (*xiao* 孝) is one of the most important and prestigious merits in Chinese traditional culture. Conventionally, caring for the elderly is undoubtedly the responsibility of their children. Filial piety is a virtue that means not only caring for one's own parents but also showing love, respect, and support for all older people. Hence, in the official discourse, a reconstruction of family and piety culture is generously praised:

> A recent competition for 'Star of filial piety' which selects the person who has been most filial to parents and dutiful to the elderly, is quite unique and deserves our praise. The 'Star of filial piety' contest, literally, has the core merit of 'filial piety'. For instance, one of the winners, Han Shihe, an employee from Hangu Saltworks, is taking care of his grandmother, parents-in-law, and aunt with all his heart and all his strength … Appreciation of filial piety is definitely the main trend in our society and matches the willingness of most of our population. Although there are defiant peoples who refuse to care for their parents, they are not the mainstream. More importantly, their attitudes and actions are despised by society as a whole. Once their cases are exposed, they are denounced and disdained by the whole world. Respecting and caring for the elderly is natural in its essence. Just like parents' obligation to bring up their children, adult children have the responsibility of taking care of their elders. The pension welfare system in our country is currently incomplete, caring for the elderly still need to be based in families. Thus, filial piety is particularly important [for us]. ('Complimenting the "Star of filial piety"', Chen Fei, 1997-11-10)

In addition to cultural factors, the state stressed that older people also deserve respect and benefits from society because they have already given their time and effort to it. In addition, the younger generation should see its own future from the situation of the generation before theirs. Moreover, rationally speaking, the 'time difference' will help the social welfare system operate better. Here are some examples of these messages:

> Today's elderly were hard at work yesterday. They contribute to the development of our society in different degrees. Therefore, they deserve

to share the material and spiritual benefits brought by the country's development. Today's youth will tomorrow become the elderly. Today when they see the whole society treating old people fairly, they won't be worrying about their fate [in the future]. They will devote more to their work in the prime of life. ('About elderly issue', Hong Tianguo, He Liangliang, and Zhang Da, 1982-06-22)

And:

Social welfare reform needs to take good advantage of the 'time difference'. [It should include] more people in the social insurance scheme … because most of these people are still young or middle aged and the promise (of a pension) can only materialise 20–30 years ahead. By the time they get old, the social insurance trust will have been accumulated to quite a size and will certainly be able to afford pension and health insurance for these people.[1] In this case, the new social insurance scheme, the realisation of past promises, and the social insurance trust will form a strategic triangle and the lapse of time will be valuable. Taking full advantage of the time difference, our social welfare system will be on the winning side. Because the gap in time will give us enough time to reduce holding shares and realise state-owned assets,[2] increase the funding of the national social insurance trust, and boost the confidence of the participants in our social insurance scheme. ('Building a new platform of social insurance', Gao Shusheng, 2003-04-08)

The logic in the discourse on redistribution was fairly simple, revolving around *contributions and rewards*, and *rights and obligations*. The old enterprises deserved to be funded by the new enterprises through the coordinated social pension funding, because they had contributed to the start-up of industrialisation. The rural areas deserved to have transferred public finance because they had contributed to the development of urban areas. Rural migrants deserved fair treatment (more social benefits) because they had contributed to urbanisation and the construction of cities. The elderly deserved better care because they had contributed to society when they were young. The maxim 'Someone deserves reward because they contributed' can also be translated as 'Someone should be rewarded *only if* they contributed'. Social rights are distributed to anyone who has contributed to society. In this way, the rationalised subjectivity of 'I am/for everyone' and 'everyone is/for me' was highlighted in the politics of redistribution. This inclusiveness, which was always conditional on 'contributions', was especially obvious when taking the 'lagged time' into account. We can only imagine our future according to the current redistribution system; therefore, everyone is tightly constrained inside the game of '*producing and giving*'.

3.4 A renewed state–individual relationship: the 'socialised self'

Pension reforms, for whatever social group, are also a move to reconstruct the relationship between the state and the public, as some texts with policy content indicated:

> Except for some special programmes (such as insurance for occupational injury and childbirth) for which individuals do not need to pay fees according to the law or international practice, the fundraising responsibility for all other social insurance programmes should be shared by the state, enterprises and individuals. Enterprises and individuals should pay the insurance fee, while the government provides a fiscal subsidy under exceptional circumstances. Raising funds from individuals is not only helpful for expanding the funding source of social insurance but also beneficial for increasing labour's awareness of social insurance. ('Speeding up and deepening the reform of social insurance system', 1997-05-20)

Accordingly, in this section I investigate the issue of 'shaping citizens' expectations' of state action in the official discourse. What should citizens expect to get from the government when faced with social risks such as unemployment, illness, and ageing? What is the proper relationship between citizens and state regarding welfare responsibility?

I generated the classification data by dividing the documents into these sub-categories:

- 'locus of responsibility'
- 'praise', or 'denounce'
- 'national conditions', and
- 'international experiences'

according to their content. The locus of responsibility includes five types of responsibility allocation regarding care for the elderly in general (such as raising funds for pension fees, daily caring, and so on) as follows: 'no clear direction of locus', 'state/party', 'individual/family', 'enterprise', and 'social coordination'. Since many documents contain more than one topic and sometimes refer to various kinds of message, my coding of the locus of responsibility is based on the most obvious direction of responsibility that can be perceived or identified from the content. Classifying the tone of a document as one of 'praise' or 'denounce' is useful as these are covariates in addressing the issue of 'what has been endorsed by the government'. The categories of 'national conditions' and 'international experience' are important in identifying whether the whole document emphasises the local situation of China or Chinese characteristics

Table 3.2: Descriptive statistics of document categories

Category	Not present	Yes present	Yes %
Praise	2,996	394	12
Denounce*	3,343	47	1
Stress national conditions	3,278	112	3
Stress international experiences	3,282	108	3

Notes: 'praise' and 'denounce' measure the tones of the articles in general; 'national conditions' and 'international experiences' measure whether the article shows highlights of national conditions or international experiences. The variation of the variable 'denounce' is small and not significant. Accordingly, the results of covariates in the analysis below does not include the statistics of 'denounce'-related results. They are presented in Appendix A3.

or draws lessons from overseas experience. The main results in the following discussion use the Naïve Bayes classifier; in Appendix A3, Figure A.8, I present the flowchart of the coding and validation of different classifiers' performances. Table 3.2 shows the descriptive data for each category from the classification results. Documents that are categorised as 'praise', 'denounce', emphasising 'national conditions' or 'international experiences' are coded as present (1) in the data, or not present (0) otherwise.

Unfolding the locus of responsibility: topic-based promotions

The promoted locus of responsibility regarding elderly care in general (such as fundraising to meet pension fees, daily caring, and so on) varied according to topic. Figure 3.5 presents on the x-axis the expected proportions of each topic in different covariate levels of responsibility. The results are quite intuitive. Within the first chart for Topic 4 (SOE Reform and Marketisation), it is clear the related documents are more likely to be coded as promoting the role of social coordination in solving the problem of care for the elderly, while the topic proportion is smaller in the class of government/party responsibility. For Topic 19 (EE Pension Plan), shown in the third chart, the pattern is quite similar. Although the main target of the EE pension reform was to ease the burden for SOEs and the government, there was not much significance in the signals from the official discourse showing that the government was promoting only individual responsibility, or at least that could not be directly perceived by the readers.

By contrast, the topic that refers to the laid-off workers, shown in the second chart, has a much higher proportion at the covariate class of

Figure 3.5: Topic by covariate: different types of responsibility emphasised

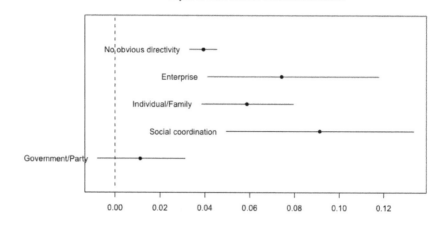

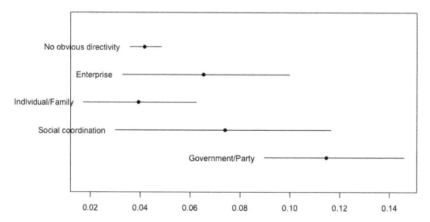

Figure 3.5: (Continued)

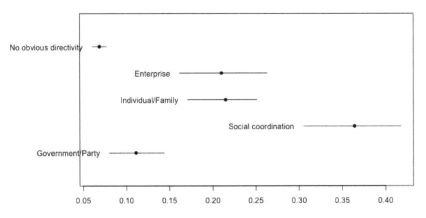

Topic of Enterprise employees' pension reform

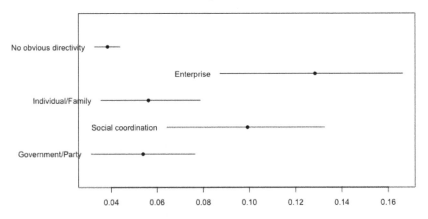

Topic of Pension fees

Note: The x-axis shows the proportion of each class of responsibility.

Figure 3.6: Some other topics by covariate: different types of responsibility emphasised

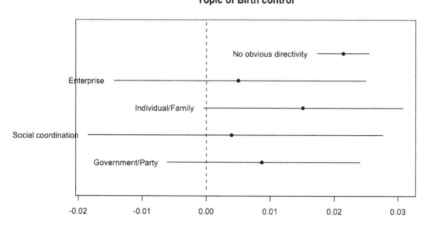

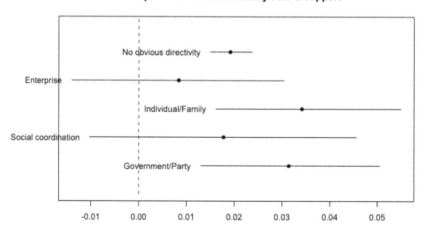

Figure 3.6: (Continued)

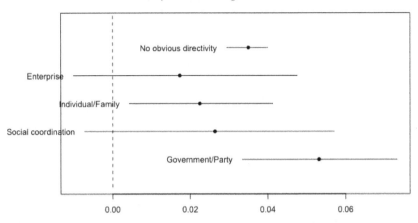

Topic of rural migrants

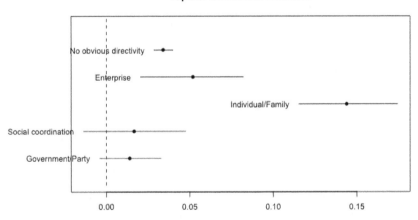

Topic of Commercial insurance

Note: The x-axis shows the proportion of each class of responsibility.

government/party responsibility. This link was clearly reasonable, because the laid-off workers were the ones who were sacrificed for the economic reform and SOE reform, and so these employees needed to be reassured that the government was not giving up on them. The last chart refers to Topic 29 (Retired/ Pension Fee). This differs from Topic 19 (the EE Pension Plan, next to it) in that it mainly refers to the fundraising problem in pension reform. As was to be expected, the highest proportion of covariates concerned in the class for enterprise responsibility (and its proportion in the class of social coordination follows). The more commonly used discourse is 'shared responsibility' between the state, the unit/enterprise, and individuals, as the accountable source of employees' pensions moved away from simply being the state and the work unit. A proper interpretation of the 'shared responsibility' discourse within its time shows that it was about increasing the individual's responsibility for and contribution to the pension system.

One question that might arise is, if it truly wanted to lighten its own burden, why did the government not directly highlight 'individual responsibility', rather than using the obscure discourse of 'shared responsibility'? The reasons for not directly urging such a clear reallocation of welfare responsibility are complicated. First of all, the government official discourse had created its own dependency. The socialist discourse of 'an omnipotent state' had become ingrained in official habits and even internalised as second nature by state organs. So, it is unlikely that the tone could change quickly or call directly for individual responsibility for welfare. Another easily identified reason is public expectations. Even if the government wished to change the direction of the official discourse, people who used to enjoy considerable benefits from their work unit and government support were (and still are) less likely to accept the reallocated social responsibility. There was a risk of alarming or enraging the target group – enterprise employees, especially employees of SOEs – at the beginning of the EE pension reform if the official discourse abruptly changed its tone. I give more illustrations in Chapter 4's analysis of official propaganda.

For topics that relate to other pension reforms, shown in Figure 3.6, the covariate class of responsibility also fits the design and intention of the policy. The proportions for all the covariate class of responsibility (again shown on the x-axis) are quite low for Topic 16 (Birth Control) in the first chart, and the highest class here is 'no obvious directivity'. This is reasonable, since this topic directly relates to a demographic policy, and not specifically to a pension policy. Moreover, the pension pilots for rural residents are scattered experiments initiated by local authorities. The main reason why the pension policy is mentioned in association with this topic is that the government wanted to trade the pension benefit for people's willingness to practise birth control. The second chart covers Topic 5 (Old-Age Care), which refers to home-based elderly care/support, where the top two main responsibility covariates are shared by the individual/family and the government. The main content of this caring approach again does not directly address the pension issue: instead, the key theme was that elderly people should be encouraged to stay in their homes, where the local street government would help them to take care of everyday problems as they arise. Covariates for the issue of rural migrants are shown in the third chart. The government is the top category, because (as noted above) it wanted to convince the urban residents that rural migrants deserved better social welfare, in view of their contributions to the urbanisation. Equally, the government also wanted to appease migrants' anxieties and assure them that the government would do the job. Finally, the last chart shows the isolated topic of commercial insurance, or the right to purchase insurance against social risks. The top covariate shows that this was obviously related to the responsibility of the individual/family.

Table 3.3 presents a summary of the models for several selected topics by covariate responsibility, which can display more information about the magnitude of each coefficient. In dealing with the issue of EE Pension Plan (Topic 19), the responsibility of the government/party, the individual/family, the enterprise, and social coordination were all significantly emphasised in the official discourse. However, when we check the magnitude of the coefficients, the role of 'social coordination' had the highest correlation with this topic. For the issue of 'Laid-Off Workers' (Topic 9), government/party responsibility was positively (and significantly) related, while the individual/family was negatively related. For Topic 25, 'Rural Migrants', the related welfare responsibility was also focused on the role of the government/party. As for 'Commercial Insurance' (Topic 2), this was mainly individual/family contributions, while the role of government/party was negatively related to this topic.

In addition to the classification of responsibilities, the other coded classifications, such as national condition, foreign experience, praising, and so on, can reveal more details about the discourse employed. For instance, what kind of sentiment is related to each responsibility allocation? Which topic (and cor-

Table 3.3: Topic proportion by covariate: types of responsibility

	Enterprise Employees' Pension Reform	Laid-Off Workers	Rural Migrants	Commercial Insurance
Government/party	0.063***	0.078***	0.021	−0.022*
	(0.015)	(0.013)	(0.011)	(0.009)
Individual/family	0.146***	−0.006	−0.016	0.098***
	(0.017)	(0.01)	(0.009)	(0.011)
Enterprise	0.158***	0.029	−0.017	0.014
	(0.025)	(0.016)	(0.013)	(0.017)
Social coordination	0.296***	0.027	−0.010	−0.019
	(0.031)	(0.019)	(0.015)	(0.016)

Note: *p<0.05; **p<0.01; ***p<0.001.

responding policy) is more likely to be promoted using examples from other countries? In Table 3.4, I present the topic proportion estimation by multiple covariates. For both Topics 19 (EE Pension Plan) and 9 (Laid-Off Workers), there is a positive correlation between the topic proportion and a document being coded as 'praise'. In other words, the pension reform for enterprise employees and the government's efforts in taking care of the laid-off workers are more likely to be reported and promoted in a positive tone. However, the interaction between an enterprise's responsibility and praise is negatively significant. It seems that in the official promotion of pension reform for enterprise employees, the documents that mention the enterprise's responsibility were less likely to be praising. Also, looking at the national situation or international

Table 3.4: Topic proportion by multiple covariates: types of responsibility and other categories

	Enterprise Employees' Pension Reform	Laid-Off Workers	Rural Migrants	Commercial Insurance
Government/party	0.061**	0.097***	0.015	−0.017
	(0.021)	(0.017)	(0.013)	(0.013)
Individual/family	0.155***	0.003	−0.013	0.108***
	(0.018)	(0.012)	(0.01)	(0.015)
Enterprise	0.179***	0.028	−0.014	0.005
	(0.028)	(0.019)	(0.015)	(0.017)
Social coordination	0.313***	0.041	−0.009	−0.023
	(0.034)	(0.024)	(0.018)	(0.017)
Praise	0.063***	0.046***	0.002	−0.015
	(0.015)	(0.012)	(0.009)	(0.01)
National condition	−0.024	−0.021	0.007	−0.03*
	(0.019)	(0.012)	(0.015)	(0.014)
Foreign experience	−0.014	−0.032*	−0.024*	−0.008
	(0.021)	(0.014)	(0.012)	(0.014)
Government/party × Praise	−0.054	−0.081**	0.01	0.003
	(0.035)	(0.025)	(0.022)	(0.021)
Individual/family × Praise	−0.067	−0.046	−0.000	0.014
	(0.047)	(0.03)	(0.026)	(0.039)
Enterprise × Praise	−0.177**	−0.072	−0.012	0.079
	(0.066)	(0.047)	(0.039)	(0.054)
Social coordination × Praise	−0.109	−0.091	−0.017	0.032
	(0.084)	(0.047)	(0.037)	(0.044)

Note: *$p<0.05$; **$p<0.01$; ***$p<0.001$.

In all the models, the mode of uncertainty is set as 'Global'.

experience codings, Topics 9 (Laid-Off Workers) and 25 (Rural Migrants) were less likely to be related to international experience, while commercial insurance (Topic 2) was negatively correlated with the national condition.

Promoting shared responsibility: the glory of being employed and the common interest

What are the desired attributes of a 'good and responsible citizen' when the government is promoting shared responsibility for social welfare? From the text corpus, one attribute that is highly praised and promoted is the glory of being employed: a liberal and free labour force – the fundamental ideas of occupational pension and welfare capitalism in liberal economics. The idea is also similar to those in the reforms of other former communist countries. In Ukraine and Russia, despite the widespread suffering caused by the reforms, there was still a belief in the early 2000s that the liberal recipes of marketisation and privatisation could work, if they were properly implemented (Lane 2007). Even the traditional left wing there accepted the neoliberal rhetoric and private ownership driven by the reform policies. Mary Gallagher (2011) deciphered some similar phenomena in China's reform era and found that individual merit was highly encouraged, while 'waiting, relying, and demanding' with regard to governmental help was criticised. The official propaganda promoted the notion that 'the market economy doesn't pity the weak' and people should take responsibility for their fate.

On this theme, looking at the typical articles for Topic 9 (Laid-Off Workers) from the *People's Daily*, some encouraged laid-off workers to change their mind regarding work, especially the idea of 'relying on the state/unit'. Former SOE employees, indeed the whole society, should change the idea of the 'iron rice bowl' and put more effort into their own attempts in the job market:

> Jinan city offered 261 charity positions especially for the '40/50' population. However, there are more than 100 positions that have lain idle since mid-August. One laid-off employee said, 'The job of an urban management officer is just too demanding, [will] entail too much outdoor work, and 420 yuan is definitely not worth it' ... [This illustrates the idea that] 'relying on the state in seeking a job, relying on a post for life'. Many people are just too comfortable with 'waiting, relying, demanding', and expect the government to find a position for them ...

> [The idea that] 'the only real employment is when you have an *iron rice bowl*' is very common in society. Following the trend of socio-economic development, since we are now in a market economy, 'contractual employment' has been promoted on a large scale. Self-motivated job searching, career building, and fluid employment have not only set the conditions of the job market, but also are an inevitable outcome of social

progress. In other words, whether for government employees or enter-prise employees, the position is no longer the so-called 'iron rice bowl'. The most reliable 'iron rice bowl' should be your skills and capacities; [people] should create and develop their own career by their honest work. ('Talking about ignored vacancies', Jiang Nanke, 2003-09-01)

In another example text shown below, a responsible citizen is expected to enjoy the opportunities offered by the marketisation reform. The main idea was to urge enterprise employees to move on from the 'old planned economy' and embrace the new efficiency-based, contribution-based market economy. The text specifically addressed three common ideas in society that inhibited people undertaking a self-motivated search for a job – that only getting another 'iron rice bowl job' was genuine re-employment; that looking for work was demeaning; or that waiting for reassignment was the only route to another job. Instead, those who could seize the chance through skills of their own would be valued:

The deepening reform of the SOEs and the process of 'reducing staff and boosting efficiency' inevitably leads to some laid-off workers ... Laid-off workers should change their attitude of reliance to independence and try all ways of expanding their capacity to find a job. The idea of 'only the iron rice bowls is counted as re-employment' has very deep roots (in this society). Indiscriminate egalitarianism and the iron rice bowl were the products of the planned economy, and have become less and less [popular] since the start of the economic reform and the building up of a social-ist market economy. Breaking down indiscriminate egalitarianism is the request of all the enterprise employees and will bring benefits to us; [while] discarding the iron rice bowl is the inevitable outcome of deeper reform ...

The idea of 'seeking a job for myself makes [me] lose face' needs to be changed. This idea was born in the old planned economy and in circum-stances where all the housing, health care, and pension provision of SOE employees were covered by the state. Nowadays, following the reform of social welfare, the difference between the SOE employees and people who have obtained a job by their own efforts is smaller. The old idea should be abandoned along with the abolishment of old (economic) system. Mean-while, we should see that the new socialist market economy brings eve-ryone the opportunity of choosing a career and a position that can show her/his capacity in line with her/his own willingness, skills, and interests. People should treasure such opportunities. As long as they are allowed to reveal their abilities and work happily while contributing to the society, the [position that they hold] will be the most glorious one [for them].

Believing that 're-employment means waiting for job re-assignment' is a 'waiting, relying, demanding' kind of attitude ... It is not possible to wait [for the state] to reassign one's job. Rather than waiting, it may be better to walk into the job market or seize an opportunity of creating your own employment. The creation of jobs is the realisation of self-value and a contribution to the society: the more you create, the more you contribute. ('Expanding the employment possibilities in changing our minds', 2002-05-31)

Another method of persuasion in official discourse was highlighting the need for common goods, encouraging people to work for better benefits, and emphasising the spirit of collectivism. For instance, in the next textual example there is a consolidated discourse that the pension reform for urban and rural areas combines rights and obligations – so, everyone should contribute to the well-being of the whole society. Meanwhile, it is also necessary to recognise the 'unavoidable' differentiation inside society, and individuals' personal endowments are given their proper value by the contribution-based differentiation in social benefits:

These following principles and tasks need to be highlighted when building the social welfare system that covers both rural and urban residents. First of all, 'coordinating the rural–urban development while maintaining differentiation'. The progress of the social welfare system in urban and rural areas is unbalanced. The rural pension system is lagging behind and the health system is incomplete. In urban areas, there are some social groups not yet covered by the social welfare system. We need to coordinate the development of both the urban and the rural welfare system and hit the target of 'covering the risks that need to be covered'. For the situation of migrating workers in the urbanisation process, we need to design policies that connect the anomalous standards across welfare schemes. Meanwhile, we need to keep in mind the urban–rural dual structure and the different social and economic levels. Our social welfare schemes designed for each area should reflect these differences.

Second, as regards 'enforcing governmental responsibilities while emphasising the obligations of units and individuals', we need to highlight the effect of social welfare on social fairness, while considering the efficiency of our system. We need to strengthen the government's management of social welfare and make use of the government's function of redistributing income, defending social justice, and providing equalised public services. We also need to consistently match 'rights' with 'obligations' by making the units and individuals fulfil their social responsibility and fundraising obligations. ('Constructing a social welfare system that covers urban and rural residents', Tian Chengping, 2007-09-30)

[We should] clarify several misunderstandings about the social welfare system. First of all, we can't regard the social welfare system as identical with 'robbing the rich to help the poor', nor as a new version of 'indiscriminate egalitarianism'. The goal of the social welfare system is to defend social fairness and share the fruits of development with all the members of the society … Second, we cannot simply insert the principle of efficiency from the market economy into the social welfare system … we need to prevent potentially bad outcomes brought by some irrational marketisation of the welfare system. Third, we cannot exclude migrant workers and rural residents by treating the welfare system as the special possession of urban residents. However, we cannot ignore the current stage of our national development and try to pursue a universal welfare system too fast. We need to gradually build a unified welfare system through diverse, multilayered institutional arrangements based on the principle of fairness and interest-sharing. ('Social welfare construction in the harmonious society', Zheng Gongcheng, 2005-09-16)

Conclusions

This chapter and Chapter 2 have addressed one crucial segment in answering my overarching question about how the modern state maintains compliance from the governed in a period of rapid social and economic transformation, and how the logic of its governmentality changes accordingly. In these two chapters, I have investigated the logic of 'whom to govern' and 'how to govern' through a decomposition of the design, implementation, and promotion of the pension reform in China, paying special attention to the way that social problems are identified, the way distinctions are defined, and the knowledge that is produced to persuade the public.

At each point in history the promotion of different key topics in pension reform closely interacted with and served the most salient issues in the social and economic reform. For instance, the documents that addressed the topics of laid-off workers and their pension plans was closely connected to the SOE reform. Official discourse pushing demographic control described the pension plan in rural areas as a 'son' that could 'take care of' the elderly. The propaganda also imported the discourse of social justice and harmony when urbanisation and migration were flourishing. The rationale of reconstructing public knowledge and expectations of the redistribution of social benefits, and the allocation of welfare responsibility between the state and individuals mainly focused on the reiteration of the principles of: 'contribution and rewards' and 'rights and obligations'. (Technically speaking, persuasions that related to enterprise employees – regardless of the socially coordinated solution to pension fundraising, or the individual's responsibility to contribute to the pension scheme – were more likely to use the discourse of profit-oriented 'efficiency'.) Meanwhile, the messages related to rural residents and other urban residents – such as birth control, rural migrants, home-based elderly care and so on – were more likely to borrow moral arguments from traditional Chinese culture.

Individuals' personal lives, therefore, were socialised, and initiated in a broader system rather than the previous unit-based and localised system. Everyone's personal interest was materialised and combined with the performance of the whole society, the whole state. Only by contributing to others could people receive rewards. The subjectivity was reconstructed among persons who were directly or indirectly involved in the production process as self-motivated, self-regulated, and self-sufficient in caring. More interestingly in the official discourse is the frequent absence of 'action initiators'; the suggestions, appeals, and logical persuasions are commonly unidentified but appeal to 'us': *we should*, *'we need to'*, *'our target/job/tasks'*, and so on. The anonymity of initiators, in fact, imposes an effective substitution on the readers, and turns them into an 'activated-self', and then a 'responsible-self'.

The analysis prompts a follow-up question: 'to what extent were the state's advocacy tactics effective in changing public opinion?' In the next chapter, I use causal inference to empirically unlock the mixed effect of the government's strategies of combining experimentation and propaganda in a specific policy reform, which was conducted through several waves of policy experimentation in the late 1990s and early 2000s. Data from social surveys provide empirical evidence on changing public attitudes, especially among the target social group for this specific policy reform, under the influence of policy experimentation and related official propaganda.

Notes

1 Ironically, a piece of news reported on 12 April 2019 was that, with the current payment rate, the accumulated surplus pension fund would run out by 2035 according to the 'Actuarial Evaluation of China's Pension' published by the Social Insurance Research Center in the Chinese Academy of Social Science. https://perma.cc/L2SG-C6MG

2 To subsidise pension funds, in the late 2000s China also resorted to another means: selling off stock shares and privatising some of its state-owned enterprises (Frazier 2010).

References

Cai, Y. (2002). 'The resistance of Chinese laid-off workers in the reform period'. *The China Quarterly*, vol. 170, 327–344. https://doi.org/10.1017/s0009443902000219

Chan, K. W.; and Buckingham, W. (2008). 'Is China abolishing the hukou system?' *The China Quarterly*, vol. 195, 582–606. https://doi.org/10.1017/s0305741008000787

Dean, M. (2010). *Governmentality: Power and Rule in Modern Society*. Sage publications.

Foucault, M.; Davidson, A. I.; and Burchell, G. (2008). *The Birth of Biopolitics: Lectures at the Collège de France, 1978–1979*: Springer.

Frazier, M. W. (2010). *Socialist Insecurity: Pensions and the Politics of Uneven Development in China*. USA: Cornell University Press.

Gallagher, M. E. (2011). *Contagious Capitalism: Globalization and the Politics of Labor in China*. Princeton University Press.

Garnaut, R.; Song, L.; and Fang, C. (2018). *China's 40 Years of Reform and Development: 1978–2018*. ANU Press.

Glasberg, D. S.; and Shannon, D. (2010). *Political Sociology: Oppression, Resistance, and the State*. SAGE Publications.

Grimmer, J.; and Stewart, B. M. (2013). 'Text as data: The promise and pitfalls of automatic content analysis methods for political texts'. *Political Analysis*, vol. 21, issue 3, 267–297. https://doi.org/10.1093/pan/mps028

Grün, B.; Hornik, K.; and Grün, M. B. (2018). Package 'topicmodels'.

Hopkins, D. J.; and King, G. (2010). 'A method of automated nonparametric content analysis for social science'. *American Journal of Political Science*, vol. 54, issue 1, 229–247. https://doi.org/10.1111/j.1540-5907.2009.00428.x. OA: http://nrs.harvard.edu/urn-3:HUL.InstRepos:5125261

Jefferson, G. H.; and Rawski, T. G. (1994). 'Enterprise reform in Chinese industry'. *Journal of Economic Perspectives*, vol. 8, issue 2, 47–70. https://doi.org/10.1257/jep.8.2.47

Lane, D. (2007). 'Post-state socialism: A diversity of capitalisms?' *Varieties of Capitalism in Post-communist Countries*, 13–39. Springer. https://doi.org/10.1057%2F9780230627574_2

Li, J. (2019). Package 'tmcn'.

Lucas, C.; Nielsen, R. A.; Roberts, M. E.; Stewart, B. M.; Storer, A.; and Tingley, D. (2015). 'Computer-assisted text analysis for comparative politics'. *Political Analysis*, vol. 23, issue 2, 254–277. https://doi.org/10.1093/pan/mpu019. OA: https://dash.harvard.edu/handle/1/38057808

OECD. (2005). *Organisation for Economic Co-operation and Development (OECD) Annual Report*. Retrieved from https://www.oecd.org/about/34711139.pdf

Roberts, M. E.; Stewart, B. M.; and Tingley, D. (2014). stm: R package for structural topic models. *Journal of Statistical Software*, vol. 10, issue 2, 1–40. https://doi.org/10.18637/jss.v091.i02

Roberts, M. E.; Stewart, B. M.; and Tingley, D. (2016). Navigating the local modes of big data. *Computational Social Science*, vol. 51. https://doi.org/10.1017%2Fcbo9781316257340.004

Scharping, T. (2013). *Birth Control in China 1949–2000: Population Policy and Demographic Development*. Routledge. https://doi.org/10.4324%2F9781315027777

Svallfors, S. (2007). *The Political Sociology of the Welfare State: Institutions, Social Cleavages, and Orientations*. USA: Stanford University Press. https://doi.org/10.11126%2Fstanford%2F9780804754354.001.0001

Maximising support for pension reform using policy experimentation, and the potential to backfire

With the emergence of market orientation, the socialist and post-socialist countries were confronted by the challenge of conducting proper reforms to their welfare systems and retrenching the demands that their legacy arrangements imposed on the state. However, because the Chinese public had not reached a consensus regarding the relative shares of the state and the individual in welfare responsibility, movements contradicting the previous image of the state–individual relationship were potentially controversial.

In addition to its propaganda for change, reviewed in Chapter 3, an essential element of the Chinese government's statecraft was a strategy of regional *experimentation* with shared welfare responsibilities. Regional pilot schemes were deployed to facilitate the public understanding of shared welfare responsibility on the pretext that the public had not reached a social consensus. Meanwhile, the official propaganda of local governments emphasised government omnipotence, which assisted them in managing public faith in regime capacity and governance.

In this chapter, I take advantage of a quasi-experimental pilot policy in China, referred to as the 'pension insurance pilot scheme in urban areas', to explore the case of hybrid responsibility of welfare provision. This empirical analysis offers a counterfactual analysis of the effect of policy intervention and official propaganda on the attitude of welfare responsibility allocation and regime support of the general public by taking advantage of the pilot policy launched by the central government in selected provinces. With the help of two nationwide surveys ('*Chinese Attitudes toward Inequality and Distributive Injustice*') conducted in 2004 and 2009, I collected over 5,000 randomly pooled cross-sectional data results for residents in eight treatment and 12 control provinces.

How to cite this book chapter:
Wang, Yan. 2022. *Pension Policy and Governmentality in China: Manufacturing Public Compliance*. London: LSE Press, pp. 91–127.
DOI: https://doi.org/10.31389/lsepress.ppc.e. License: CC BY

The empirical results show that the pilot policy launched by the Chinese central government significantly affected the citizens' understanding of shared responsibility and privatised social risks in general and that the public apparently accepted the underlying accentuation of the individual's responsibility for pension contributions. The length of time that the policy has been in force amplified the attitudinal change in individuals' perception of the government's role. Local official propaganda, which emphasised the image of an 'omnipotent government', moderated the treatment effect of the pilot scheme on the public's understanding of shared responsibility. In other words, local propaganda helped the regime to maintain the public's faith in the government's capacity and responsibility for social welfare provision, while gradually implementing the experimentation policy.

Beyond the attitudinal change toward individual welfare responsibility, I also find that the influence of policy propaganda interfered with the pilot policy, as shown by the contradictory finding about the public's political trust. Controlling for other factors, short-term exposure to the local propaganda – which praised the government's efforts to respond to people's expectations and improve people's living standards – increased the public's confidence in institutions. However, the disjunction of the policy content, which set out to share with individuals the responsibility for welfare – and content of the propaganda actually backfired on the authorities regarding institutional trust in the long term. Thus, the strategies used by governments were influenced by the conditional and practical aspects of policy promotion and the local governments' handling of the perceived role of the government for public. A mismatch between the policy content and propaganda details is likely to be noticed by the public – especially by members of the target population (enterprise employees) who are more likely to expect a 'big government' that can take care of their social risks – and to weaken their support for the institution.

4.1 Risks in the pension reform and the statecraft of policy experiments

As a special form of society, state socialism adopts a distinct structure of institutions and rules regarding development, production relations, and welfare provision (Polanyi and MacIver 1944). The basic principle of state socialist regimes is that material resources are distributed through central planning and a system of political identification. Take the example of China. Before the reform and opening up in the late 1970s, the state organised and governed individuals through work units (*danwei*) in urban areas and people's communes (*renmin gongshe*) in rural areas. However, the redistributive principle posed serious challenges to governance continuity. In particular, collective ownership hindered production efficiency, while the offering of incentives for productive improvements and the scarcity of resources cultivated a sense of 'manipulated equality' among privileged groups (Kornai 1992; Szelenyi 1978). The unsustainability of such institutionalised settings pressured state socialist countries in the late 20th century to pursue market reforms (Szelenyi and Szelenyi 1994). The emergence of market power during the reform led to the change in distributional principles, the return rate of capital and human capital, social structures, and so on (Bian and Logan 1996; Nee 1996). At the same time, the boundaries of the state, market, and society in these state socialist countries were redrawn and negotiated across different sectors, especially in Eastern Europe, eastern and south-eastern Asian countries, and the former Soviet Union. Szelenyi and Kostello (1996) argued that market competition, as opposed to state mechanisms, began to play a greater role in Eastern Europe in 1980–89 and in China after 1985. Subsequently, among the East European countries after 1989, the privatisation of public enterprises became a key state policy.

The transitional process caused profound changes in the social welfare provision in China. Market-induced competition led the state and urban collective enterprises to reduce or renege on pensions, medical costs, and housing for employees (Guthrie 2012; Song and Chu 1997). The responsibility for welfare provision shifted from state institutions to society (including families) and this scheme was identified by the Chinese central government as the 'socialisation of social welfare' (State Council 2000a). This special concept captures the change from state-led welfare provision to a welfare system with multiple contributors, in which the state, the market, the sectors of society, and families all share welfare responsibility, and the work units no longer take on the welfare function. To match the socialist market economy, the government promoted joint responsibility as the practical method of funding, service provision and social welfare regulation (Li and Zhong 2009; Wong and Ngok 2006).

This process was similar to the 'retrenchment' and 'risk privatisation' process in Western welfare states and the emergence of a hybrid welfare system there, in which individuals were given flexibility but increased responsibility for handling the various social risks related to their personal lives, such as 'unemployment, death of a spouse, retirement, disability, childbirth, [and] poverty' (Hacker 2002, p. 245). From the mid-1970s onward, welfare states faced rising unemployment rates, high levels of inflation and low economic growth, along with demographic changes that made the social policy increasingly costly and unsustainable. Welfare systems were burdened with extensive problems over 'low-wage, low-skill labour with low work incentives', which were severe in the case of 'welfare without work' (Anderson and Ebbinghaus 2011; Pierson 2001). Meanwhile, 'big government' in welfare provision was recognised as over-committed and underperforming (Mashaw 2006). In these crises, Western policymakers decided to address the new social and economic situation by adopting a neoliberal modernisation strategy (Hall 2001). The welfare regimes in Western Europe, therefore, opted for the retrenchment of welfare provision, including:

> policy changes that either cut social expenditure, restructure welfare
> state programs to conform more closely to the residual welfare state
> model, or alter the political environment in ways that enhance the prob-
> ability of such outcomes in the future. (Pierson 1994, p. 17)

In addition to the cutbacks in public spending and other fiscal rearrangements, certain countries started to reconsider citizens' social right in order to legitimise the welfare reforms. For instance, rather than the universal entitlement to social rights for every qualified citizen, welfare support should be provided for the population that truly needs it (Béland 2005; Cox 2001).

Models that offered a choice, such as the contracting-out and welfare-mix model, were popular in developed countries and also used frequently in less developed countries. For instance, the private pillar in the pension system was adopted in the 2000s in countries such as Chile, Mexico, and Uruguay, with varied proportions of public to private (Mares and Carnes 2009). In East Asia, countries such as Korea and Malaysia also expected a fast-expanding private market in social services (Gough 2001). Haggard and Kaufman (2008) located their discussion in the context of the global economic crisis and identified attempts to retrench social policies in Latin America and Eastern Europe driven by the economic crisis and liberalisation, leading to extending a hybrid welfare system in which social welfare responsibilities were shared between the state, the market, and individuals (Benish, Haber, and Eliahou 2017). Individuals now faced long working lives and redefined responsibility in a state-led welfare-mix system where they enjoyed enhanced 'flexibility' and increased 'responsibility'.

As the 2010s began, welfare reform in China gradually stopped its previous pursuit of marketisation and socialisation. The official discourse about social policy now focused on expanding 'welfare coverage' to rural and non-salaried urban residents. Certain scholars have labelled this new trend in the welfare format 'state capitalism' or a 'state paternalistic capitalism' (Gao, Yang, and Li 2013). In this chapter, I focus on the period of 'welfare socialisation' in the 1990s and 2000s, when the main pension reform for enterprise employees was aligned with the marketisation of state-owned enterprises (SOEs). This period was an important stage in which the ideas of 'a welfare system with hybrid contributors' and 'shared responsibility for facing social risks' were developed and actively promoted by the state. Only after the reconstruction of the public's understanding of shared responsibility could the state be confident in diffusing its attempts to expand welfare coverage without reincurring huge burdens similar to those in the state socialist period.

Existing studies have carefully examined the details of the pension policy in this period, such as the return rate, coverage, and return on investment of pension trusts (for instance, Li and Ge 2010; Li and Wang 2009; Lin and Ding 2007; Yang, Wang, and Zhang 2010). However, the effects of the transitional process on *social beliefs*, especially public perceptions of the state–individual relationship and the function of institutional dependency in shaping people's political attitudes, have not been fully investigated. The rhetoric of 'socialism' itself describes the state or state-managed public bodies acting as sources of social welfare – in schemes similar to a social contract – with the cost of low salaries and limited social mobility (Haggard and Kaufman 2008). For instance, work units in urban China before 1978 were subsidised by the state so as to provide not only jobs to individuals but also to generate pensions, housing, education, and health care to employees and their dependents (Lu and Perry 1997). In the rural areas, funds were also allocated for the basic education and medical support or health care of residents (Wong 2005). The socialist institutional setting cultivated a strong image of an omnipotent government, in which the state was expected to superintend the social welfare of the public, especially among urban enterprise employees, who were expected to be cared for 'from cradle to grave' (i.e. with generous welfare benefits). The legacy of this socialist policy was a population with a strong sense of state dependency, attachment to the welfare state and organised stakeholders favouring the welfare setup (Cook 2013).

However, the cognitional inertia of the public's assumptions about welfare responsibility arising from socialist traditions may pose considerable challenges when neoliberal reforms come to be implemented. For instance, Cook (1993) found that workers from the former Soviet Union expressed discontent and to a certain extent jeopardised state legitimacy when the social contracts that used to guarantee their economic welfare broke down. Denisova et al. (2012) analysed data from a survey held in 2006 involving 28,000 individuals from 28 post-socialist countries. They found that transition-related difficulties influenced respondents' support for privatisation reforms, given the preference for state agency and concerns regarding the legitimacy of privatisation. Evidence from East Europe suggested that, when 'literally over a single night, all the things that had been taken for granted were no longer valid', many individuals suffered from 'serious identity crisis' (Ekman and Linde 2005, p. 357).

Apart from cognitional dependency, two other factors weakened welfare reforms that were intended to rebalance state–individual accountability. First, when the market principle was introduced in social and economic matters, the ruling party in China did not relinquish the claim of communist ideology. Perry (2007; 2017) indicated that its resilience in power was endorsed by its skilled employment of the communist revolutionary legacy and of symbols from traditional culture. Slogans were presented, such as 'serve the people' and 'the party represents the benefit of the overwhelming majority of the people'. By combining the destiny of the party and the welfare of the people, these repeated and solemnly vowed ideological claims in fact aided the formation of the 'common interest' of society and became an important element of the 'inertial thinking' of the public when it had to face external changes. In other words, people in former socialist states are more likely to treat the government as the bearer of ultimate liability for all social and economic problems. But, at the same time, they are more likely to accept social or policy changes 'for the sake of the common interest'.

Second, the shadow of other previous public policies also shaped the expectations of the people. For instance, the demographic 'one-child' policy posed a specific quandary for the care of older people in China because its demand for the obligatory compliance of the people in reducing the number of their descendants went against perceptions of children as being the main form of old-age support in the traditional context of filial piety. So, to gain leverage and make a morally and politically fair request, the government had to take charge of elderly welfare there. Despite this fairness rhetoric, urban residents suffered more than those in rural areas, because the one-child policy was strictly enforced in urban areas.

To sum up, China's welfare reforms during the 'socialisation process' in the 1990s and 2000s may have induced a failure of consensus between the state's conduct and individual perceptions regarding the role of government in welfare provision. The difference may also have endangered state legitimacy by the public's sense of betrayal. To avoid a legitimacy crisis caused by the above consensus gap, the Chinese government needed to seriously consider the public's expectations and anticipate their feedback in its policymaking process, especially during dramatic transitions in the social welfare provision. A parallel statecraft of social policy experimentation and official propaganda was created to address the consensus gap and resolve the dilemma of combining privatised social risks and shared responsibility during the pension reform process.

In China, policy experimentation is a core tool of an incremental policy process, a matter of 'crossing the river by feeling the stones'. Such experimentation is very important for maintaining state legitimacy while avoiding radical policy changes at the national level. In a huge state like China, a process of conducting moderate and manageable policy changes allows enough space for the central government to learn from 'trial and error' (Heilmann 2008b). Policymakers of the central government could determine the types of experimentation to undertake, look at the results, and decide what aspects of successfully implemented experimentation could be adopted at the national level (Heilmann 2008a; Mei and Liu 2014; Zhu and Zhao 2018a). Provinces, cities, or regions could participate in the selection of pilot sites. Within the process of pilot policymaking, local governments could benefit from conditional and limited autonomy if the central policies permitted. Apart from the unified policy guidelines proposed by the central government, local authorities could localise and reinterpret the policy details on the basis of their specific local conditions (H. Huang 2013). In such a structure, local governments could also employ strategies, such as the construction of rhetoric, enhancing certain policy elements to popularise the policies when they sense potential obstruction from the public.

I propose that policy experimentations in the field of social welfare were used as a tactic for *dialogue* with the general public to demonstrate the legitimacy of a reform. The idea of experimentation as a dialogue tactic differs from the conventional understanding of policy experimentation in the theoretical spectrum. The traditional wisdom on policy experimentation has mainly focused on policymakers at the central and local levels, but has paid little attention to the recipients of social policies – the public. Conventional theories either highlight the autonomy of local authorities, arguing that decentralised federations contribute to economic leapfrogging (Montinola, Qian, and Weingast 1995; Weingast 1995) or accentuate the full control of the central government, whose experimentation serves to demonstrate that policies are workable (Heilmann 2008b), identify errors (Zhu and Zhao 2018a), or delimit competition (Cai and Treisman 2006). I emphasise that the government can integrate the public's expectation into the policymaking process around policy experimentation and employ a feed-forward effect (Schneider and Sidney 2009) to minimise any undesired impacts on society. If the central government pushes for an across-country reform that contradicts its omnipotent stature (which is generally interpreted by the public as being a 'caring and accountable' government), then the difficulties for the public of identifying and accepting the new situation can be considered risky, given the cognitional dependency discussed above. By distributing policy changes in selected regions through policy experimentation, the government can measure and test the potential feedback and the limits of the public in turn, and contain the public's expectations about the general process of policymaking. Moreover, policy experimentation provides effective channels for the government to further influence public opinion by engaging individuals in dialogue.

The central government can wield power via several mechanisms. First, the experimentation depends upon the fiscal division between China's central and local governments, where the central tier controls the fiscal resources and allocates transfer payments to local governments, and the local governments are motivated to accomplish or improve pilot programmes so as to gain financial resources and cope with welfare expenditure (Zhu and Zhao 2018b). This interactive loop helps the central government find the most appropriate policy instrument to develop as the much broader version of the experimental reforms. Moreover, the central government can establish its legitimacy by modestly implementing the reform process (Zhu and Zhao 2018b). Second, the general public may change its perceptions, mainly through an experiential process, in the context of external experimental interventions. Gradual reforms based on policy experimentation instil in the public the belief that a new policy may be cancelled if it does not work. In the regions chosen to pilot the new welfare policy, the public may have derived benefits and observed deficiencies – but with less anxiety. Therefore, the central government can promote new policies without the need to obtain large-scale prior approval from the general public as a whole; rather, it can persuade people by informing them of the pros and cons of the policies as the experimentation proceeds. An incremental pilot scheme facilitates the building of public attitudes, in which the most preferred outcome corresponds to the policy design, especially when a controversial policy is involved. During the buffer period of policy experimentation, the public may either accept the permanence of the controversial policy or signal their discontent in ways that are not too radical for the government. So, experimentation can be a useful tool in letting the central government initiate dialogues with the public.

It should be noted here that the risks of policy failure and legitimacy crisis in the piloting of welfare reforms are unevenly distributed between the central and the local governments. In China, local governments are more likely than the central government to be blamed by the public for deficiencies in social policies, whereas the central government can claim credit and obtain rewards from warmly accepted policies more easily than the local governments can (Shi 2014). Central government generally possesses a higher degree of political trust than local governments do, which is referred to as 'hierarchical political trust' (Lü 2014; Shi 2014). This is partly because local governments are the ones that implement the rules and provide the services and their proximity leads the public to focus on their deficiencies and misbehaviours. Cultural factors also matter because Chinese people tend to look up to a 'just and upright lord' and believe that most of the local problems are the results of distortion by local officials. Additionally, social instability caused by public discontent may threaten the political career of local officials. As a precaution, local governments may either actively initiate localised innovations when the experimentation scheme allows it, or promote central government-instructed policies with carefully designed messages (Zhu and Zhao 2018b).

In the design process for public policy, official discourse is commonly recognised as effective statecraft, helping any government to convince their subordinates regarding new policies and eliminate the possibility of a legitimacy crisis (Beetham 1991). For instance, in liberal democracies' electoral politics the core principle of making politics work is to mobilise the 'majority' of the population. Schneider and Ingram used the theory of 'social construction of target groups' to describe the process in developed countries whereby the election elites use certain portrayals to maximise voters' support and minimise electoral costs by identifying the target population of the policy whom they want to promote (Boushey 2016; Schneider and Ingram 1993; Schneider, Ingram, and DeLeon 2014). Political elites in competing parties sacrifice the interests of a smaller group of people while promoting a reallocation of welfare resources through the rhetorical construction of certain weak and marginalised target populations – those who lack effective political power to engage and change the policy process. This can be effective, so long as the policy is constructed to be legitimate for the majority (Goode and Ben-Yehuda 1994; Schneider and Ingram 1993). These constructions are formed from social values, emotions, or stereotypes of the target population. As an example, when policymakers intend to impose a new welfare burden or retrench welfare benefits for a certain group of people, the target population may be constructed as 'undeserving' and 'selfish' – and hence eligible to be denied certain social assistance (Hynes and Hayes 2011;

Maynard-Moody, Musheno, and Musheno 2003). By such devices, an elected government can legitimise its proposed policy and alter the expectations, perceptions, and even behaviours of the citizens (Donovan 2001; Lawrence, Stoker, and Wolman 2013; Schneider and Sidney 2009).

In developing and non-democratic regimes, institutional differences mean that the logic of social construction in public and social policy changes. In these regimes, the government is perceived to be likely to directly issue a policy with or without majority consent, and to have less motivation to construct portrayals that would do enough to meet the citizens' expectations. However, in practice, we still find numerous cases where policy promotion delivers rhetorical messages not directly related to the policy itself, or contains specific information that is highly sensitive and salient to certain social groups. In this chapter, I find a strategy that is similar to the situation in democracies' electoral politics, but is more specific and tailored to the constraints in developing countries without mature democratic elections, and where policies targeting a certain population do not need voting approval from the whole population. The pressure on policymakers mainly comes from possible discontent among the targeted population that lose out, because any instability caused by their collective resistance can lead to a legitimacy crisis for non-democratic authorities (Lipset 1959). Thus, welfare retrenchment that is designed to reallocate the responsibility between the state, the market, and the target population requires the policymakers to try hard to ensure that the image and the actual working logic of a policy are congruent. In this case, policymakers can strategically construct the policy content to gain the acceptance of the target population and avoid the risk of legitimacy crisis from the incongruence of the welfare policies. The ideal achievement of such constructional efforts by government might be a cognitional change in the target population to adapt to the design of the policy, together with greater general trust from the entire population, if possible.

In practice, for the authorities to attain the goal of social construction – persuading the public of the advantages of policies and the credibility of governments – they must use the acknowledged tool of propaganda through the public media (Easton 1975; Shirk 2011). The incumbent authority can effectively defend or promote its policies and guide or mobilise public opinion by using its own media (Di Tella, Galiani, and Schargrodsky 2012; Keefer and Khemani 2011). Many specific components of constructive propaganda are used by governments to help promote policy changes. For instance, propaganda can be designed to magnify the necessity and urgency of policy changes, particularly by connecting them to short-term social problems (Cox 2001). Propaganda can also emphasise the part of the message in which a government's duty and credibility are enhanced, while neglecting other parts where the government has begun to withdraw from its former role. Some propaganda models glorify and exaggerate to the public the benefits of new policies, especially to the target groups of certain policies (Schneider and Ingram 2019). Regarding the efficiency of official propaganda, Huang's paper (2015; see also 2018), on a government's indirect provision of information, identified 'subtle and sleek propaganda' as something likely to have a highly persuasive effect, whereas 'hard propaganda' may backfire and alienate citizens from the policy.

In the case of China's social welfare areas, where an extensive socialist legacy persists amid the transition in socio-economic conditions, efforts by local governments to promote welfare reform require careful social construction tailored to the target population of the reform. In the case of a pension pilot for enterprise employees led by the central government, I observe that the local governments' promotion of the reform described the piloted policy as something closely associated with the generosity of the state. It may be asked why, if the government as a whole intended to share responsibility for pensions with individuals (society) and enterprises in its broader reform, its propaganda did not use relevant discourses, such as connecting the pilot reform directly with individual responsibility. One reason why official propaganda about the pilot reform still connected the policy with the state's generosity is partly because of the citizens' dependence on the socialist media pattern of official discourse. As in other communist counterparts, in the pre-reform period China's official propaganda was famed for its 'formalistic, ritualistic and ideological' content (H. Huang 2015). The state-owned media usually exaggerated the omnipotent role of the state, avoided negative messages/information, and signalled the capacity of state power (see, for example, McQuail 1987; Siebert, Peterson, and Schramm 1956). The authority in non-democratic regimes also tends to take a 'paternalist role' in public welfare provision (Beck 1997; Leung and Nann 1995). Thus, the state is unlikely to change its habits completely in its official discourse. Another, more important reason in this case is that the local governments were also trying to avoid the risks that the reform might bring. The promotional content of the propaganda emphasised the role of the government in appeasing public anxiety, especially since the social welfare reform involved incremental changes to a more individually based type of responsibility. I further analyse local government's motivation to use selective discourse in the following section.

The reform of China's urban pension insurance in the 2000s is an especially apt case to demonstrate the strategy of combining social policy experimentation with official propaganda. The central government led the promotion of a new pension scheme for a certain population in some selected provinces over three main waves, which was ideal for investigating the exposure effects of the policy treatment on the public. This reform was also an important segment of the overall reconstruction of welfare responsibility, moving away from the state socialist welfare model and towards 'socializing the social welfare' (Ringen and Ngok 2017; Shi and Mok 2012). And to study propaganda in this chapter I focus on local official discourses published by local provincial party committees, rather than that of the central government such as the *People's Daily* (analysed in Chapter 3). On the one hand, local official propaganda followed the basic tone of central government in promoting certain policies. Yet, on the other hand, local governments could vary their propaganda efforts (in volume, coverage, emphasis, and so on) according to their understanding of the reform's direction, policy details, and local conditions. Especially with regard to policy experimentation, local governments were allowed to make localised changes under the general direction of central government. Therefore, local governments' varied efforts in promoting the government's image and the policy reform provide a good case model for analysing the effects of constructive propaganda.

Before the economic reform in 1978, the 'creation of a socialist egalitarian society [promised] a relatively stable livelihood at the expense of economic development' (Leung and Xu 2015, p. 33). In urban areas this meant that work units acted as administrative social integration sections, as well as public goods providers (Lu and Perry 1997). Urban work units provided not only jobs for life but also pensions, housing, education, and health care to employees and their dependants. More than 80% of the urban labour force was covered by the *danwei* system (Leung and Wong 1999). The state's patriarchal role was a collective welfare mechanism that collectively secured citizens' social rights at the stage of state socialism (Xie 2016).

As economic reforms gathered pace and the state promoted social reforms that helped to cut its welfare burden and boost efficiency, there were massive implications for lifetime employment, pensions, health, and the housing system in urban areas (Li and Zhong 2009; Wong and Ngok 2006). Large numbers of employees in state-owned enterprises were laid off in the process of liberalisation and marketisation. Furthermore, the newly established basic health insurance scheme also required contributions from individuals and employers. The functioning of hospitals started to employ market-competition principles. The total welfare contribution from individual workers accounted for quite a large proportion of their salaries (Ringen and Ngok 2017). Certain areas of welfare provision would be transferred to local government, to society, or even back to the family.

China's pension plan for urban enterprise employees changed dramatically after the retraction of the 'iron rice bowl' and the reformation of SOEs in the 1980s. Beginning from the 1990s, what used to be a pay-as-you-go system of pension insurance gradually changed to a mixed two-tier system comprising social and individual accounts. The reformation officially started in 1997 when the State Council issued Document no. 26, entitled *Decision on Establishing a Unified System of Basic Pension Insurance for Enterprise Employees* (State Council 1997). According to this, the responsibility for raising funds for the new pension system should be shared by enterprises, employees and the government (Gao 2006), although the action was not de facto compulsory. The document proposed that each individual account be maintained at 11% of an employee's salary, to which individuals needed to contribute up to 8% of their salary (i.e. starting at 4%). To this, employers were expected to cover the shortfall in individuals' accounts (i.e. the remaining 3% of an individual's salary) while separately contributing at most 17% of the payment (i.e. the enterprise's total contribution should not exceed 20% of an individual's total wages) for the social account.

However, individual accounts were often 'empty' owing to insufficient fund allocation and the diversion of funds to the social accounts. which were originally designed to cover the needs of retirees. This situation also caused a 'common pool' problem, in which current pension contributors always expected the social account to cover everyone's pensions, although their individual accounts might have been used up. To further clarify the division between the pooling of individual and social accounts, and to cover the deficit in individual accounts, the central government issued Document no. 42 in December 2000 to promote a new reform, *Fully Funding the Individual Accounts* (State Council 2000). This pilot policy reform was first implemented in Liaoning Province in 2001, and it specified that all contributions to individual accounts must be handled solely by employees and the 8% rate must be set from the contributory wage. In 2003, the pilot policy was extended to Heilongjiang Province and Jilin Province. These two provinces adopted similar policy schemes that differed only slightly in terms of the regulations regarding the contribution rate. The three provinces in north-eastern China comprised the first wave of pension insurance reform for urban enterprise employees. In 2005, the central government issued *Decision on Improving the Basic Pension System for Enterprise Employees* (State Council 2005) and added eight more provinces that would form the second wave of pilots: Tianjin, Shanxi, Shanghai, Shandong, Henan, Hubei, Hunan, and Xinjiang, beginning in January 2006. Jiangsu and Zhejiang Province joined as the third wave in 2008. Thus, overall 13 provinces took part in the reform's pilot scheme. Later on, the 10-year pilot scheme gradually faded away as the 2010s began, the main reason being cited as the unsolved problem of 'empty individual accounts' (Zheng 2016).

Social welfare provision was generally considered a local affair under the pre-reform arrangements, financed by local tax receipts. In general, provincial governments could retain up to 84.5% of their fiscal revenue and most of the funds were diverted to reinvestment and development instead of the provision of social welfare for local residents. Following the 1994 fiscal reform, the central–local relationship was redefined as a tax share between the two tiers because the balance leant towards the central government. Under the new system, the central government took 75% of the value-added tax, one of the most important fiscal resources for government revenue. However, the expenditure on social welfare remained a local matter, especially at the prefectural and county levels, where fiscal revenue had already gone through the process of recentralisation (Y. Fan 2015). The situation was worse if we consider that the social welfare index was not even included in the promotion criteria for local authorities until the late 2010s. In other words, local governments were expected to provide social welfare but did not have enough capacity or motivation to provide it. Nevertheless, they were more likely to be held responsible by the public and blamed for a policy that was unwelcome. Therefore, local governments were motivated to take precautions against the possible negative effects of implementing policies when the central government attempted to promote a hybrid type of welfare reform.

In local official newspapers, we find that articles reporting the pilot policy were associated with the omnipotent role of the state. The articles were full of the following messages: the government's generosity, efficiency, and conscientiousness ensured social justice; the framing of 'good government', and the government's taking 'people's livelihood into account' – all these messages are consistent with the socialist rhetoric. For example, one of the local official newspapers described the pilot policy as follows:

> This policy aims to support the basic pension and social old-age insurance systems by reforming the methods of calculating the basic pension and allowance. We are ensuring the punctual granting of pensions for retired enterprise employees whilst expanding the coverage of the old-age insurance system for everyone included in the scheme. This requires the government to renew its efforts to collect insurance funding and tighten the supervision and management of it. Moreover, we should also improve and integrate a pluralistic approach of fundraising in order to fully fund individual accounts. (*Shanxi Daily*, 2006. Originally in Chinese; my translation.)

Another widely employed approach in local official newspapers was to magnify the necessity and urgency of the reform by connecting it to general social benefits, where it is consistent with the central government's repertoire of knowledge construction methods covered in Chapter 3. For instance, one report addressing the 2005 State Council no. 38 decision argued:

> This decision (*Decision on Perfecting Basic System of Pension Insurance for Enterprise Employees*) is a significant one made by the central authority on the basis of the overall socio-economic development of our country. The decision is vital for the healthy and sustainable development of the economy as well as for the long-term safety of our nation. It is also essential for protecting the well-being of our prefecture's citizens (*Tianjin Daily*, 2006)

4.2 Policy effects on how the public sees the locus of responsibility for pension contributions

To examine the causal relationship between the trajectory of welfare reform from state socialism for shared responsibility and changes in individuals' perceptions, I propose a set of hypotheses made testable by the quasi-natural experiment created by the pilot scheme for pensions for enterprise employees in the 2000s. The main research interest is the effectiveness of statecraft regarding changes in individuals' attitudes to the locus of responsibility (LoR) of certain welfare provisions, and regarding the trust given to political institutions across regions and periods. Individual perceptions of welfare responsibility are sensitive to changes in social policies (Im and Meng 2015; Lü 2014) and are of great importance in understanding political support in general. As a market-oriented policy that resonated with the privatisation of the SOEs in the late 1990s, the pension insurance reform had as one of its goals the sharing with individuals, the market, and society of the responsibility for social pension insurance contributions. For the central government, the ideal micro-level outcome of the reform would be that the target population should recognise their responsibility as individuals for pension contributions, thereby achieving a sustainable system of pension contributions for future retirees. Accordingly:

Hypothesis 1: The implemented pilot experimentation of the basic pension insurance reform increased the popular acceptance of individual responsibility for elderly care. The longer the public experiences the pilot experimentation, the more intensely they become affected by and adapted to the reform.

The new emphasis on incorporating individual responsibility in welfare provision differed from the egalitarian–socialist period practice stressing the duty of the state to provide elderly care in the form of either pensions or social insurance. So, local governments were strongly motivated to take precautions to offset the potential negative effects of the policies – the anxiety of the public (especially the target population) over losing the state's support/benefit. Meanwhile, the local governments did not want to be blamed for the reform, as they would have been if the public distributed blame/trust in its usual hierarchical fashion, given the special central–local relationship in China. A countervailing stratagem against this risk was for the local governments to use official propaganda to send messages in the course of the basic pension insurance reform emphasising the omnipotent role of the state. I found qualitative evidence of the propaganda efforts of local official newspapers focusing on the public's faith in the government's devotion to duty and responsibility. Drawing on these arguments, I test the following hypothesis:

Hypothesis 2: Policy propaganda emphasising the omnipotent role of the government offset the pilot policy's effect on public perception and shifted the people's perception to governmental responsibility.

I recognise the short-term effectiveness of official propaganda in maintaining the public's faith. However, in the long term, individuals will be likely to distinguish the real target of the policy and even to resist its implementation (Chen and Shi 2001; H. Huang 2018; Kennedy 2009). In the case of the pension insurance policy reform, although its description in the official media highlighted the government's efforts to improve the public pension system, individuals reportedly had to increase their individual contributions to their pension, and once in retirement they encountered difficulties in claiming benefits. People who conscientiously planned their monthly income and expenditures were deeply influenced by the implications of governmental retrenchment as part of the policy design. Thus, in the event, the reform dramatically changed the individuals' disposition of their salary and their expectations of risks as they aged, social welfare and the state–individual relationship. This contradiction between policy propaganda and policy experimentation may over time undermine the public's confidence and trust on government institutions. Thus, I propose the following hypothesis regarding the concurrent effect of the propaganda and pilot policy on the public's political trust:

> Hypothesis 3: In the short term, local official propaganda regarding the pilot policy increased the public's support for the regime. However, in the long term, local official propaganda regarding the pilot policy can reduce the public's support.

To measure the dependent variables (DVs) here I draw on two rounds of household surveys called 'Chinese Attitudes toward Inequality and Distributive Injustice', which were conducted by teams led by Marty Whyte and Mingming Shen in 2004 and 2009. The two surveys used randomised spatial sampling under the global positioning system (GPS sampling). The sample pool of the national adult population involved respondents aged 18–65. The total number of observations from the two surveys is over 6,100, as shown in Table 4.1. Since the three provinces in north-eastern China started the pilot policy before 2004, we dropped the samples of these three provinces from the dataset, thus constraining the analytical samples within the window of the two surveys (2004 and 2009). This modification left the analysis with 5,280 observations from 20 provinces.

The main independent variable in this study is the different waves of pilot policy. The full pilot policy started in 2001–3 and expanded in 2006 and 2008, respectively involving three, eight, and two pilot provinces. Figure 4.1 shows the provinces in the three waves. The construction of treatment variables is explained in the model identification section.

The two core questions in the survey that were used to construct the DVs for hypothesis testing are as follows:

> (DV for Hypothesis 1): 'Between the government and the individuals, who should take greater responsibility for elderly pension provision?'

> (DV for Hypothesis 2): 'Do you trust the central/provincial/local governments?' (asked as separate questions)'

Table 4.1: Descriptive data of two rounds social survey respondents

Province	Survey year 2004	2009	Total samples	Pilot year	Pilot wave
Shandong	486	453	939	2006	2
Hubei	251	291	542	2006	2
Heilongjiang	239	212	451	2003	1
Guangxi	242	206	448	—	0
Liaoning	205	183	388	2001	1
Anhui	177	184	361	—	0
Guangdong	164	181	345	—	0
Shanghai	233	87	320	2006	2
Beijing	121	136	257	—	0
Henan	122	110	232	2006	2
Shanxi	112	104	216	2006	2
Xizang	94	108	202	—	0
Zhejiang	90	111	201	2008	3
Yunnan	137	63	200	—	0
Jiangsu	88	107	195	2008	3
Fujian	87	71	158	—	0
Shaanxi	67	73	140	—	0
Jiangxi	42	84	126	—	0
Hunan	54	68	122	2006	2
Hainan	58	54	112	—	0
Hebei	58	44	102	—	0
Ningxia	25	37	62	—	0
Samples (total)	3152	2967	6119		

Notes: Martin Whyte served as the principal investigator for the project, which also involved Albert Park (Oxford University), Wang Feng (University of California-Irvine), Jieming Chen (Texas A&M University-Kingsville), Pierre Landry (Yale University), and Shen Mingming (Peking University), with Jie Yan, Tianguang Meng, and Chunping Han as research assistants. The initial project was held in 2004.

Figure 4.2 presents the provincial variation of the dependent variable – the locus of (welfare) responsibility from two rounds of survey data. In addition to the dependent variables, the two-round survey also provides demographic information about the respondents. These variables are then used as control variables in our models and comprise (among others): age, gender, educational

Figure 4.1: Visualisation of three waves pilot policy

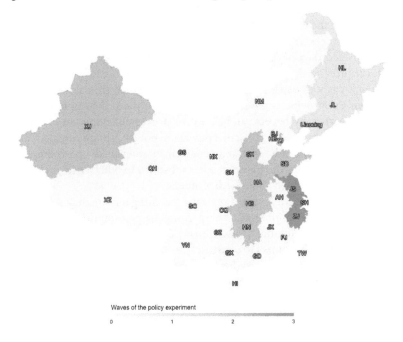

Figure 4.2: Provincial variations of the dependent variable: locus of responsibility perception

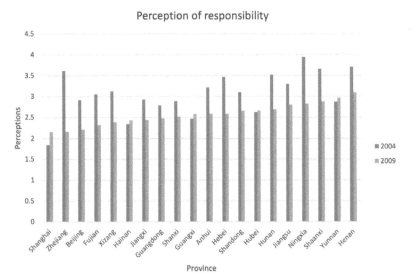

attainment, marital status, party membership, household income level, and residential registration (*hukou*) status.

To measure the independent variable of local official propaganda, I collected newspaper articles from the 'China Knowledge Resource Integrated Database',[1] which covered data beginning in 2000. The official newspapers published by the local provincial party committees were selected, because these were the provincial party newspapers that generally highlighted propaganda information from the provincial government. Moreover, the propaganda rhetoric of provincial party newspapers can help to construct public opinion in the provinces. Officials' attitudes to the current welfare policy that are revealed in provincial newspapers can be spread and appear in other media platforms across a province. So people who do not read or subscribe to official provincial newspapers are also informed about such attitudes.

The collection of data involves keyword searching and manual selection. To capture the intensity of propaganda regarding the pension insurance reform, I collected articles containing the exact name of the pilot policy (e.g. 'fully funding the individual accounts') to construct the variable 'policy propaganda', and I used the ratio of the variables rather than absolute numbers. Figure 4.3 presents the provincial variation of local official propaganda efforts (as the article rate) on the pilot policy. Moreover, I calculated the accumulated ratio in three or five years $\left(Ratio = \frac{\Sigma(Article\ of\ Pilot\ Policy)_t}{\Sigma(Total\ News\ Articles)_t}\right)$, where t equals three or five years before the two survey years of 2004 and 2009, respectively) to capture the long-term effects of the propaganda.

To compare the provincial-level covariates between the treatment provinces and the rest of the country, for the period covering 2000 to 2010 I collected from the National Bureau of Statistics[2] provincial-level statistical data on social and economic variables – which can influence the possibility that certain provinces will be selected as pilot provinces and the public's perception of pension insur-

Figure 4.3: Provincial variation of local official 'policy propaganda' efforts

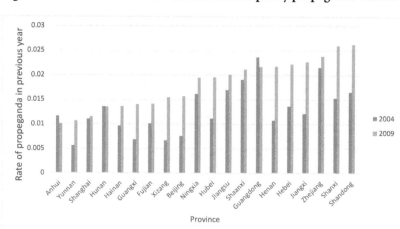

ance. The selected social and economic variables included regional economic performance, demographic characteristics, fiscal revenue and expenditure distribution, the implementation and participation rate of pension insurance, and so on. The nature of the two rounds of survey data permits us to adopt the difference-in-differences (DID) model for estimating the average policy effect on individuals through counterfactual inference. The detailed justification of the counterfactual DID design is presented in Appendix A, Section A4, including parallel trends and individual and regional balance.

In the DID model, I define the treatment group as all the samples from the provinces that participated in the pilot policy, with other provinces used as the control group. The baseline model is to estimate the difference between the treatment area and the control area before and after the policy experimentation.

$$LR_{it} = \alpha + \beta_1 Pilot_i + \beta_2 Post_t + \beta_3 Pilot_i Post_t + \beta_4 X_{it} + P_i + \varepsilon_{it} \quad (1)$$

where LR_{it} denotes the individuals' attitudes regarding the LoR of pension insurance;

$Post_t$ is a dummy variable that equals 1 for year 2009 and 0 for year 2004;

$Pilot_j$ is the treatment variable that equals 1 for samples in the piloted provinces and 0 otherwise;

the β_3 of the interaction term between $Pilot_j$ and $Post_t$ is the average treatment effect on individuals;

X_{it} is an array of control variables that is employed to capture minor imbalances in demographic factors that can interfere with the outcome of interest; and

P_i is a a dummy variable for the provinces.

Given that the pilot sites were selected at the provincial level, I included a dummy variable P_i for provinces to ensure that the selections did not lead to an overestimation of the treatment effects. By taking advantage of the condition that the policy was targeted at urban enterprise employees, I further analysed the occupational and residential differences by using different subsamples.

In addition to the dualistic treatment-or-control variable, I also coded a continuous variable denoted by *Duration* to capture the gradual feature of the policy implementation by substituting the variable *Pilot*. This variable on *Duration* corresponds to the length of time that each treatment province had experienced the new pension arrangements by 2009, the time that the post-treatment survey was conducted: so its value was set at 0, 1, or 3. *Duration* also captures the slight policy differences between two different waves.[3] The model including '*Duration*' as the explanatory variable is similar to Model (1).

$$LR_{it} = \alpha + \beta_1 Duration_i + \beta_2 Post_t + \beta_3 Duration_i Post_t \\ + \beta_4 X_{it} + P_i + \varepsilon_{it} \quad (2)$$

where $Duration_i$ is the length of time for which each sample experienced the pilot policy.

In investigating the mixed effect of the pilot policy and the local official propaganda, I further constructed the difference-in-difference-in-differences (DDD, or triple difference) model as follows:

$$
\begin{aligned}
LR_{ijt} = {} & \alpha + \beta_1 Pilot_i + \beta_2 Post_t + \beta_3 Propaganda_j + \beta_4 Pilot_i Post_t \\
& + \beta_5 Pilot_i Propaganda_j + \beta_6 Post_t Propaganda_j \\
& + \beta_7 Pilot_i Post_t Propaganda_j + \beta_8 X_{ijt} + P_i + \varepsilon_{ijt}
\end{aligned}
\tag{3}
$$

where '*propaganda$_j$*' represents the individuals' direct exposure to the pilot policy. The coefficient β_7 of the interaction of *pilot effect (Pilot × Post)* and *propaganda* thus caught the concurrent effect on the outcome variable. I contained the same control variables of X_{it} and province dummy P_i.

To test the short-term and long-term effects of the local policy propaganda on the public's political trust, I employed the question in the 2009 survey measuring the level of Chinese citizens' trust in the central government, provincial government, and local government (county or district). (There were no questions related to political trust in the 2004 survey – so I can use only the 2009 survey for data on political trust.) Short-term and long-term propaganda were identified with the accumulated ratio of articles that contained the exact name of this pilot policy in the previous year, three years and five years. I constructed the following model by using the interaction between pilot policy and local propaganda to capture the marginal effect of official propaganda on the public's political trust in the treatment provinces:

$$
\begin{aligned}
Trust_{ij} = {} & \alpha + \beta_1 Pilot_i + \beta_2 Propaganda_j \\
& + \beta_3 Pilot_i Propaganda_j + \beta_4 X_{ij} + P_i + \varepsilon_{ij}
\end{aligned}
\tag{4}
$$

where the marginal effect of local official propaganda on political trust was calculated as

$$
\frac{\partial\left(Trust_{ij}\right)}{\partial\left(Propaganda_j\right)} = \beta_2 + \beta_3 Pilot_i
\tag{5}
$$

Thus, the coefficient $\beta_2 + \beta_3 \times 1$ indicates the estimated marginal propaganda effect on the public's political trust in the pilot provinces. Here, the dichotomous variable *Pilot$_j$* can be replaced as the continuous variable *Duration$_i$* (to be discussed in the empirical section), which then turns the measurement into the marginal effect of propaganda on political trust for one additional year. Using *Duration$_i$* helps us identify the long-term and short-term effects of propaganda in spite of the stepwise pilot policy.

I present the DID regression results of the public's attitude to the LoR on pensions by using *Pilot*, *Post* and the interaction between *Post* and *Pilot* (pilot effect), along with other control variables, in Table 4.2. Clustered standard errors at the provincial level are reported in parentheses. The coefficient of the

Table 4.2: Where people see the locus of government responsibility for pensions by policy effects

Variables	Treatment vs control			Policy duration		
Pilot effect (DID)	0.126**	0.123*	0.091			
	(0.060)	(0.068)	(0.068)			
Duration effect (DID)				0.085***	0.083***	0.073***
				(0.020)	(0.023)	(0.023)
Demographic controls	No	Yes	Yes	No	Yes	Yes
Provincial dummies	No	No	Yes	No	No	Yes
Year dummies	Yes	Yes	Yes	Yes	Yes	Yes
Observations	4,921	3,790	3,790	4,921	3,790	3,790
R-squared	0.025	0.069	0.148	0.027	0.071	0.150

Note: *$p<0.1$, **$p<0.05$, ***$p<0.01$. The table presents ordinary least square (OLS) results. Clustered standard errors at the provincial level are reported in parentheses. The estimates of treat, post, duration, demographic controls – which include age, age squared, gender, educational attainment, marital status, party membership, household income level, and *hukou* status – are not reported. The estimates of constants, provincial dummies, and year dummies are not reported either.

pilot effect (*Post × Pilot*) shows a significant positive effect (0.126), which indicates that the policy in the treatment provinces after the pilot increased the public acknowledgement of individual responsibility on pension insurance. After controlling for province, year and individual demographic variables, the effect remains positive (0.091) but insignificant. This mixed effect is partly addressed in the following section by discussing the propaganda effect.

The interaction between *Duration* and *Post* (duration effect) has a significant and positive effect (0.073) on people's LoR attitude after controlling for the demographic factors, provinces and year dummies. This result indicates that the people in the provinces who experienced longer pilot policy experimentation had higher levels of acceptance of individual responsibility on pension insurance. Thus, our Hypothesis 1 is supported.

As shown in Table 4.3, after controlling for the demographic features and province dummies, policy propaganda was shown to have a contrary effect on the public's LoR conditioning in pilot situations. In other words, people affected by the pilot policy were likely to have a higher impression of governmental responsibility when exposed to stronger local official propaganda. The result from the decomposed subsample indicated that the 'pulling back' function of the policy propaganda was significant for the target populations of

Table 4.3: Effect of pilot policy and policy propaganda on the locus of government responsibility

Variables	All samples	Urban samples	Rural samples	Enterprise employees (target population)	Public sector employees (urban)
Pilot effect (DID)	0.500***	0.557***	0.379**	0.523	2.245***
	(0.117)	(0.168)	(0.176)	(0.339)	(0.722)
Pilot effect × Policy propaganda (DDD)	−0.105***	−0.184***	0.018	−0.161**	−0.552***
	(0.029)	(0.041)	(0.043)	(0.080)	(0.197)
Policy propaganda	0.017***	0.045***	−0.021**	0.038***	0.029
	(0.006)	(0.008)	(0.009)	(0.012)	(0.024)
Policy propaganda × Pilot	−0.026*	−0.066***	0.012	−0.082	0.142
	(0.014)	(0.018)	(0.021)	(0.052)	(0.140)
Policy propaganda × Post	0.079***	0.139***	−0.009	0.123**	0.261**
	(0.025)	(0.036)	(0.035)	(0.061)	(0.120)
Observations	3,790	1,947	1,846	729	207
R-squared	0.156	0.164	0.149	0.191	0.260

Note: *p<0.1, **p<0.05, ***p<0.01. All models include demographic controls and province and year dummies.

the reforms, namely, the enterprise employees (−0.161) and the public sector employees (−0.552) in urban areas. Meanwhile, rural residents who had largely been alienated from the policy were weakly influenced by the propaganda, as shown by the slight increase in their confidence (0.018) on the omnipotent role of the government. Hypothesis 2 is thus supported. Along with the pilot policy, local governments' official propaganda in defending the governmental image in welfare provision (as well as the justification of joint responsibility to a certain extent) attenuated people's faith – especially that of the target population of enterprise employees – in the 'glorious government'. In other words, official propaganda acted as a moderator for the treatment effect of the pilot scheme and kept the government from 'losing face' (faith).

4.3 The concurrent effects of experiments and media campaigns on political trust

Despite the image construction of a 'caring and accountable' government that may have effectively swayed public opinion in the short term, the case presented here shows that the divergence between the propaganda images and the benefits derived by individuals from the pilot policy would probably result in political distrust in the long term. The results of the marginal effect of propaganda on the public's political trust in the pilot provinces are shown in Table 4.4. The coefficient of the interaction between treatment and policy propaganda indicates that local official propaganda in pilot areas significantly increased the public's trust in local governments by 0.286 (=0.497−0.211) and in provincial governments by 0.132 (=0.298−0.166) in the short term (one year), calculated using Equation (5). The effect on the public's trust in the central government (0.012) is not as significant as the effects on trust in the local and provincial governments. Meanwhile, in the long term (three years), official propaganda significantly but negatively affected the public's trust in the local and provincial governments (−0.279 and −0.129, respectively). The effect on the public's trust in the central government (−0.012) was not significant. The coefficients of accumulated policy propaganda for five years indicate a similar pattern: policy propaganda affected the public's trust in local and provincial governments (−0.131 and −0.060, respectively) in a significant and negative way, while the effect on trust in the central government was very weak (−0.006). The effect on the central government was clearly not statistically evident, which is reasonable, considering that the statistically measured propaganda and the above discussion on pilot policy took place only at the provincial level. So Hypothesis 3 was also supported.

In this result, I also distinguished a possible confounding variable to capture the self-interest factor under the policy effect: the number of older family members who needed to be taken care of (as shown in Table 4.4). The coefficients of this variable in the various models suggest that the direct self-interest factor has limited influence on the public's political trust.

A logical concern over the difference between the short-term and long-term effects of propaganda on political trust may arise if we consider the different waves of policy implementation in the treatment provinces. Therefore, I added another test to show how the effects of propaganda varied in the different waves, shown in Table 4.5. Here I replaced *Pilot* with *Duration* in Equation (4). The marginal effect of propaganda on the individuals exposed to the pilot policy for different years is calculated with $\beta_2 + \beta_3 \, Duration_i$. The results, which are consistent with those in Table 4.4, further validate our hypothesis on the effect of incremental experimentation.

For individuals in the treatment provinces that started their pilot policy in 2008, the duration of experience of the reform is one year. Therefore, the estimation of the effect of the one-year propaganda on the public's trust in the 2008 wave of pilot provinces is −0.045 (=−0.211+0.166×1). Individuals in these provinces in the 2006 wave of policy experimentation with a three-year pilot exposure show significant and positive change in their trust on the local government by 0.287 (=−0.211+0.166×3), different from the weak negative effect on the ones under the intensity of one-year official propaganda. For provincial governments, the pattern is similar: short-term official propaganda shows

Table 4.4: Effect of pilot policy and policy propaganda on political trust (2009 data)

	Political trust in different levels of government								
	Model 1			Model 2			Model 3		
Variables	Local gov	Province gov	Central gov	Local gov	Province gov	Central gov	Local gov	Prov-ince gov	Central gov
Pilot	−0.956*** (0.222)	−0.620*** (0.185)	−0.309** (0.124)	0.721 (0.627)	0.125 (0.514)	−0.269 (0.409)	−0.037 (0.482)	−0.308 (0.401)	−0.397 (0.299)
Policy propaganda (1 yr)	−0.211** (0.088)	−0.166** (0.075)	−0.088* (0.053)						
Pilot × Policy propaganda (1 yr)	0.497*** (0.150)	0.298** (0.124)	0.101 (0.096)						
Policy propaganda (3 yrs)				−0.053** (0.022)	−0.042** (0.019)	−0.022* (0.013)			
Pilot × Policy propaganda (3 yrs)				−0.226* (0.119)	−0.087 (0.096)	0.010 (0.077)			
Policy propaganda (5 yrs)							−0.069** (0.029)	−0.054** (0.024)	−0.029* (0.017)

	(1)	(2)	(3)	(4)	(5)	(6)	(7)	(8)	(9)
Pilot × Policy propaganda (5 yrs)							-0.062 (0.062)	-0.006 (0.051)	0.023 (0.040)
Enterprise employee	0.051 (0.056)	-0.050 (0.051)	-0.112** (0.051)	0.051 (0.056)	-0.050 (0.051)	-0.112** (0.051)	0.051 (0.056)	-0.050 (0.051)	-0.112** (0.051)
Public sector employee	0.038 (0.085)	-0.021 (0.079)	-0.086 (0.075)	0.038 (0.085)	-0.021 (0.079)	-0.086 (0.075)	0.038 (0.085)	-0.021 (0.079)	-0.086 (0.075)
#Old age people in the family	0.015 (0.017)	0.015 (0.014)	0.001 (0.015)	0.015 (0.017)	0.015 (0.014)	0.001 (0.015)	0.015 (0.017)	0.015 (0.014)	0.001 (0.015)
Observations	1,549	1,529	1,555	1,549	1,529	1,555	1,549	1,529	1,555
R-squared	0.076	0.099	0.106	0.076	0.099	0.106	0.076	0.099	0.106

Note: * $p<0.1$, ** $p<0.05$, *** $p<0.01$. All models include demographic controls and province dummies.

Table 4.5: Effect of policy duration and policy propaganda on political trust (2009 data)

| | Political trust in different levels of government | | | | | | | | |
| | Model 1 | | | Model 2 | | | Model 3 | | |
Variables	Local gov	Province gov	Central gov	Local gov	Province gov	Central gov	Local gov	Province gov	Central gov
Pilot duration	-0.319*** (0.074)	-0.207*** (0.062)	-0.103** (0.041)	0.240 (0.209)	0.042 (0.171)	-0.090 (0.136)	-0.012 (0.161)	-0.103 (0.134)	-0.132 (0.100)
Policy propaganda (1 yr)	-0.211** (0.088)	-0.166** (0.075)	-0.088* (0.053)						
Duration × Policy propaganda (1 yr)	0.166*** (0.050)	0.099** (0.041)	0.034 (0.032)						
Policy propaganda (3 yrs)				-0.053** (0.022)	-0.042** (0.019)	-0.022* (0.013)			
Duration × Policy propaganda (3 yrs)				-0.075* (0.040)	-0.029 (0.032)	0.003 (0.026)			
Policy propaganda (5 yrs)							-0.069** (0.029)	-0.054** (0.024)	-0.029* (0.017)

	(1)	(2)	(3)	(4)	(5)	(6)	(7)	(8)	(9)
Duration × Policy propaganda (5 yrs)							-0.021 (0.021)	-0.002 (0.017)	0.008 (0.013)
Enterprise employee	0.056 (0.056)	-0.048 (0.051)	-0.112** (0.051)	0.056 (0.056)	-0.048 (0.051)	-0.112** (0.051)	0.056 (0.056)	-0.048 (0.051)	-0.112** (0.051)
Public sector employee	0.044 (0.085)	-0.018 (0.079)	-0.085 (0.075)	0.044 (0.085)	-0.018 (0.079)	-0.085 (0.075)	0.044 (0.085)	-0.018 (0.079)	-0.085 (0.075)
#Old age people in the family	0.019 (0.017)	0.017 (0.015)	0.001 (0.015)	0.019 (0.017)	0.017 (0.015)	0.001 (0.015)	0.019 (0.017)	0.017 (0.015)	0.001 (0.015)
Observations	1,549	1,529	1,555	1,549	1,529	1,555	1,549	1,529	1,555
R-squared	0.076	0.099	0.106	0.076	0.099	0.106	0.076	0.099	0.106

Note: * p<0.1, ** p<0.05, *** p<0.01. All models include demographic controls and province dummies.

a weak and negative effect (−0.067) for individuals who resided in provinces with a short exposure to the policy, whereas the effect is positive (0.131) for individuals who resided in provinces with a long exposure of the policy. If we accumulate the propaganda effect for the longer terms (i.e. three and five years), then the negative effect on local and provincial governments becomes extremely high as the exposure to the pilot policy lengthens. As shown in Table 4.4 and Table 4.5, which both use 2009 survey data, the long-term decline of the public's political trust is related to propaganda and of the disjunction of policy from propaganda, rather than the policy itself. Therefore, we can exclude the alternative explanation that the possibility of policy failure caused the long-term distrust we observed.

No matter whether it is called 'social construction', 'frames', or 'discourse', the idea of official propaganda does have a risk of failure. In many cases, unsuccessful alterations of either the image of the target population or the discourse of the policy agenda may lead to a failure to promote the policy. For the pension pilot for enterprise employees in the early 2000s, the key potential problem was the 'mismatch' between the promoted pilot policy content and the local government's official discourse. Such mismatching partially results from the discourse dependency of the communist state-owned media; it also comes from local governments' efforts to maintain the general face (faith) of the 'state' before its population. The 'mismatch' can be captured by the public in a longer period, such as three or five years, and it diminishes their political trust.

In addition to the main results, as robustness checks, I also exploited the design of the pilot policy to explore the marginal effect of propaganda on the policy's target population. I conducted regression modelling of the official propaganda on political trust with the urban samples, and the results are shown in Table 4.6, focusing on the targeted group for the policy reform, enterprise employees in the piloted provinces. Columns 1 to 3 show the short-term effect of the propaganda on urban residents and its marginal effect on enterprise employees, while columns 4 to 6 present the comparable effect of propaganda over the long term. The outcome for the policy's target population was in line with my Hypothesis 3, in which local official propaganda has incremental effects on political trust in the short term and has reductive effects on the public's confidence in the long term. In particular, short-term propaganda significantly increased the target population's trust in local (country/district) governments by 0.365 (=0.368−0.003) and in provincial governments by 0.267 (=0.272−0.005). (Since all of these are interactive terms, the real estimations are the combination of two coefficients relating to the specific variable: for instance, the 0.365 is calculated by adding up 0.368 and −0.003.) The effect on the target population's trust in the central government 0.015 (=0.017−0.002) was positive but insignificant. Long-term propaganda, measured as either accumulated over three years or five years, led to a significant loss of public trust in local and provincial governments among the target population. In particular, the three to five years of official propaganda exposure diminished the trust of enterprise employees in the local government from −0.293 (=−0.292−0.001) to

Table 4.6: Short-term and long-term propaganda effects on directly targeted group in piloted provinces (2009 urban data)

	Model 1			Model 2			Model 3		
	Political trust in different levels of government								
Variables	Local gov	Province gov	Central gov	Local gov	Province gov	Central gov	Local gov	Province gov	Central gov
Enterprise employee	0.056 (0.097)	−0.008 (0.092)	−0.070 (0.095)	0.044 (0.121)	−0.092 (0.124)	−0.134 (0.130)	0.100 (0.142)	−0.076 (0.144)	−0.107 (0.151)
Policy propaganda (1 yr)	0.368*** (0.122)	0.272** (0.112)	0.017 (0.107)						
Enterprise employee × Policy propaganda (1 yr)	−0.003 (0.011)	−0.005 (0.011)	−0.002 (0.010)						
Policy propaganda (3 yrs)				−0.292*** (0.097)	−0.211** (0.088)	−0.009 (0.085)			
Enterprise employee × Policy propaganda (3 yrs)				−0.001 (0.010)	0.005 (0.010)	0.005 (0.010)			
Policy propaganda (5 yrs)							−0.556*** (0.185)	−0.403** (0.168)	−0.020 (0.161)
Enterprise employee × Policy propaganda (5 yrs)							−0.006 (0.011)	0.004 (0.012)	0.002 (0.012)
#Old age people in the family	0.068*** (0.022)	0.077*** (0.020)	0.037* (0.021)	0.068*** (0.022)	0.076*** (0.020)	0.037* (0.021)	0.069*** (0.022)	0.077*** (0.020)	0.037* (0.021)
Observations	729	711	733	729	711	733	729	711	733
R-squared	0.088	0.111	0.099	0.088	0.111	0.100	0.088	0.111	0.099

Note: $p<0.1$, $p<0.05$, $p<0.01$. All models include demographic controls and province dummies.

−0.562 (=−0.556–0.006) and the provincial government (from 0.206 to 0.399) using similar calculations. The results show that, with long periods of local official propaganda, the target population's political trust in local and provincial governments regarding the pension pilot policy consistently declined, reversing from positive to negative. In general, we may conclude that the negative effect of long-term local official propaganda on local regime support does not vary among different social groups.

More robustness tests, including results with order logit model, multilevel model, models with intergenerational difference, and other confounding variables can be found in Appendix A, Section A4.

Conclusions

Policy experimentation can help downplay controversial reforms by slowing down policy implementation and minimising the confusion and reaction of the public. In cases where the authority wishes to evaluate the potential trade-off between opportunities and challenges of conducting social and economic reforms (social change), policy experimentation is useful to buffer the associated risks. Meanwhile, it is vital for the authority to promote its intentions, construct knowledge, and shape a population's ideology by propaganda. Hence, a combination of incremental piloting of policy and relevant constructed propaganda helps the government to manage any chance of public discontent and build a consensus for the reform.

A government always needs to make the greatest possible effort to promote a potentially controversial policy, especially during a time of socio-economic transition. After the 'socialisation' period, the welfare reform in China entering the 2010s exhibited substantial diversity in policy design, under increasing pressure from the people over the social justice of redistribution and the sustainability of the welfare system. The government proposed reforms such as postponing the retirement age, integrating the rural and urban pension schemes, and allowing the social security fund to be listed. However, the steady progress of these follow-up adjustments relied on a consensus over the sharing of welfare responsibility between the state and individuals.

Evidence in this chapter shows that China's pension reform for urban enterprise employees is a combined tactic of policy experimentation and official propaganda. However, although the socialisation of welfare provision relieved the government of its complete responsibility, the transition may also reduce the public's confidence on government capacity and accountability. Therefore, the central government used policy experimentation for the pension reform as a dialogue mechanism between the state and the public for building up social consensus on a welfare system with hybrid contributors. Local governments employed official propaganda to socially construct and persuade the public by projecting an omnipotent image of the government as a way of maintaining the public's faith about regime capacity.

The empirical results based on two rounds of survey data and local propaganda data show that the pilot policy decreased the public's perception of governmental responsibility on elderly welfare in general. Moreover, the longer that individuals experienced the pilot policy, the greater the attitudinal change was. However, along with the pilot policy, local governments' use of official propaganda to maintain the government's image amid welfare provision and justify shared responsibility *reduced* the public's faith in the omnipotent role of the government to a certain extent. Moreover, the disjunction of policy propaganda and policy experimentation seems to have been recognised by the public and this phenomenon led to a decrease in the perceived credibility of the governments in the long term.

These conclusions align well with those in many studies focusing on the transitional role of governments in welfare reforms. Despite China's policy experimentation and propaganda both being useful at the onset, the political attitude of the public in general later seems to have been influenced by the mixed information arising from the various approaches. As in other cases, their support for the regime may lessen unexpectedly – or even reverse – in the long term. Facing the state's well-designed statecraft, an individual's options are limited but not null. People are capable of identifying the potential inconsistency in policy details and the propaganda, so should the state be seen to (in a broad sense) 'go back on its word' this might lead to loss of public confidence. Therefore, in Chapter 5 I move beyond looking only at pension reforms to further unpack the wider state–individual power interactions, from the perspective of individuals and the possibilities they have for counter-conduct.

Acknowledgements

Chapter 4 received strong support from Prof. Xufeng Zhu (Tsinghua University) on data collection and valuable feedback on framing, and a related collaborated article is under review with disciplinary journals.

Notes

1 The dataset does not include the official newspaper data of Shandong Province and thus is complemented by another newspaper database, that of 'Wisenews' (http://wisenews.wisers.net) [accessed July 2016].

2 'National Bureau of Statistics' (http://www.stats.gov.cn) [accessed July 2016].

3 The pilot policy was conducted in three waves. The full scale of funding the individual accounts by local governments and the financial subsidies from the central government varied somewhat across these three waves.

References

Anderson, K.; and Ebbinghaus, B. (2011). *The Varieties of Pension Governance. Pension Privatization in Europe.*

Beck, H. (1997). *The Origins of the Authoritarian Welfare State in Prussia: Conservatives, Bureaucracy, and the Social Question, 1815–70.* University of Michigan Press. https://doi.org/10.3998%2Fmpub.13913

Beetham, D. (1991). 'Max Weber and the legitimacy of the modern state'. *Analyse & Kritik*, vol. 13, issue 1, 34–45. https://doi.org/10.1515/auk-1991-0102

Béland, D. (2005). 'Ideas and social policy: An institutionalist perspective'. *Social Policy & Administration*, vol. 39, issue 1, 1–18. https://doi.org/10.1111/j.1467-9515.2005.00421.x

Benish, A.; Haber, H.; and Eliahou, R. (2017). 'The regulatory welfare state in pension markets: mitigating high charges for low-income savers in the United Kingdom and Israel'. *Journal of Social Policy*, vol. 46, issue 2, 313–330. https://doi.org/10.1017/S0047279416000593

Bian, Y.; and Logan, J. R. (1996). 'Market transition and the persistence of power: The changing stratification system in urban China'. *American Sociological Review*, 739–758. https://doi.org/10.2307/2096451

Boushey, G. (2016). 'Targeted for diffusion? How the use and acceptance of stereotypes shape the diffusion of criminal justice policy innovations in the American states'. *American Political Science Review*, vol. 110, issue 1, 198–214. https://doi.org/10.1017/s0003055415000532

Cai, H.; and Treisman, D. (2006). 'Did government decentralization cause China's economic miracle?' *World Politics*, vol. 58, issue 4, 505–535. https://doi.org/10.1353/wp.2007.0005

Chen, X.; and Shi, T. (2001). 'Media effects on political confidence and trust in the People's Republic of China in the post-Tiananmen period'. *East Asia*, vol. 19, issue 3, 84–118. https://doi.org/10.1007/s12140-001-0011-3

Cook, L. J. (1993). *The Soviet Social Contract and Why It Failed: Welfare Policy and Workers' Politics from Brezhnev to Yeltsin*, vol. 86. Harvard University Press.

Cook, L. J. (2013). *Postcommunist Welfare States: Reform Politics in Russia and Eastern Europe.* Cornell University Press. https://doi.org/10.7591%2F9780801460098

Cox, R. H. (2001). 'The social construction of an imperative: Why welfare reform happened in Denmark and the Netherlands but not in Germany'. *World Politics*, vol. 53, issue 3, 463–498. https://doi.org/10.1353/wp.2001.0008

Denisova, I.; Eller, M.; Frye, T.; and Zhuravskaya, E. (2012). 'Everyone hates privatization, but why? Survey evidence from 28 post-communist countries'. *Journal of Comparative Economics*, vol. 40, issue 1, 44–61. https://doi.org/10.1016/j.jce.2011.11.001

Di Tella, R.; Galiani, S.; and Schargrodsky, E. (2012). 'Reality versus propaganda in the formation of beliefs about privatization'. *Journal of Public Economics*, vol. 96, issue 5–6, 553–567. https://doi.org/10.1016/j.jpubeco.2011.11.006

Donovan, M. C. (2001). *Taking Aim: Target Populations and the Wars on AIDS and Drugs*. Georgetown University Press.

Easton, D. (1975). 'A re-assessment of the concept of political support'. *British Journal of Political Science*, vol. 5, issue 4, 435–457. https://doi.org/10.1017/s0007123400008309

Ekman, J.; and Linde, J. (2005). 'Communist nostalgia and the consolidation of democracy in Central and Eastern Europe'. *Journal of Communist Studies and Transition Politics*, vol. 21, issue 3, 354–374. https://doi.org/10.1080/13523270500183512

Fan, Y. (2015). 'The centre decides and the local pays: Mandates and politics in local government financial management in China'. *Local Government Studies*, vol. 41, issue 4, 516–533. https://doi.org/10.1080/03003930.2014.968706

Gao, Q. (2006). 'The social benefit system in urban China: Reforms and trends from 1988 to 2002'. *Journal of East Asian Studies*, vol. 6, issue 1, 31–67. https://doi.org/10.1017/s1598240800000035

Gao, Q.; Yang, S.; and Li, S. (2013). 'The Chinese welfare state in transition: 1988–2007'. *Journal of Social Policy*, vol. 42, issue 4, 743–762. https://doi.org/10.1017/s0047279413000329

Goode, E.; and Ben-Yehuda, N. (1994). 'Moral panics: Culture, politics, and social construction'. *Annual Review of Sociology*, vol. 20, issue 1, 149–171. https://doi.org/10.1146/annurev.so.20.080194.001053

Gough, I. (2001). 'Globalization and regional welfare regimes: The East Asian case'. *Global Social Policy*, vol. 1, issue 2, 163–189. https://doi.org/10.1177/146801810100100202. OA: https://eprints.lse.ac.uk/43959

Guthrie, D. (2012). *China and Globalization: The Social, Economic and Political Transformation of Chinese Society*. Routledge.

Hacker, J. S. (2002). *The Divided Welfare State: The Battle over Public and Private Social Benefits in the United States*. Cambridge University Press. https://doi.org/10.1017%2Fcbo9780511817298

Haggard, S.; and Kaufman, R. R. (2008). *Development, Democracy, and Welfare States: Latin America, East Asia, and Eastern Europe*. Princeton University Press.

Hall, P. A. (2001). 'The evolution of economic policy'. *Developments in French Politics*, vol. 2, 172–191.

Heilmann, S. (2008a). 'From local experiments to national policy: The origins of China's distinctive policy process'. *The China Journal*, vol. 59, 1–30. https://doi.org/10.1086/tcj.59.20066378

Heilmann, S. (2008b). 'Policy experimentation in China's economic rise'. *Studies in Comparative International Development*, vol. 43, issue 1, 1–26. https://doi.org/10.1007/s12116-007-9014-4

Huang, H. (2013). 'Signal left, turn right: Central rhetoric and local reform in China'. *Political Research Quarterly*, vol. 66, issue 2, 292–305. https://doi.org/10.1177/1065912912443874

Huang, H. (2015). 'Propaganda as signaling'. *Comparative Politics*, vol. 47, issue 4, 419–444. https://doi.org/10.5129/001041515816103220

Huang, H. (2018). 'The pathology of hard propaganda'. *The Journal of Politics*, vol. 80, issue 3, 1034–1038. https://doi.org/10.1086/696863

Hynes, B. O. D.; and Hayes, N. (2011). 'Who benefits from early childcare subsidy design in Ireland?' *Journal of Poverty and Social Justice*, vol. 19, issue 3, 277–288. https://doi.org/10.1332/175982711x597017. OA: https://arrow.tudublin.ie/cgi/viewcontent.cgi?article=1034&context=cserart

Im, D.-K.; and Meng, T. (2015). 'The policy–opinion nexus: The impact of social protection programs on welfare policy preferences in China'. *International Journal of Public Opinion Research*, vol. 28, issue 2, 241–268. https://doi.org/10.1093/ijpor/edv013

Keefer, P.; and Khemani, S. (2011). *Mass Media and Public Services: The Effects of Radio Access on Public Education in Benin*. The World Bank. https://doi.org/10.1596%2F1813-9450-5559

Kennedy, J. J. (2009). 'Maintaining popular support for the Chinese Communist Party: The influence of education and the state-controlled media'. *Political Studies*, vol. 57, issue 3, 517–536. https://doi.org/10.1111/j.1467-9248.2008.00740.x

Kornai, J. (1992). *The Socialist System: The Political Economy of Communism*. Oxford University Press. https://doi.org/10.1515%2F9780691228020

Lawrence, E.; Stoker, R.; and Wolman, H. (2013). 'The effects of beneficiary targeting on public support for social policies'. *Policy Studies Journal*, vol. 41, issue 2, 199–216. https://doi.org/10.1111/psj.12014

Leung, J. C.; and Nann, R. C. (1995). *Authority and Benevolence: Social Welfare in China*. Chinese University Press.

Leung, J. C.; and Wong, H. S. (1999). 'The emergence of a community-based social assistance programme in urban China'. *Social Policy & Administration*, vol. 33, issue 1, 39–54. https://doi.org/10.1111/1467-9515.00130

Leung, J. C.; and Xu, Y. (2015). *China's Social Welfare: The Third Turning Point*. John Wiley & Sons.

Li, B.; and Zhong, Y. (2009). 'How did China's transitions impact people's welfare benefits in the reform era?' *Journal of Contemporary China*, vol. 18, issue 62, 813–829. https://doi.org/10.1080/10670560903174606

Li, J.; and Ge, K. (2010). 'Review of pension insurance individual account studies'. *Social Security Studies*, vol. 2, 21–26.

Li, Z.; and Wang, H. (2009). 'Return rate and replacement rate of individual account in basic pension insurance'. *Journal of Public Management*, vol. 6, issue 4, 45–51.

Lin, D.; and Ding, Y. (2007). 'New pension policy: Replacement rate comparison of new-old pension insurance policies'. *Population and Economy*, vol. 1, 69–74.

Lipset, S. M. (1959). 'Some social requisites of democracy: Economic development and political legitimacy'. *American Political Science Review*, vol. 53, issue 1, 69–105. https://doi.org/10.2307/1951731

Lü, X. (2014). 'Social policy and regime legitimacy: The effects of education reform in China'. *American Political Science Review*, vol. 108, issue 2, 423–437. https://doi.org/10.1017/s0003055414000124

Lu, X.; and Perry, E. J. (1997). *Danwei: The Changing Chinese Workplace in Historical and Comparative Perspective*. Me Sharpe.

Mares, I.; and Carnes, M. E. (2009). 'Social policy in developing countries'. *Annual Review of Political Science*, vol. 12, 93–113. https://doi.org/10.1146/annurev.polisci.12.071207.093504

Mashaw, J. L. (2006). 'Accountability and institutional design: Some thoughts on the grammar of governance'. *Public Law Working Paper*, vol. 116, 115–156. https://ssrn.com/abstract=924879

Maynard-Moody, S. W.; Musheno, M.; and Musheno, M. C. (2003). *Cops, Teachers, Counselors: Stories from the Front Lines of Public Service*. University of Michigan Press. https://doi.org/10.3998%2Fmpub.11924

McQuail, D. (1987). *Mass Communication Theory: An Introduction*. Sage Publications.

Mei, C.; and Liu, Z. (2014). 'Experiment-based policy making or conscious policy design? The case of urban housing reform in China'. *Policy Sciences*, vol. 47, issue 3, 321–337. https://doi.org/10.1007/s11077-013-9185-y

Montinola, G.; Qian, Y.; and Weingast, B. R. (1995). 'Federalism, Chinese style: The political basis for economic success in China'. *World Politics*, vol. 48, issue 1, 50–81. https://doi.org/10.1353/wp.1995.0003

Nee, V. (1996). 'The emergence of a market society: Changing mechanisms of stratification in China'. *American Journal of Sociology*, vol. 101, issue 4, 908–949. https://doi.org/10.1086/230784

Perry, E. J. (2007). 'Studying Chinese politics: Farewell to revolution?' *The China Journal*, vol. 57, 1–22. https://doi.org/10.1086/tcj.57.20066239. OA: https://dash.harvard.edu/bitstream/1/11595641/1/farewell.pdf

Perry, E. J. (2017). 'Higher education and authoritarian resilience: The case of China, past and present'. Harvard-Yenching Institute Working Paper Series. OA: https://dash.harvard.edu/handle/1/30822717

Pierson, P. (1994). *Dismantling the Welfare State?: Reagan, Thatcher and the Politics of Retrenchment*. Cambridge University Press. https://doi.org/10.1017%2Fcbo9780511805288

Pierson, P. (2001). 'Post-industrial pressures on the mature welfare states'. *The New Politics of the Welfare State*, vol. 1, 80–105. https://doi.org/10.1093%2F0198297564.003.0004

Polanyi, K.; and MacIver, R. M. (1944). *The Great Transformation*. USA: Beacon.

Ringen, S.; and Ngok, K. (2017). 'What kind of welfare state is emerging in China?' *Towards Universal Health Care in Emerging Economies*, 213–237. Springer. https://doi.org/10.1057%2F978-1-137-53377-7_8

Schneider, A. L.; and Ingram, H. M. (2019). 'Social constructions, anticipatory feedback strategies, and deceptive public policy'. *Policy Studies Journal*, vol. 47, issue 2, 206–236. https://doi.org/10.1111/psj.12281

Schneider, A. L.; Ingram, H.; and DeLeon, P. (2014). 'Democratic policy design: Social construction of target populations'. In P. Sabatier and C. Weible (eds), *Theories of the Policy Process*, 3rd edn, 105–149.

Schneider, A.; and Ingram, H. (1993). 'Social construction of target popula-tions: Implications for politics and policy'. *American Political Science Review*, vol. 87, issue 2, 334–347. https://doi.org/10.2307/2939044

Schneider, A.; and Sidney, M. (2009). 'What is next for policy design and social construction theory? 1'. *Policy Studies Journal*, vol. 37, issue 1, 103–119. https://doi.org/10.1111/j.1541-0072.2008.00298.x

Shi, S. J.; and Mok, K. H. (2012). 'Pension privatisation in Greater China: Insti-tutional patterns and policy outcomes'. *International Journal of Social Wel-fare*, vol. 21, S30–S45. https://doi.org/10.1111/j.1468-2397.2012.00875.x; https://doi.org/10.1111/j.1468-2397.2012.00875.x

Shi, T. (2014). *The Cultural Logic of Politics in Mainland China and Taiwan*. Cambridge University Press. https://doi.org/10.1017/CBO9780511996474

Shirk, S. L. (2011). *Changing Media, Changing China*. Oxford University Press.

Siebert, F. S.; Peterson, T.; and Schramm, W. (1956). *Four Theories of the Press: The Authoritarian, Libertarian, Social Responsibility, and Soviet Communist Concepts of What the Press Should Be and Do*. University of Illinois Press.

Song, S.; and Chu, G. S. F. (1997). 'Social security reform in China: The case of old-age insurance'. *Contemporary Economic Policy*, vol. 15, issue 2, 85–93. https://doi.org/10.1111/j.1465-7287.1997.tb00468.x

State Council. (1997). *Decision on Establishing a Unified System of Basic Pension Insurance for Enterprise Employees (State Council [1997] No.26)*. Retrieved from http://www.gov.cn/ztzl/nmg/content_412509.htm.

State Council. (2000a). *Opinions on Accelerating the Process of Social Welfare Socialization*. Retrieved from http://shfl.mca.gov.cn/article/zcfg/200809 /20080900019761.shtml.

State Council. (2000b). *The Notice of Issuing the Pilot Program of Urban Social Security System (State Council [2000] No.42)*. Retrieved from http://www .gov.cn/xxgk/pub/govpublic/mrlm/201011/t20101112_62507.html.

State Council. (2005). *Decision on Perfecting Basic System of Pension Insur-ance for Enterprise Employees (State Council [2005] No.38)*. Retrieved from http://www.gov.cn/zwgk/2005-12/14/content_127311.htm.

Szelenyi, I. (1978). 'Social inequalities in state socialist redistributive econo-mies'. *International Journal of Comparative Sociology*, vol. 19, issue 1–2, 63–87. https://doi.org/10.1177/002071527801900105

Szelenyi, I.; and Kostello, E. (1996). 'The market transition debate: Toward a synthesis?' *American Journal of Sociology*, vol. 101, issue 4, 1082–1096. https://doi.org/10.1086/230791

Szelenyi, I.; and Szelenyi, B. (1994). 'Why socialism failed: Toward a theory of system breakdown—Causes of disintegration of East European state social-ism'. *Theory and Society*, vol. 23, issue 2, 211–231. https://doi.org/10.1007 /bf00993815

Weingast, B. R. (1995). 'The economic role of political institutions: Market-preserving federalism and economic development'. *Journal of Law, Eco-nomics, & Organization*, 1–31. https://doi.org/10.1093/oxfordjournals.jleo .a036861

Wong, L. (2005). *Marginalization and Social Welfare in China*. Routledge. https://doi.org/10.4324%2F9780203982990

Wong, L.; and Ngok, K. (2006). 'Social policy between plan and market: Xia-gang (off-duty employment) and the policy of the re-employment service centres in China'. *Social Policy & Administration*, vol. 40, issue 2, 158–173. https://doi.org/10.1111/j.1467-9515.2006.00482.x

Xie, Y. (2016). 'Understanding inequality in China'. *Chinese Journal of Sociology*, vol. 2, issue 3, 327–347. https://doi.org/10.1177/2057150x16654059. OA: https://europepmc.org/article/MED/29854420

Yang, Y.; Wang, W.; and Zhang, M. (2010). 'Operational safety of social insurance fund: Experience from fully funding the individual accounts'. *Chinese Public Administration*, vol. 5, 61–66.

Zheng, G. (2016). *Evaluation of China's Social Protection Policies*. Retrieved from https://www.euchinasprp.eu/images/documents/Component1Cn/2017-assessment-eport/EvalSSCn.pdf

Zhu, X.; and Zhao, H. (2018a). 'Experimentalist governance with interactive central–local relations: Making new pension policies in China'. *Policy Studies Journal*. https://doi.org/10.1111/psj.12254

Zhu, X.; and Zhao, H. (2018b). 'Recognition of innovation and diffusion of welfare policy: Alleviating urban poverty in Chinese cities during fiscal recentralization'. *Governance*, vol. 31, issue 4, 721–739. https://doi.org/10.1111/gove.12332

CHAPTER 5

Falsification of 'manufactured compliance' and wider legitimation and governmentality issues

Although China is experiencing tremendous social and economic changes, the Chinese government reports considerable public endorsement from many kinds of survey results – all of which suggest people's praise of the current authority together with a strong sense of belonging and solidarity. Of course, the government uses many tactics to manufacture public consent and minimise the possibility of challenge from the governed with the case of pension reforms, as earlier chapters have shown. However, people can also reflect on and reshape the idea of the 'state', 'politics', and the 'state–individual relationship' in their interactions with governmental power. In other words, despite the well-designed statecraft of the government, *there are risks for the authorities of falsified compliance/consent from the people.*

These individual-level reflections and (undisclosed) second thoughts – or ideological rebellions or modifications – play an important role in shaping the long-term expectations and superficial compliance of the general people. Many studies have highlighted the constant bubbling up of collective actions from the bottom of society in China, which obviously contradict the orderly scene on the surface. Chapter 4 also showed empirically that, while in the short term people may express contentment with a controversial policy, in the long term there is a decline in political support as the real impact of the policy on their everyday lives fails to match with the official propaganda. This situation makes China an interesting field for studying the possibilities of falsified compliance and its implications for state governmentality.

Explaining why people do not do something is always complex and needs to take account of several different factors. I begin by considering the idea of 'falsification' by individuals of their views and what methods might help in detecting it. The second section looks at different aspects of people's compliance,

How to cite this book chapter:
Wang, Yan. 2022. *Pension Policy and Governmentality in China: Manufacturing Public Compliance*. London: LSE Press, pp. 129–179.
DOI: **https://doi.org/10.31389/lsepress.ppc.f**. License: CC BY

and especially words left in the shadows. Section 5.3 explores the idea that there is a dual track of political knowledge, allowing people to hold ideas in tension at the same time. The fourth section looks at ignorance, apathy, and collective conservatism as underpinnings for the status quo. Section 5.5 examines the impact of education, generations, and social heterogeneity on individuals' attitudes. The final section examines the likely actions people could take in such scenarios.

5.1 'Falsification' and methods for exploring it

The concept of 'falsification' is used here as a convenient label for a situation where people construct their public images/attitudes/preferences in a way that may not be exactly the same as their privately held images/attitudes/ preferences. Most commonly, a falsification in public compliance or consent usually describes the situation when people hide their true attitudes/preference. The population's falsified compliance could reshape and even distort the social order and public knowledge, and could be especially dangerous for the authority where it may lead to an unexpected 'cascade' (Kuran 1991; Kuran 1997). This chapter sets out to dig into the seemingly paradoxical situation that, on the one hand, the Chinese people report high public consent regarding authority, while on the other there is empirical evidence of discontent in private. A lack of confidence in the claims of the official publicity seems to have led to numerous collective activities around specific issues and people 'voting with their feet'. So, why and how do citizens disentangle their reported consent from private attitudes/choices? How do different mechanisms work for different social groups? Owing to the complexity of the research question, I combine observation and in-depth interviews to investigate the black box of the subjectively constructed public political attitudes of the people in an authoritarian regime.

Attitude falsification occurs when people are unwilling or unable to truthfully reveal their actual preferences (or attitudes), and so intentionally (or unintentionally) construct preferences that can be publicly reported. The notion of 'constructed attitudes' has its roots in social psychology studies and is sometimes used by the critics of social surveys. It is also an idea frequently used when describing public political attitudes in authoritarian regimes, as either 'falsified compliance' or 'preference falsification'. Social science scholars have devoted considerable effort to identifying examples and mechanisms whereby people falsify their ideas. In everyday social interaction, people tend to convey specific information about themselves (which may not be true in private) to others, in order to influence the audience's perceptions and judgements (Goffman 1978). The motivation of self-performance or impression management is to either to match one's own self-image or to match audience expectations and preferences. In these practices, individuals can achieve high social value (which is also called 'face') or satisfaction with themselves.

Social interaction therefore occurs when a person 'can be relied upon to maintain himself as an interactant, poised for communication and to act so that others do not endanger themselves by presenting themselves as interactants to him' (Goffman 2017, p. 155). The capacity to present oneself in the way one wishes is in practice distributed very unequally across the population. It may be determined by people's resources, experiences, personalities, and so on. Individuals' intentions and actions in constructing social images not only change the way that they express themselves but also exert a certain social pressure on others and change their behaviours (Bursztyn and Jensen 2017). In spite of the fact that self-presentation itself is investigated by many scholars, the prevalence of impression management causes inevitable problems in social science studies and opinion polls before elections/referendums. Since empirical social science research relies heavily on interviews and surveys, individuals' self-presentation can distort the results of empirical evidence. Researchers have identified many conditions involving the 'social desirability bias', such as the 'interviewer effect' in interviews and the 'pressure of social expectation' in social surveys (Edwards 1957; Nederhof 1985).

Research about the falsification of political preference was especially salient when the social scientist Tim Kuran proposed a theory to explain the unexpected revolutions in East European countries in the late 20th century. He defined falsification as the difference between people's public preferences and private preferences; 'preference falsification' occurs when an individual's public preference diverges from the one that he holds in private (Kuran 1991). Building on impression management, Kuran described a situation when individuals have several public preferences on a given issue, each tailored for a particular audience. He presented a vivid example of a Soviet citizen admitting to 'six faces' under communist repression: 'one for my wife; one, less candid, for my children, just in case they blurted out things heard at home; one for close friends; one for acquaintances; one for colleagues at work; and one for public display' (Kuran 1997). These 'faces' differed from each other in that the faces for his family could be very private and sincere, while the ones worn for colleagues and the public could be disguised. There are some extreme examples (such as during the Maoist period in China) when everyone had to perform in a politically correct way, even in private, because close family members could turn people in to the authorities for some casual 'wrong' word or action.

As opposed to spontaneity, performance and impression management are fairly common in societies of all kinds, where people are connected with others and receive rewards/punishment from 'others' – be they other individuals, social groups, or certain institutions. For instance, people with unorthodox views may fear revealing themselves in public owing to the social pressure in their community. Some candidates running for an election may seek to 'buy off' anyone who does not support them in the first place. The state apparatus can also force dissenters to show compliance, notwithstanding their strong discontent in private. What is fascinating for social scientists is to investigate the interaction of powers beneath the norm-enhancement, support, and compliance. Among the institutions and arenas that may generate falsification, authoritarian states (that are generally recognised as intolerant) attract much attention.

Public opinion or public support is crucial for political stability and even for the survival of the authority. Scholars are especially curious about changes of public opinion in authoritarian states, including the distribution of public opinion, the directions of any changes, and factors that shape changes in these regimes. More importantly, observers are often keen to assess how far the state is perceived by the citizens to be legitimate. Even more intriguing are unexpected events, such as the fall of the Soviet Union and the communist authorities in East Europe – when there was no clear sign of a revolution before the event (Kuran 1991). Falsification of public opinion may be one of the main factors to blame:

> [People] knew that to criticize their governments openly could derail their careers or land them in jail … even in the absence of formal sanctions, there is the universal human desire for approval, which often prevents people from voicing minority opinions. (Frank 1996, p. 115)

In this way, the discontent of the public can be disguised beneath the fake flourish of praise for the status quo. When the time comes, however, private non-compliance may turn into collective public non-compliance.

Studies about falsification in China have been undertaken, although of course the fall of the state has not occurred. It is commonly agreed that the political trust reported from survey data is very high. Tang's work (2016), along with many others', attributes this high political support to China's economic growth, the state's effective promotion of Chinese nationalism, the individual's external efficacy based on the government's responsiveness to public demands, and the cultural tradition of conformity. However, it is also widely admitted in China studies that people in Chinese society do hesitate to report discontent, especially when it concerns political authority. Scholars who do not think that people do not report their political trust in a sincere/truthful way also tend to believe that, as a typical communist and Asian regime, China's high political support derives from people's fear of the authority, or from the patriarchal and hierarchical culture of society and its politics (Fuchs 2007; Rose 2007; Rose, Mishler, and Munro 2006).

Yet, although falsifying compliance has been broadly discussed and recognised by plenty of theoretical arguments, empirical studies that provide evidence of 'preference falsification' in authoritarian regimes are scarce. Currently, several published or working papers have been produced. Jiang and Yang's paper (2016) took advantage of the political fall of one high-profile official in Shanghai, China, and constructed a semi-natural experiment to examine which people would lie about their attitude to corruption and the government.

Their result showed that the falsification was most intense among the groups that had access to alternative information but were vulnerable to political sanctions (Jiang and Yang 2016). Frye and his colleagues used a list experiment to test Putin's political support among Russian people and found counter-intuitive evidence: the high approval of Putin in Russia was genuine (Frye et al. 2017). Tang's work (Tang 2016) used a similar design and found similar 'true support' in China's case. Other empirical work includes Tannenberg's working paper manipulating the affiliation of the survey – government, academic institute, or NGO – to see whether or not people would falsify their answers (Tannenberg 2017). Shen and Truex's (2018) working paper considered existing social surveys and compared the abnormal 'no answer' replies to sensitive questions and to non-sensitive questions.

Many factors that could exacerbate the falsification of ideas in general social interactions and in the context of authoritarian regimes. Falsification in public attitudes may stem from inner utility, external temptations, or pressure. For instance, people may find it rewarding to falsify their opinion so as to follow the crowd, or find it frightening to reveal their true feelings in public. In some cases, people simply feel content or happy to present themselves with a certain public image. Generally speaking, there are several recognised sources of falsification in public political attitudes.

The most obvious ones are the 'reward' (or patronage resources, in many studies) and 'punishment' associated with one's reported preference (Magaloni 2006; Wedeen 1999). Reward is seen as a common tactic for the authority to exchange for loyalty and votes from the public (Lane 1984; Lust-Okar 2006; Pepinsky 2007; Zhao 2001). People who have fewer endowments and little bargaining power may be bought off more easily and then controlled by the authority (Blaydes 2006). Sharing benefits can also silence people who may not be pleased with those in power. So long as they display compliance, they may still be entitled to the benefits of being a member of the club. Punishment is another common factor that causes political attitudes to be falsified. People who voice their discontent and disloyalty may be punished by violence or must have their voices censored. Authoritarian governments find it easier to mobilise resources to buy loyalty and carry out punishment; people are thus more likely to disguise their true feelings/preferences, lest they seem unacceptable or undesired by the authority.

Some indirect sources are also identified in explaining the falsification in public opinion. For instance, individuals may overestimate or underestimate the conditions of public opinion, which is sometimes termed 'pluralistic ignorance'. For example, some members of the public could reject certain norms in private but mistakenly assume that most others accepted them (O'Gorman 1986; Noelle-Neumann 1993). A famous early lab experiment in social psychology (Asch and Guetzkow 1951) showed that individuals tended to obey a false consensual judgement rather than risk being isolated as deviants. Using a computational simulation, Centola and his colleagues (2005) carefully discussed the equilibrium in pluralistic ignorance, whereby few people would actually enforce a norm but no one realises this. They found that, if agents' horizons are limited to their immediate neighbours, highly unpopular norms can be enforced by both true believers and non-believers. Another explanation for possible (ignorant) falsification in public attitudes is the effect of socialisation and education. For example, students in high school may present a politically correct opinion for questions about politics, simply because they know the 'right' answer and have not reflected on it. These two indirect sources are more or less unconscious falsifications compared to the types of falsification brought about by rewards and punishments. However, they may still be useful for the authority and manipulated by state power through information segregation and educational cultivation.

When the state acts as a central source of power, both 'totalizing' and 'individualizing' power (Foucault 2009), a phenomenon in Chinese political attitudes in line with the effective governmentality can be identified: the involution of people's political attitude. The concept of 'involution' – meaning internal shrinkage, turning in, or closure, as the opposite of external growth – was originally used by Clifford Geertz to describe the process in Java where agriculture appeared to intensify rather than change under the external economic pressure from the Dutch rulers and the internal population (Geertz 1963). Later on, the concept was borrowed by Philip Huang to describe the rice economy of the Yangzi Delta, which he argued was locked in a pattern of 'involutionary growth' with little or no improvement in per capita output and living standards and a pattern of declining labour productivity (Huang 1990). Another school stretched the concept of 'involution' to apply to state theory; for example, Prasenjit Duara (1987) took China's example in the early 20th century and introduced 'state involution' as an imperfect state-making process wherein:

> an expanding state structure penetrating levels of society untouched before, subordinating, co-opting, or destroying the relatively autonomous authority structures of local communities in a bid to increase its command of local resources, appeared to be repeating itself in late imperial and republican China. (Duara 1987, p. 132)

Entering the 1990s, the concept of involution was widely used in social science writing on China to describe the phenomena of the social economy or cultural system exhibiting 'increased inertia'. Both external restrictions and internal factors are possible reasons for such involution. For instance, in explaining the operational logic of the state-owned enterprises, Li and Zhang (1999) argued that the SOEs followed two contradicting objectives: optimising the efficiency of the enterprise while maximising the welfare of the employees. The two objectives dragged the SOEs in the direction of functional involution and staffing intensification and led to the standstill of enterprises. Some other works have addressed the involution of dictatorship, the involution of *guanxi* (social connections), and the involution of social class in Chinese society. Generally speaking, it can be used to refer to all kinds of communities or situations where transformation fails and the inner complexities proliferate without new inputs.

I introduce the notion of 'involution' here to capture the increasingly obvious trend in Chinese political attitudes formed in a situation where the state as a central source of power can construct the knowledge (political or social) in whatever form is most suited to maintaining its power. Individuals who have limited access to alternative explanations of social facts are less likely to interpret the environment in a different way. In the long term, even when citizens are provided with a new possibility, they are not capable of accepting a different version of the story, or reaching out on their own initiative (as shown in Chen and Yang 2019). To be sure, social knowledge is still increasing in society, thanks to the diversity of the population and the historical trend that keeps moving forward. However, it increases without questioning past or current stories, and therefore is leading to an involution of the population's 'hard knowledge' (Kuran 1997). In the following section, I demonstrate with more substantive evidence the 'involution' process as regards social knowledge and public opinions.

Is there any chance of breaking the cycle? A Foucauldian understanding of counter-conduct can be found in all kinds of power relation: struggles against exploitation, domination and subjection. Foucault did not use concepts such as 'revolt', 'disobedience', 'insubordination', 'dissidence', and 'misconduct' because they were, in his view, 'either too strong, too weak, too localized, too passive, or too substance-like' (Foucault 2009, p. 200). Conduct and counter-conduct emphasises the idea of the same thing being *utilised and reutilised* in state–population interaction, analogous to describing the state's strength and its circular working through the population's well-being. In Foucault's example of techniques of Christianity, he argued that one of the most important aspects of Christianity's 'pastoral' power was that it had a sophisticated understanding of the congregation's imagining of the world, their inner secrets, their expectations of reality. The respective counter-conduct against the pastoral power similarly relies on the form of the tactical elements being used in conduct. The struggle against subjection requires individuals to make an effort to break out of the subjectification imposed by the state through the process of self-formation and self-understanding. My exploration of the individual's subjective rebellion against the involution of political attitude in authoritarian regimes begins with two different but overlapping approaches: either through falsified compliance (intentionally or non-intentionally) or through active reflection on subjectivity, power and the current state–individual relationship. Of these two approaches, reflection is more difficult to achieve, but more meaningful in breaking the 'involution' of public/private knowledge.

In this research, I take falsified compliance in authoritarian regimes as the hidden discontent with and disdain for the authorities in people's voiced consent. Compliance includes political trust of the government and the incumbent leader. Acceptance regards political uncertainties during the reform, approval of the official propaganda, and so on. It is not easy to find people's real attitudes, especially in answers to questions that may be quite sensitive. Therefore, I use a combination of observation and in-depth interviews to address this problem.

Observational data are valuable for painting a preliminary picture of the population. Combining with the relevant literature, they are also important for researchers constructing basic assumptions and hypotheses. I actively participated in the social life of Beijing during my fieldwork from September to December 2018. I also keep track of changes in public opinion through Chinese social media and make notes on important texts accordingly, as evidence to reflect on. Observational evidence provided a solid foundation for my follow-up research design and data collection; it also worked as a useful source of cross-validating references in my final analysis.

Face-to-face interviewing is a useful tool that allows researchers to observe the interviewees' reactions and add tailored follow-up questions (Seidman 2006). The emotions, the choice and the lengths of pauses and reactions during an interview are good pointers to the unnatural situation of an interviewee. For the first round of interviews, I conducted 10 face-to-face in-depth interviews with four male and six female interviewees from various backgrounds. Their ages ranged from early 20s to late 60s, and their occupations covered government officials, retired enterprise employees, public institutional employees, private sector employees, unemployed young people, students at school, and so on. Five of the interviewees were recruited through my own social network (such as a friend of my parents, a remote relative, the parent of a college friend, who might have willingness to reveal their true attitudes to me), while the other five were recruited through a local community in collaboration with a municipal social science research institute. Each interview lasted at least one hour, rising sometimes to five hours, depending on the situation. To help them relax and feel secure in talking about politics, all the interviewees were informed in advance that the whole conversation would not be recorded and notes would not be taken during the interviews (with permissions to use the anonymised content of our dialogue in the book). Thus, quotations from the interviews given here are not verbatim records of what the interviewees said, but recalled versions, noted after the interviews and translated for inclusion here.

The first-round interviews focused on the interviewees' experiences, ideological changes, and the politics in their daily lives. We discussed such topics as how they perceived the current political situation, the past 40 years of transformation (reform) and the future possibilities of society; their view of a desirable state–individual relationship; whether they believed the rhetoric and discourses promoted by the authority; and what they thought about the potential challenges of the state. In some conversations, I asked directly about falsified public attitudes in general and their opinion of falsification. In addition to these in-depth interviews, during the fieldwork period I discussed the above topics with more than 15 social scientists from various academic institutions in

China in private talks, workshop panel discussions, and so on. These materials provided me with primary evidence of the falsification in public political attitudes. Combining them with the existing theories and the research questions underlying my whole book, I narrowed down some hypotheses, which were designed to be further discussed and explored with a second-round interview.

The first set of hypotheses relates to the existence and different types of falsification of political consent. It has been constantly argued in both theoretical and empirical works that general (or diffuse) political support is substantially different from specific political support, since Easton's (1965; 1975) work on the multiple dimensions of this concept. People may show different levels of compliance regarding different branches of the current political institutions. They may have specific complaints regarding certain polities and may even have special expectations of certain politicians. Thus, my investigation of the heterogeneity of falsification in people's political support starts from the varied features related to politics.

The political support for the Chinese state's institutions already has considerable internal variations. Many of my interviewees had a sense that 'the state is good and sincere [to its people], [it's] just local authorities twisting the policies and instructions'. The *state* here is more than central government; it is also an abstract idea of the grand governors who rank above local officers. For ordinary Chinese people, the idea of the 'state' is a vague concept that mixes the notion of country, nation, government, and sometimes even the Communist Party. Chinese people in general never seem to fear the expansion of the state – as long as they can get benefit and convenience from the expansion (Xiang 2010). In this sense, the state–individual relationship reveals some duplicity. On the one side, the 'state' as an abstract image is moralised and is given legitimacy by its nature in good faith. Yet, on the other side, the public is highly suspicious about the specific actions of state institutions: the interaction between individuals and the branches of government/officials relies heavily on the exchange of benefits. With such Janus-faced attitudes in mind, it is easy to explain hierarchical political trust (T. Shi 2001), as well as the rule consciousness in China's contentious politics (L. Li 2010). People trust the central government more than the local government and would blame the local government for 'not following directions from the centre'; and, when people perceive 'injustice' from local government, they tend to appeal for 'just and right' supervision from a higher authority. Examples of treating local officials/government as scapegoats when a policy fails, but respectfully addressing the top leader as 'Chairman Xi', are not uncommon in my interviews, either.

To better understand the complexity of political support revealed in my interviews and the theoretical arguments, I first hypothesise about the potential differentiation of falsified compliance directed at the various types of state representative: the local authority, the central government, the Chinese Communist Party (CCP), and the incumbent president Xi Jinping as top leader. The public's criticism of these state representatives differs in the freedom of discourse that is allowable: the lower in the hierarchy is the subject discussed, the less controlled the speech is. Thus, the deficiencies of local government furnish the least sensitive context. My first hypothesis is about the heterogeneity of falsification of political support: people falsify their compliance regarding the central government, the party, and the top leader, but will reveal their true discontent regarding local authorities.

The objects that I use to test the varieties of compliance include a multilevel measurement. The first – *attitudinal* – level covers questions about whether the respondents would agree with various statements (which might not be 100% true) about social conditions under the promotion (endorsement) of different state representatives; for example, 'under the leadership of CCP, education brings a higher possibility of social mobility', or 'under the leadership of the central government, the dual track social pension system [covered in Chapter 3] has been largely reduced'. The second – *cost* – level refers to the individual level of cost that people are willing to bear at the request of different state representatives. Here I distinguish two kinds of cost: the cost of common goods (taxes imposed on individual goods to protect the environment) and the cost of national requests (income/consumption degradation to help China win in the trade war with the US). The underlying rationale here is that people are more willing to express their true feelings in response to questions that are less sensitive to them.

As indicated in the duality theory of the state, Chinese people are quite capable of disentangling the policies from the policymakers – a policy is acceptable as long as it does not hurt their own interests too much. In many cases, people take their chance in the policy reform and bargain with the government (without fundamentally questioning the legitimacy of the policymakers) to gain more benefits. There are many cases of controversial policies that the interviewees criticised in our conversations, but very few of them would directly blame the incumbent central authority. When it came to specific policies, such as the property tax, education reform, and health care policies, some interviewees would open with, 'I am not saying there is anything wrong with it, just some things I think the policy could improve in a little bit' or 'The state may have an overarching design and I believe it's a good policy, but there may be some local officials who distort it when they put it into action'. For instance, with regard to the education policy of 'lifting the student's burden', young parents complained that this leads to the problem of shifting the burden of educating children from the schools to the parents. Since the primary schools are reducing the school hours and the size of the curriculum, parents have to register their children in private education institutions after school. When I probed their complaints, however, some of them identified the discontinuity and arbitrariness of the policy to a certain extent. Therefore, we may suppose that the degree of falsification is not significant for specific policies even when the policy is controversial.

The logic of people's attitudes to the official propaganda is not one-way, either. On the one hand, they are easily guided by the propaganda content (as shown in Chapters 3 and 4). On the other, I also discovered that people could identify the disjunction between official propaganda and the policy content and this disjunction sooner or later led to a loss of political trust. Existing studies suggest that the Chinese public is aware of pro-regime bias from official mouthpieces, but still trust these outlets more than other sources (Truex 2016). It is possible that the public prefers the official reports to commercial/foreign news sources, while also being able to admit that their preferences are swayed by the propaganda. In other words, people may recognise that the official propaganda only says 'good words' about the government and never says 'bad words', but still believe that these words are 'real' and 'trustworthy'. This is consistent with the model shown in Kamenica and Gentzkow's work: that the degree to which citizens are persuaded by a positive media report is negatively related to the degree of media bias (Kamenica and Gentzkow 2011). To further explore the 'cognitional duality' regarding official propaganda, I extended my exploration of falsified compliance to a third subsection: people's attitudes to the legitimacy of official news. To be more specific, I wanted to know whether people could identify the element of indoctrination in official propaganda and why they liked biased official news better than other news. The related hypothesis is that people do not falsify their acknowledgement of the social constructive nature of official propaganda. Moreover, people may be aware of the potential discontinuity in public discourse.

Apart from the existence of falsification, I was also interested in the mechanisms that could induce falsification in reported public attitudes. An inference design is not feasible with qualitative data; therefore, in this research I focused only on the details of possible reasons, rather than making causal inferences as shown in the hypotheses. As I explained in the theoretical discussion, people may choose to falsify their true political attitudes – because they are aware of the potential rewards of displaying loyalty in public, or because they are afraid of potential punishment from showing discontent, or they mistakenly perceive that the general public hold a certain 'common' viewpoint. In line with the model of statecraft used to generate compliance in Chapter 1, the state would prefer to manufacture true consent and avoid falsification brought about by fear. For individuals, I hypothesise the following relationship between the effect of punishment and rewards on displayed compliance: punishment, rather than reward indicates a higher degree of falsification.

During the first-round interviews, one factor that was not highlighted in the existing explanations was the low political efficacy people have when talking about the reason for not telling the truth or fighting for their own rights. 'There won't be anything changed even if I speak up'; 'It's just not my turn to discuss about [these political issues]'. This may be because citizens are not confident about the responsiveness of the government, or they are not confident in their own ability of making a difference, or both. To identify the role of political efficacy, one hypothesis I propose to further discuss regarding the mechanism behind the falsification is: low political efficacy might relate to a high degree of falsification.

In addition to the general scenario of falsification and the average effect of stimulation (such as the rewards for showing loyalty, or punishments for non-compliance) on the population as a whole, people with distinctive endowments may have different degrees of falsification and various degrees of elasticity regarding the spectrum of stimulation. Chapters 2 and 3 showed that the government is prepared to differentiate the allocation of benefit and construct specific knowledge for people of high or low political status. Political status and age group determine 'what pension benefits people get', as well as 'what policies/propaganda/education they receive or experience'. Consequently the cost of expressing oneself truthfully varies and the motivation to construct a public face varies a great deal. Exploring the potential heterogeneity of falsification among different social groups was valuable for unpacking the varied degrees of falsification in people's political attitudes.

Jiang and Yang (2016) also touched upon unequally distributed falsification of the attitude to corruption in different social groups. Falsification was most intense among the groups that had access to alternative information but were vulnerable to political sanctions. Shen and Truex (2018) in their working paper also showed that, when they measured the falsification with an unusual inflation of 'don't know' and 'no answer' responses to sensitive questions in cross-sectional surveys, self-censorship was more prevalent among older cohorts (who voiced extremely high levels of support for the regime), women, ethnic minorities, non-Party members, and members of the working class. The evidence of these writers thus suggests that people who are marginalised in society are more likely to falsify their political attitudes with 'don't know' and 'no answer' responses.

I highlighted the first category of heterogeneity among social groups by saying that people who are closer to the power system react more strongly (with a higher degree of falsification) to the possibility of punishment than people who are further from it. The logic is that people who are closer to the power system may enjoy more benefits and privilege, but they are also sensitive to the potential loss that they might suffer if they revealed their discontent and moved away from the 'guided road'. For instance, taking the most prestigious group, would an officer from the public sector be more prone to falsify their loyalty to the authority than a farmer? I asked one interviewee from the government sector why he did not try to use his position inside the government machine to offer a suggestion to the decision makers when he found aspects of policy that were not feasible at the local level. He replied:

> we are not like ordinary people who have nothing to lose by arguing with the government. We [government officials] all have to be very careful about picking out errors for the leaders. It's like skating on thin ice – one careless move could ruin everything. (no. 22)

Another characteristic that may determine people's ability to distinguish the problem in official propaganda and deliberately construct their public preferences is their educational level. People who are more educated are more likely to receive diverse sources of information ('alternative information', as Jiang and Yang (2016) called it) and are more likely to be critical about the current political, social, and economic situation. Meanwhile, an individual's education level may highly correlate to people's closeness with the power system, which makes them more likely to hide their discontent (if it exists). I propose the next hypothesis: people who are more educated are more likely to falsify compliance regarding nationalist requests from the authority.

In addition to the feature of 'distance from the power system' and 'educational capacity' discussed above, some other heterogeneities may be decisive for people's reported compliance regarding authority and the state apparatus. For example, would a respondent who had been exposed to a socialist education be less likely to falsify loyalty to the party? Would respondents who belong to an ethnic minority be more sensitive than other people to possible political sanctions? I investigate these questions in greater depth when I analyse the data. The final differentiation of social groups is age, or generational difference. People who have experienced more in society are in general more likely to conceal their true discontent. Hence, the last hypothesis is: people who are younger are less likely to falsify their discontent.

The 15 second-round interviews were conducted in late May and June 2019, through the video chat on the online social platform WeChat (for interviewees who were located in China) and face-to-face interviews (for the few interviewees who were in London). In order to capture the heterogeneity of the population, I invited interviewees through snowball sampling from a diverse range of ages, genders, occupations, education levels, ethnicities, and locations in China. A detailed table of interviewees' attributes is shown in the Appendix A, Section A5. Each interview lasted 1.5 to two hours. As in the pre-research interviews, the interviewees were informed in advance that the interview would not be recorded and would be anonymous. Rather than rigidly following the three blocks of hypotheses proposed above – 'falsification, mechanism, and potential actions' – the interview questions were tailored for the interviewees according to their personal situations and instant reactions to specific questions. The questions were also continually modified according to the stream of interactions between them and me.

My strategy of interviewing for falsified compliance and disguised discontent also took advantage of the changing political and social environment in the presidency of Xi Jinping. The period of Hu Jintao and Wen Jiabao's administration was widely recognised as open in political power sharing and decentralised. During their administration from 2003 to 2013, much progress was made in social welfare reforms and social events often drove the institutional reform (e.g. see Kelly 2006; Liu and Sun 2016; K. Ngok 2013). The abolition of the 'temporary residence permit' regulation is an outstanding instance. It originated from the death of one migrant worker, but it later gathered widespread attention from the whole society and hastened the change of policy on migrants (Qiu and Wen 2007). It was also the period when online social media platforms (such as Weibo, launched in 2009) and some non-official papers (such as the *Southern Weekly*) came to the forefront of the forces monitoring political power through publicity and reports (Stockmann 2013; Tong and Lei 2010).

Xi's administration, however, started with a vehement anti-corruption campaign, a recentralisation of political power, and a gradual tightening up of the societal space. Censorship on online content accelerated around late 2017 and 2018. Moreover, in early 2018, the 13th National People's Congress approved the abolition of the limited presidential term in the constitution proposed by the CPC.[1] Beginning in 2018 and intensifying in 2019, the US–China trade war posed new challenges in the domestic socio-economic situation. This 'new normality' affected everyone's daily life, directly or indirectly. Many people experienced or heard of the 'disappearance' or 'explosion' of some personal social media accounts. Some government officials or civil servants were required to use a state-issued app called 'STUDY (XI) STRONG COUNTRY' every day. All the changes could be seen by people from every background and would be assessed and compared with conditions in previous periods. Therefore, it is fascinating to make use of the theme of *transition* in objective scenarios and to investigate the subjective perceptions of ordinary people.

In my interviews, I normally started with some casual talk about the worsening trade war and invited the interviewees to evaluate its impact on their everyday lives. I asked how much they would feel like paying as a patriotic sacrifice if the state requested them to give something up in order to win the trade war. Further questions could then turn to the general socio-economic situations in China in the previous year or two and how it differed from previous years, with varied questions regarding controversial social policies (such as the education inequality brought by the *hukou* system, or the patriotic slogans all over the streets), social issues (such as the perceived loss of space for public speech, or the accusations made against teachers by students for using 'inappropriate speech' in class), and institutional reforms (such as the lifting of term limits for the top leader, or anti-corruption moves and the foundation of the National Supervisory Commission). In addition to interviewees' personal reactions, I also paid attention to public opinion and public knowledge as they perceived them.

The potential problem is that the collected interviews data are not distinctively 'public' or 'private' in the attitudes they represent. They are clearly not 'public' since the interviews are all one-to-one conversations, so the interviewees can feel the intimacy of the dialogue and it is possible for them to trust me as a friend. But nor are they purely 'private', in the sense that I as the interviewer was still counted as a semi-stranger, not in the inner circle for most of the interviewees. However, from a different perspective, this may have been useful for my analysis. By combining the interview data with observational data, I could actually construct a relatively smooth scale, which covered the observational data proper to a public space (online and offline), the interview data of the middle-distance interviewees, and the observational data of very close friends/relatives.

Table 5.1: Qualitative data collection on falsified compliance

		Institutional difference	Difference in compliance
Falsified compliance	Legitimacy of representatives of the state	Local government	Agreements on social facts descriptions; Attribution of controversial policies
		Central government	
		CCP	Controversial institutional reforms; Pay for a nationalist request
		Xi as the top leader	
	Legitimacy of public discourse	Official propaganda	
		Political Knowledge	

It should also be highlighted that, owing to the accessibility problem, the interview evidence mainly came from the group of people who were more educated or living in major cities. Even though I tried my best to reach samples with distinctive attributes and backgrounds, the analysis in the following sections has *no* intention to offer any general inferences about the whole population. The discussion all focused on interpreting the accessible data from the interviews and observations, deciphering the rationale of certain choices at an individual level and revealing the heterogeneity of political compliance across different social groups within the range of available data. To better present the structure in the analysis part, Table 5.1 is helpful.

5.2 Different faces of compliance: the words in shadow

In this section, I first present the varied political compliance for different representatives of the state with evidence from the observational and interview data, deciphering the differentiated 'distinctive faces' that people constructed and the words in shadow.

The differentiated niches of the different levels of government resulted in several observable phenomena of people's political compliance. The first and most obvious one was that people tended to blame the local government for controversial policies while not questioning the ability and good faith of higher-ranking/central government. In other words, people generally did not avoid complaining or discussing controversial policies in public, but they would be cautious over attribution. For instance, from late 2018 to early 2019, a new policy of 'clearing and unifying the billboard format' was promoted in big cities and caused large-scale debates about the appropriateness of doing so. Many people argued that there was no need to keep the same format (e.g. font, size, and background colour) for all the billboards in the street; it was unaesthetic and the government was too controlling. A propos of this controversial urban policy in an interview, one interviewee who worked in Beijing said:

> Sometimes I feel like it is the local government that tries to do something excessive to take credit and seek rewards from the upper government or the central government … The 'unifying the billboard' campaign was getting heated last winter. Our office building … used to be able to control the light outside the building … last year, the local government informed us that we need to remove the original lights and install a new set of lights and follow the unified rule for on and off. We used to show the shape of a Christmas tree in the Christmas period, but now we can only follow the general instructions. (no. 11)

Although intolerable for some, policies relating to minor aspects of urban planning such as lighting and billboards seem no big deal to others. They can certainly tolerate the seemingly nonsensical regulations. Many people find it acceptable so long as the government can give explanations, even when a plan may affect local residents' lives, such as the construction of a chemical plant, or changing the purchase constraints on the real estate market:

> The government has its own difficulties; we [the people in general] should try to give sympathetic consideration to the mountainous problems the government has to solve. If the government gives us reasons [for policies that seem controversial], we should understand and give full support and not trouble them. (no. 16)

Regarding the reason why a higher-ranking government, especially the central government, should be trusted more than the local government, some people reasoned by comparing the abilities of the officials.

> The appearance of weird/strange policies is mostly like … the central government puts forward a certain project and the executive department and the local government are responsible for implementing it. However, the policies are very likely to be distorted or twisted in the process. The governance capacity of county level governments is very worrying; the local governmental officials do not possess enough knowledge and ability to capture the whole picture. But I think the cadres and leaders in upper government have higher education and merit, they can deal with the governance problems appropriately. (no. 9)

Although the topics of government, governance, and the state were not absolutely taboo in people's daily conversations, the sensitivity of various representations of the government was varied. As discussed in the section on hypotheses, the sensitivity of political issues relating to the government, party, and top leader gets more significance in moving to the right side of the scale. People were less likely (either from will or ability) to publicly discuss issues relating to the top leader, especially after the accession of Xi. For instance, the official accounts of state newspapers would close the comment area (which was in grey and no one can leave a comment under the post) when they posted a Weibo (a Twitter-like social platform) post concerning the top leader. For topics related to the party or central government, the official account would show only certain select comments with positive content.

The regulation of the party became stricter after the large-scale anti-corruption campaign in late 2012. At the time of writing, one former member of the Standing Committee of the Politburo, two vice-chairmen of the military commission, one alleged successor in the 20th Party Congress, and more than 200 provincial-level officials were all in jail due to this unexpectedly intense and protracted campaign. Following the anti-corruption campaign, the party regulations became more and more strict and came to directly affect party members in many ways. One of my interviewees who worked in a local government office talked about her personal experience and attitude:

> I read the news quite often, but mainly focus on the items which are closely related to my work and life. In everyday work, we basically have quite limited autonomy with regard to policies … we just follow the guidance from the upper government. In recent years, especially after Xi's reign, the workload has got substantially larger, working overtime is just as common as your meals every day … I knew many cases of death by overwork [among] local government officials … Everyone faces the heavy pressure of performance evaluation [by the upper government and the inspection group from central government] and strict regulation [of your behaviour]. The inspection group from the central are just like the feudal prefectural governor (刺史, CI SHI) in the old days[2] … I am aware that this is because of the start of the anti-corruption campaign and ideological education is very necessary inside the party. We currently have many 'red education' modules, such as party history, new theory, new thoughts [proposed by Xi] and local governments organise a visit for us to the 'red-base'[3] occasionally. I mean, in the current international and domestic situation, it's necessary to have ideological unity [inside the party]. (no. 2)

Party members who do not work in a government department can also identify changes in party regulations and have their own understanding of these topics. For instance, as one of the interviewees commented,

> Since the 18th National Congress of the Communist Party of China [when Xi was elected as the Party leader], the party regulation became

a core issue, which is much stricter than in previous periods. It starts from the cadres, with the campaign against the 'four styles' [formalism, bureaucracy, hedonism and extravagance]. Then party members are encouraged to join the 'two studies, one action' [study the party regulations, study the leader's speech, be a qualified party member]. There is also the 'STUDY (XI) STRONG COUNTRY' app, so all party members are strongly encouraged to use it every day. In other words, the party regulations have been normalised … There are also campaigns for a youth league, called 'one study, one action' [study Xi's thoughts, be a qualified youth league member]. And we all know the interaction between the party and the youth league is very close. We can see that ideological education has moved to the forefront in our society. This is better – the ruler can listen to the public and help to solve the problems at the grassroot. [I think] for a party that wants to rule such a big country with so many people, that it's necessary and correct to unify its own members and regulate their behaviour. (no. 4)

Another interviewee, who was a member of an ethnic minority and worked in a university that gave professional training, had similar observations to make in and outside the party:

My own experience, from school to work, is that the emphasis on ideology is stronger now. There used to be regulations for party members, but these were not strictly followed and no one would come along and accuse you directly. Now it's getting formal … In universities, we would also organise teachers to learn the new thoughts, or new regulations. The ideology is not just about communist or red ideology as you might think, it also includes our traditional concepts such as 'kindness and love', 'respect', 'equality', and so on. We also try to include patriotic ideas in our professional courses; [the attempt] is encouraged and promoted by our city government. For instance, we would introduce the idea of 'glorious China' in our textile courses and encourage students to include more traditional beauty in their work … The existence of such things must have its proper reasons. (no. 3)

Although many people might have genuinely found the Party regulations necessary and important, other voices mentioned the conspiracy feature of the anti-corruption campaign and the Party's stringent inspection of its cadres. For instance, in informal conversations, people passed on gossip and hearsay, like: 'The anti-corruption campaign started with good intentions, but seems to have been used as a weapon that certain people used to pull their opponents out of the party.' The issues related to the party were, however, generally not very controversial and people found it easy to accept the changes as new governance tactics that would contribute to social well-being. After all, the new party regulations reduced corruption and brought better-regulated and better-behaved cadres.

When we move from the party to the top leader (of the party and the state), the related issues are less likely to be discussed openly and discontents are less likely to be disclosed. One significant move of the top leader in recent years was the removal of limits to the term a state president can serve. Under the previous constitutional regulations, the president could not serve more than two consecutive terms; this rule was obeyed from 1982 onwards. But in the 2018 National People's Congress conference this constitutional limit was lifted, with only two delegates voting against and three abstaining, out of 2,964 votes.[4] This news attracted considerable attention overseas, because the move technically allowed a person to remain president for life. There were some domestic objections from a few intellectuals, though without anything being changed. What did ordinary people think? In the interviews, I asked, directly or indirectly, 'Would you think that if a leader has enough merits, he/she shouldn't be limited by term regulations?' In some interviews, when the conversation went well, I directly asked their feelings about Xi's case and what their friends' reactions had been back in 2018. Their reactions expressed similar passive sentiments. Although they did not agree with the political move of lifting the term limits, they were already trying to accept it and find excuses for it.

> If you ask me, I would say we really need term limits for top leaders. Our society and history are all very different from the Western system. It's difficult to change a 'guanxi' society and our reliance on the assumption of upright rulers. In such circumstances, if a leader stays in power for a long time, we might expect some flaws or wrong doings. Therefore, we need to make sure that when the time comes someone else will be there to fill the position ... But currently, [regarding Xi's] move we have no power to change the situation, although we can complain in private with our friends. (no. 3)

Some interviewees resorted to the reasoning that it was 'pointless to reject', or 'doesn't affect normal life' or 'people are already finding life enough of a struggle' when they disliked strong reaction to political change. Some simply responded to such events with 'we are not trained to express our opinions' or 'we should trust the central government'. Here are several examples of interviewees' replies regarding the term limit change:

> I feel like the change of term limit is just a political game. To be fair, whether it changes or not does not make much difference. We are a one-party state, the power and the rule of the party chairman is not under the control of any other authority ... and for people in general, well, we don't really do anything about it, right? If you can't fight why don't just accept it? I can see it [the party] is moving forward, progressing ... (no. 9)

I was really worried when I heard about the [term limit] change. How-ever, when I mentioned it to my colleagues, they were, like, not anxious at all. They felt like it had nothing to do with their lives, whoever was in that position didn't matter at all. If it's something directly related to their own interests, they might complain, very probably without doing anything about it. Maybe it's because we were educated to avoid show-ing our own views when we were young. We can't parade or strike like capitalist countries; we can't unleash our anger. (no. 11)

The term-limit thing, to be fair, is something you can't change now. Peo-ple are already thinking how to adjust themselves to it. We don't really have much choice. If we did, we might not be like this; but we don't. Most people feel like the change has no direct impact on our income and living conditions ... currently the cake is large enough for almost everyone [to share], so the resentment is not strong. Even if the state censored most of the political news, people might still feel like events had no impact on their own career. Honestly, I would say that people are very tolerant about issues related to politics. (no. 5)

It's useless [to try to change it]. I would say, maybe it [the changed term limit] is for the better development of the country. We [ordinary peo-ple] should do whatever we can and not make troubles to the state and society ... the term limit change was probably a group decision [by all the central leaders] and we should fully understand and trust them. If anyone has other [different] views, it would be pointless [to voice them] and might obstruct public order. (no. 4)

It seems as though the top leader had a golden shield that excluded any criti-cism from the public. Even in private, most of the interviewees chose without much complaint to swallow their worries and discontents over the changed term limit. In later sections, I discuss further their defence of the political apa-thy in themselves and their circle in response to their weak political efficacy and nationalist ideology.

But, if the public are tolerant of undesired political moves by the leader and still willing to find excuses for it, would things change if they were asked to bear some personal cost in order to promote the state's interests? In addition to people's direct attitudes to the government, I asked questions about interest exchange by taking advantage of the ongoing trade war between the US and China[5] to see if they were willing to accept an individual burden in order to win the trade war. Most of the interviewees said they did not personally feel any direct influence of the trade war (such as domestic inflation, unemployment, or difficulties in international communication). But some mentioned that they had friends working in a factory where the trade war had reduced the number of overseas orders. One interviewee who worked for the press said that the reason why many people were not aware of the effect and the danger of the trade war was the information control:

> Now we are having the trade war and the whole economy is slowing down, everyone is stressed out. Like Huawei, directly hit by the conflict. But the central state doesn't allow much news reporting on the trade war issue – well, maybe some nationalist articles are allowed. I personally feel that the issue is actually quite serious, many companies are laying off employees, just it's not reported publicly. Any issue, whether it's a social, political or simply economic issue, if it has a chance of sparking wide public discussion is not allowed to be reported nowadays. (no. 13)

Whether directly perceived or not, if the central government encouraged individuals to bear more costs (in the form of more taxes, inflation, and so on, converting into income reduction), would they agree to accept or not, and why? Some would find it acceptable to bear some burdens if it was for the general good:

> [The trade war] doesn't have much effect at the personal level. Although, emotionally, you will feel like it's being at war and we should stand together and stay strong. In reality you can't really measure any influence, like, our schools still have their normal exchange programme with US schools. The price of daily goods may go up slightly, but it's really small and you can't perceive it, to be honest. If one day the state calls everyone to bear the cost [of the trade war], I would probably accept a maximum reduction of 5%~10% income. Anything more would affect my personal life. Although, if we really had to bear more costs more than that, I think maybe I would have to accept it. I mean, well, for most people, we just let our complaints loose when we're at home and in practice you have to bear the cost anyway. Most people don't really have a choice, or don't have the capital to make choices. (no. 3)

Some interviewees did not find the costs problematic at the individual level, since very few rational discussions were heard:

> Is the trade war really because China is doing better than the US now? I only have some ideas about the trade war because our company invited a lawyer to show us the changed regulations and further sections that we needed to pay attention to. Our colleagues were kind of patriotic for a bit, but just complained a little bit and didn't discuss it too much … We [work for] a Japanese company, so can't really do much or say much about the stand. Our colleagues do not really consciously care about it. But if you asked them to bear some costs, they might have no objection. (no. 11)

Other interviewees would refuse to make a patriotic sacrifice proposed by the state:

> Our friends may discuss the trade war a bit about when we get together for dinner or something. But they mostly focus on the things that directly relate to everyday life … generally speaking, it [the trade war] is not a good thing … About the request to bear an individual level cost, I would refuse. Why should I? I really don't like this grand storytelling. It [the trade war] is not a war about justice or injustice – it's just a Party action. I just don't like the big idea of letting state or country influence my personal life … I mean, I would be willing to devote myself or make a sacrifice, but I just don't want to do this for any big, macro concept. I hope we can make judgements from an objective and fair angle, not just some emotional and ideological perspective [calling for sacrifice] … Other people in the society, I would say, people in a different social stratum or age group may have different degrees of acceptance of nationalist requests, or ideological requests. Maybe older people may be easily motivated, but I don't think the younger generation will … (no. 10)

Another example of a refusal to take on an individual burden for the trade war insisted that no one should bear the cost because the trade war is merely a typical political game:

> [I think] no one is willing to bear the cost. I personally wouldn't … Why would anyone do so? It [the trade war] is caused by certain politicians. There shouldn't be any sacrifice or cost at the individual level. (no. 8)

Comparing people's attitudes and reasoning regarding the top leader's controversial actions and a nationalist request that might directly damage someone's personal interests, it can be identified that people were cautious about complaining over political issues that related to core politics, especially when the issues did not directly affect their benefits. However, a nationalist request that might bring about changes in personal living was more likely to be rejected, even though the topic itself was still not publicly debatable.

Throughout this research, I identify the falsification of compliance as a distinguishable difference between people's public support and private support. The change from public face to private face, however, does not seem from the interview evidence very distinctive. There are complaints that people are not allowed to publicly discuss or spread certain opinions. But the degrees of falsification differ according to whether the issue directly relates to the speaker's life, whether the issue is sensitive or not, and which level of authority the issue refers to. As common sense would suggest, people did not hesitate to reveal their true discontent regarding local authorities. People might be cautious when discussing in public issues relating to the central government, the Party, and the top leader, while in private they would be honest. From the evidence above it is clear that people's public faces were not the same as their private faces. But there is no clear line between these faces and people themselves might not necessarily have been aware of the difference.

One interviewee reflected on whether or not to publicly present discontent:

> About discontent, normally people are not willing to discuss it in public. Mostly because, if you don't have a better solution, or a constructive suggestion, I would rather not talk about it with total strangers … Don't make a fuss. If you simply want to unleash your emotions, it's pointless and will not help to solve the problem. Moreover, it might deepen the social conflicts, or social divisions. And make it difficult for the government to work. (no. 17)

Some close friends expressed their views of people's discontent and the boundary between expressing it publicly and not:

> In my opinion, in today's China, you can discuss your discontent in public, regarding politics, the government, the party or any other authority. But don't touch historical issues such as June 4th, or issues relating to the state's fate, like classified topics. If you do, it might be identified as treason; people might treat you as a traitor to the country. (no. 19)

Another obvious feature when people talked about politics, in many public discussions and even in private conversations, was that people were very keen to see things from the position of the governor and tended to explain/consider issues from his standpoint. For instance, one friend's view of ideological education ran like this:

> I would say, everyone should take care of themselves, live their own life. Don't make trouble for the state or the government … When the international and domestic situation gets tough and tense, like the trade war, it's totally necessary to emphasise the ideological education from the state's point of view. Or you might say we need special policies in special times. (no. 21)

The smooth transformation of people's public and private attitudes made it difficult to capture the moment when people began to hide their true discontent intentionally. However, this observation enriches the theoretical discussion of falsified compliance and constructed political attitudes by highlighting the elusiveness of varied compliance and the way in which the cautiousness of political sensitivity is embedded in daily life. In later sections, I investigate further how people manage the discontinuity (and continuity) between different faces.

5.3 The dual track of political knowledge

In addition to the varied attitudes to different state representatives, another field in which people may have perceptions in private that are unlike their public discourse is political knowledge. People's social knowledge is shaped by various agents. School, family, public education, and past experiences are all effective in establishing or changing the way that individuals perceive, describe, and understand their situation. How, then, do people think about the shaping agents of their knowledge? Moreover, is there any possible difference between their public knowledge and private knowledge?

The public media have been recognised as main sources in shaping people's knowledge, preferences, and desires. As noted earlier (Chapter 1), authoritarian and communist countries rely heavily on ideological legitimation, through tactics such as knowledge construction and media censorship. Chapters 3 and 4 also elaborated on the content of knowledge construction in official propaganda and the effect of the media on individuals' welfare preferences. The question then arises: are people themselves aware of the power of the official media in shaping their political attitudes? And do they find information censorship tolerable or not?

The interview data along with observational data show that people did not falsify their acknowledgement of the socially constructive nature of official propaganda. They acknowledged the shaping power of official propaganda and were also aware of the possibility of the state to use biased discourse. However, they would argue that discourse construction is a necessary to maintain the rule of the authority.

> The state is very cautious about changes in public opinion. You can't mention certain issues in public, for sure ... The whole propaganda system, or the official voice is a bit harsh now, I admit, kind of leaning to the left. But I would also say that 80% of the opinions that were censored or deleted had inappropriate content, or twisted the facts. From the viewpoint of the government, our government is led by the party, no question, so when it feels like its interest is harmed, it will surely take action, like using propaganda, or just censoring wrong opinions ... As individuals, we all only have so much energy every day, so we would definitely be influenced by the official discourse. (no. 4)

> I think most people are quite obedient in public and do not publicly criticise the authorities, no matter which social stratum you come from, upper level or lower level ... I think we all have similar perception of the nature of politics. It's all about governance and rule. So, it's natural that the official media will only say good things about the country. I totally understand that sometimes the [official] media will avoid tackling social or political issues head on. (no. 1)

One press editor who had worked for several commercial presses in China for 10 years also admitted that the educative nature of the public press had never changed:

> We all know that the press in China is nothing but propaganda. Even the commercial press is just some platform that puts forward official decisions or policies. Well … several years ago, there was still some space, but now we can feel it getting tighter and tighter. But no matter whether it was years ago or yesterday, the nature of the press in our socio-political scenario has never changed. It's beyond question a tool for the state to manage its governance. (no. 13)

Some attributed the necessity of news control to the weakness of the Chinese population, arguing that the state needed to lead the trends in public opinion in order to keep society moving forward.

> There are some things the government prefers us not to know. I think it might be because Chinese people are not intelligent enough to digest some information properly. There are many social conflicts in our society, so people are quite easily led by inappropriate opinions … About the official propaganda, I think the starting point must be good and the intentions are good. I believe the leaders still want to serve the people and the think tanks are not dumb, they definitely know how to govern the country. In many cases we may see the emotions being set above the rational. But we all understand that we are a huge country with 1.4 billion people, that is very difficult to govern. We have a very complex population structure so every move of the government needs to be very cautious … I know there are historical cases that the party does not want to mention or explain, but they have no effect on our domestic development … When we get strong, all our actions and choices will be understood [by the world]. (no. 15)

It was quite common for people to be aware of the problem of information control while also having very limited optimism about other approaches of obtaining information due to the limited freedom of expression. One interviewee who had experienced the pre-reform period compared the current information control to former times:

> Currently the control on free speech is quite tight. But the sky won't fall if you let people say something. Now I know there are some local platforms, if you say 'too much', your post will be censored. The situation is somehow similar to that in Mao's time. Only good and positive things can be publicly discussed, only things that are beneficial to the state and the party … other approaches exist [if you want to solve problems other

than resorting to the press], for instance, you can write to a government office or something of the kind, but it won't help much. (no. 12)

From the interview evidence and observational evidence on the social media, people were aware of the shaping power of official propaganda and the constructed official discourse when they described the situation. However, many accepted that they were thus influenced and seemed not to be too worried about the extensive role of the state. How is this discontinuity sustainable for them?

Even though China experienced so many reforms in the short period after 1978, whether politically, socially, or economically, the official discourse was quite consistent regarding the institutional nature of the state. The public description of the political system is still 'socialism with Chinese characteristics' and the economic system remains a socialist market economy. However, as many scholars have identified, the economic system in China is more like state capitalism (Huang 2012; Naughton and Tsai 2015) and the so-called 'socialist' structure has largely been changed since the reform. So how does the general population interpret the ideological position and the nature of the current economic system in China? Is private knowledge consistent with or variance with the public discourse? One of the interviewees who worked in a private equity company expressed concerns about the disjunction between the perceived situation and the public discourse:

In our current [economic] system, I think the state of affairs and the public propaganda don't match. The state-owned economy serves political ends, but does nothing to improve the market efficiency ... Some people admire the state's capacity to use collective resources to solve big problems. I certainly don't doubt it, but I'm not quite convinced.

[Interviewer: Would you agree that different kinds of market economy and governance rationale exist?]

I don't think so. I know many people argue that there are different forms of market economy, such as the ones with Chinese characteristics. I don't agree. There is one single concept of a market economy and there is only one governance rationale with respective to it, which consists of the market, democracy and the rule of law. If the state claims that it is serving the interests of the people, the only object of people's interest is to have a living standard comparable to that in the developed countries ... A market economy and the rule of law are indispensable. I agree there are local scenarios for each country. We all have our peculiarities and should definitely try to find our own path. But what I was talking about is the ideal type, the 'should be' type, the one we all want to reach in the end. (no. 8)

Unlike the view from a respondent that 'there is only one type of governance rationale', I more commonly noted opinions (in public and in private) that emphasised the special situation in China and the country's own institutional rationale with Chinese characteristics. For instance, one interviewee paid attention to tradition and history in discourse about possible institutional routes for the state:

> I think the cleverest people are among the government officials. In their minds, the so-called capitalist-socialist division is just a conceptual classification. No matter what the form of the politics, the ultimate aim is to rule. The state is essentially a force machine and the nature of human beings is selfish. So, they must have institutions that can rule the population. Different countries have their different culture and history. The Chinese or Asian culture is so different from those in Europe and North America. Europeans have the accumulated political culture of democratic decision-making, but we have a long history of one-man decision-making, or dictatorship, as some might call it. I would personally support a parliamentary system if I could choose, but I would not prefer a parliamentary system which only had the format and lacked the spirit. Look how Taiwan has gone. We have a quite different history and culture and communication with other countries and systems will surely help us to find a way that suits us. (no. 9)

Another interviewee made a similar judgement when discussing leftist or rightist positions on the politico-economic spectrum and their indication of the direction that economic reform would take in China:

> I would say, we are in a situation where it doesn't matter whether it's leftist or rightist, so long as it's useful. In recent years we see clearly that the 'the state enterprises advance, the private sector retreated', which is definitely a left turn in the Chinese context ... We have a system called socialism with Chinese characteristics, which literally means that whatever is useful and effective for the authority's rule can be employed by the authority – without completely crashing the economy, society and people's lives, surely. From my point of view, the left-right argument doesn't really matter, and this is also consistent with my observation of the society. (no. 13)

These opinions suggest a pragmatic logic similar to that in political compliance towards the state's representatives. Constitutional change does not matter, information restriction does not matter, ideology position does not matter, as long as they are useful to society and development.

Supporting such pragmatic logic, the wider crisis or problems of liberal democracy in recent years caused confusion for many Chinese people who used to firmly doubt the official discourse and believed that China should aim to have democratic politics. As one interviewee said,

> In the old days when our country was still struggling for food, we may have been quite lost about the direction of the political reform. Recently, we have gained some knowledge of a political way out. However, watching how the US and the EU has got on lately, I'm not really sure if we want to follow in their footsteps any more … quite disappointed about democracy, to be honest. (no. 11)

One noticeable feature of individuals' political attitudes from the examples above is that they are full of conflict. It seems that people recognise the misbehaviour of the authority, but also assume that it has kind intentions; some are aware of and feel uncomfortable about the heavy pressure of party regulations and performance evaluations, but still find it necessary to have the rules tightened. Interviewees sometimes noted that it was unacceptable to ask someone to check on a teacher's talk in class, while also agreeing with the idea that they 'would rather go further "left" than further "right"'. And some people argued that the government stretched its hand too far into society/the market, while complaining about the government's inaction regarding the high cost of housing.

Psychological studies have noted that people tend to avoid cognitive dissonance (Festinger 1962). However, as Tim Kuran identified in his work on preference falsification:

> the models that an individual applies to an issue need not be mutually consistent. A person may subscribe to conflicting models, for instance, a 'big government' model that justifies lower taxes together with an 'educational crisis' model that calls for more government services. (Kuran 1997, p. 159)

In most cases, individuals were learning to use a coherent supermodel consolidated from multiple explanatory models. People might not have been aware of the costs of inconsistency between distinctive models, so long as these models 'yield[ed] reasonably satisfactory choices and generate[d] fairly accurate predictions' (Kuran 1997, p. 179).

In China's case, one formula that individuals used to justify seemingly controversial statecraft and public discourses that were not consistent with personal knowledge was: 'It's common in every country to find the state needing to rule the population in many areas. Countries merely differ in specific actions, but essentially, we are the same.' Also: 'It's all for the state's governance, all about legitimacy.' By dissolving the division between the role of the state and of society and seeing things with the ruler's eyes, individuals can find ways of living with the inconsistency in their minds. At the same time, a smooth change between the political attitudes belonging to different faces allowed individuals a little space in which to buffer themselves from the external shocks that might have challenged their original beliefs.

5.4 Ignorance, apathy, and collective conservatism

The reason why people assume different faces in public and in private and construct a public preference for public display has been examined by scholars from different areas of social science. Explanations such as fear of punishment, desire for reward, ignorance of the general opinion, or the motivation of fitting in have been identified separately or simultaneously. In authoritarian regimes, the mechanism of compliance as falsified by the general public can be explained similarly, but has some specific features. For instance, in China's case, many people who work in the public sector receive more respect from society and treat this reputation as a reward from the Party, thus creating more loyalty. Rewards for them can either be conducive to the individual's self-interest, such as higher living standards, or take the form of a long-term payback that can be extracted from the state's stability and development. Some scholars have argued that socialist education has a strong influence on the individual's action preference to express loyalty and conceal discontent. My interview evidence, combined with the observational data, shows that the mechanisms in people's choosing to falsify their public compliance are complicated, intertwined, and sometimes contradictory.

People's actions or preferences are strongly directed by social norms and by their past education. Their knowledge about society and the desired social behaviours that people have encountered in the past are crucial motives of their choices. In understanding Chinese people's preference for political participation and political attitudes, we should address the core features of its political culture. The traditional Chinese culture, which is selectively promoted by the state, emphasises concepts such as the 'middle course' (*zhongyong*, 中庸), 'tolerance' (*rongren*, 容忍), and 'ethics' (*daode*, 道德). These notions can still be identified in today's Chinese politics. For instance, 'LI' (礼) in traditional political culture is a layered and societal concept. It can be interpreted as ethics, manners, and rules; it can only be established when the whole society accepts and obeys it. Therefore, it nurtures the culture of collectiveness, in which the community rather than the individual is treated as the ultimate principle of achievement. All individuals can realise their personal value only when they have fulfilled society's requirements. With such cultural incentives, collectiveness and conservatism are prevalent in China's contemporary political culture.

The consistency of Chinese history for more than 3,000 years also leads to the phenomenon that people still (consciously or unconsciously) use concepts or terms from Chinese history to describe the conditions or institutions in the contemporary world. One example is the term 'CI SHI', which was used by one interviewee to describe an inspection group from the central government during the anti-corruption campaign period (explained in endnote 2 of this Chapter). The idea of a 'crown prince', which is used to refer to the successor of a top leader, is also a concept from the period of monarchy. These terms were attached to a systematic 'ruler and ruled' ideology. Although people often use them unconsciously, they still indicate the enduring shadow of admiration of authority and obedience to it.

Even though the CCP came to the fore by breaking the chain of (worthless) traditional culture and promoting the revolutionary spirit, cases of the state's promotion of traditional values so as to maintain its authority have actually become very common in recent years. One example is the concept of the 'harmonious society', which was introduced by the then president Hu Jintao in his ideology, or 'thoughts', during the 'Scientific Development Concept' around the mid-2000s, before being written into the constitution in the National People's Congress Conference of 2005. The idea of a 'harmonious society' (which strongly discourages any attempts by the public to 'make a fuss/trouble') was a response to the increasing outbreaks of social unrest in the early 2000s due to economic inequality and the flaws and injustice of government actions. Ironically, over the years, the notion of 'harmonious society' has developed into a substitute for 'stability at all costs', and what was 'harmonised' actually referred to what had been censored on the online platforms. In Xi's presidency, the central authority also was in favour of 'enhancing the national cultural heritage … and building up our cultural confidence'.[6] As indicated above, borrowing ideas from traditional culture also magnifies the structural features behind it. It reveals the way that the authority imagines its population and the approach it finds (thinks) most appropriate for persuading the public.

Some interviewees attributed compliance falsification to the socialist education. One remarked: 'I don't think the public choice of staying silent comes from the traditional culture; it's implanted in the education we've received through the past 70 years.' Other qualitative evidence from interviews also suggested that such core concepts as 'people's democratic dictatorship', 'leadership core',[7] and 'maintaining social stability' were unconsciously accepted and used in daily dialogue. Existing studies also confirm that the part played by education (such as the high school politics curriculum) shaped students' political attitudes (Cantoni et al. 2017). The socialist education led to a belief in collectivism and meritocracy and dismissed personal appeals and universal values such as freedom and democracy.

In spite of the ideologies, social memories brought about by core historical events also shaped the population's political preference in the long term. In his work, Kuran used a thought experiment to reveal that small events can be responsible for the establishment of a particular equilibrium of public opinion and are not averaged out over time (Kuran 1997). Moreover, once an event has tipped public opinion toward one equilibrium or another, subsequent events do not necessarily weaken its impact. In China's case, there are many specific actions from the revolutionary period that were still carried out at the time of writing, such as reporting speech that one dislikes to higher-level supervisors (such as the upper government, or the school, or the administrator of an online forum). Other past events, such as the Cultural Revolution or the June 4th movement, had become terms that could not be mentioned either in public or in private conversation.

No matter whether the cautiousness of political preference came from the traditional political culture, the socialist education, or past events, once the intentional concealment of certain individual attitudes (or the meticulous avoidance of certain topics) is established, the interaction of certain preferences with everyday rituals forms a circle that constantly reinforces itself in the long run – see the discussion of this 'circle' in relation to 'ideological involution' (Section 5.1).

In addition to the pressure brought by social knowledge and historical events, external pressure from state coercion and censorship was also frequently observable in my qualitative evidence. For instance, from early 2019 the pressure on public speech had accelerated, as many interviewees identified from their own experience:

Recently many public accounts on WeChat have been blocked, sometimes you just don't know why and where you have stirred up a sensitive point in your words. (no. 6)

There are many restrictions online, like certain topics, issues, certain people and even certain dates. It feels like most people are quite afraid to say something meaningful … If you do [have a serious discussion] your post will probably be censored or your account will be blocked. We all treasure the Weibo or WeChat accounts which we devoted much effort to maintain, so after several attempts, everyone gets to be docile in their behaviour. (no. 5)

One interviewee described the everyday regulations on an editor for a commercial press:

On average I would receive about 30 messages or emails [from the relevant supervision departments] per day with instructions on what I should or shouldn't do. It's regulations on every hand. Sometimes the instructions can refer in detail to the words, or phrase corrections in the articles … We have a massive bureaucracy which specialises in media management. If you want to join the bureaucracy you need to pass the proper exam … I know most of the officials in the system genuinely agree on the idea that the propaganda is the tool for the ruler. (no. 13)

When I asked, 'How does a press, like your institution, find the line between publishable and unpublishable issues', he replied:

> [T]hrough careful trying and summarising the existing cases. Like, recently one self-media site got censored on the topic of the 'trade war'. After communication, we found that it was because they had directly cited a report from the *New York Times*. So we realised that even on the most heated topic, we are not expected to cite the foreign press directly. It would be safer to cite official reports in that case.

Another interviewee who worked for a new media institution faced similar supervision from the government in the selection of content.

> This year we have a special digital column which is designed to deliver one poem every day to our audience. On June 4th, we published a short one with a title that roughly reads 'There isn't a day in our life'. We didn't initially intend to signal a memorial or anything special and we didn't even realise the title had some relevance for this special day. But soon after it was published on our website, I received a call from our leader and got reproved for not being careful enough. I didn't get a chance to explain … We can't control people's interpretation though … The selection of topics needs extra care when it relates to issues of the party, minorities and religions … Strict external inspection [by the government] surely leads to stricter self-censorship. (no. 10)

The control on information had a considerable impact on people's public knowledge about current society and shaped people's attitudes in the form of the attitude desired and expected by the authority. For instance, one event in June 2019 that attracted the headlines in media all over the world was the anti-extradition bill protests in Hong Kong.[8] The protest there was the most significant political protest since the Umbrella Movement in 2014; nearly 2 million people turned out to demonstrate. However, all information about this protest was blocked in mainland China. One of my interviewees who went to school in Hong Kong and then worked in Beijing told me that, even though she personally used a VPN (virtual private network) sometimes to access external news, she learned about the massive protest only after several days. Until then, most of her colleagues still had no idea what was going on in Hong Kong.

> To be honest, even I, who still have the knowledge and ability to occasionally climb the wall [the Great Firewall[9]] and get access to the external world, was a day or two late in discovering the situation in Hong Kong. There hasn't been a single mention of Hong Kong in the mainland's social media. (no. 11)

Several days after the protest, the official government account issued a statement that identified the nature of the protest as a 'riot' and supported the Hong Kong government's 'sensible treatment'. The statement told a one-sided story of the Hong Kong movement and left no space for argument or defence. My interviewee told me that after she read news and reports of Hong Kong's protest she tried to explain the complexity of the Hong Kong issue and the appeals of the Hong Kong people to her colleagues and they seemed to be very open to this information and recognised that the protest was not simply the riot that the central authority had claimed. But she still could not discuss these issues openly online.

> Recently bloggers have complained of the many rules about public discussions and the many topics/issues are not allowed to be discussed. Feels like the restriction has tightened up and the list of sensitive words is somehow extended.

Not everyone felt this pressure, however. Some voices still argued that: 'I don't think that the so-called pressure on free speech will affect daily life too much; most of the pressure still comes from the struggle to live without overspending in this competitive society.'

In spite of the structural factors that may have shaped or constrained people's choices to express opinions, or signal their preferences, there were many mechanisms that relate to internal reasons on the personal level.[10] For instance, when the interviewees were asked why they would not say something about the issues that they felt to be unfair, they would often reply, 'For what?' and 'What would be the point? It won't change anything.' Problems such as weak political efficacy, or sometimes incorrect evaluations, in the general view, also led to reluctant political expression and further appeals for social change.

Political apathy normally refers to a situation where individuals lack interest in participating in political activities. In China's case, many interviewees mention the scenario that people are not interested even in talking about social or political issues.

> In my current working environment, in which most of my colleagues have a background in science education, most of them have no clue about the social or political issues. They kind of live in their own small space, and will even blame you for not 'having your feet on the ground' if you bring up some socio-economic topics. They basically care about their own lives, just trivial things really. (no. 3)

Why would this happen? The unaccountability of the authority regarding social issues tends to weaken the intention to take part in politics. The weakened external efficacy interacts with and reduces people's internal political efficacy.

For instance, one interviewee recalled the days when many people still hoped to participate (in whatever forms) so as to push the government or policy to change and when disappointment gradually led to silence:

> In the past, like 10 years ago, people still believed that crowds of onlookers could somehow change society, or China's politics someday. The internet provided a great opportunity for everyone to pay attention to and support people who were miles away when they were suffering injustice. The logic was, crowd attention can bring pressure on the authority and force them to make changes. But now it's totally useless. You can't change anything. Meanwhile, everyone is so pre-occupied by the struggles in their own lives, they barely have enough energy to really engage in social issues. It really takes time, energy and passion and watching things end inconclusively definitely kills the crowd's enthusiasm. (no. 6)

One radical explanation given regarding the public's weak political efficacy was that ordinary people were not capable of discussing the political issues seriously and we should trust the wisdom of the government.

> Things are much more complicated than we thought. For instance, for the events of June 4th, there has been much criticism at home and abroad. Some people ask why the government doesn't just make the archives public and then all the criticism and puzzles will be clear. I would say, the Zhongnanhai[11] must have thought about this solution and they definitely have a reason for not choosing to do so. There are many things we ordinary people have no clue about, so we can't really comment on them. (no. 4)

Although it seemed as if most people care nothing about the political issues, some studies have mentioned that the Chinese make a cult of political rumours (H. Huang 2017). Many local websites gossip about such things as political factions and conflicts, the direction of international or domestic policies, and even the personal lives of government leaders. However, some interview comments denied the role of these rumours in Chinese politics: 'All this gossip and rumour is just natter. China's politics is 100% closed-door politics' (no. 23).

In addition to the changes in political efficacy, the benefit that each person had received or perceived also determined their chosen attitudes. Hence, another common reason for not discussing political issues was that some Chinese people felt that life was much better and there was no need to change the current system further or criticise the politics. The self-interest to which this refers is not some dramatic benefit from the current system but a simple and everyday convenience that one may derive from interaction with current system.

I think our country is doing very well lately, especially since Xi's rule. In the old days, we had an old version of 'official accountability', but it turned out to be nothing but swagger and exaggeration. The new version nowadays is more solid. Each level of government takes its role and the general secretary takes full responsibility. Any officials who are not doing their part get punished. For example, in the past when you wanted to be reimbursed from the health insurance scheme, you had to go through many offices and counters. Now the whole process is simplified and the officers are friendly to our patients … This is what I call satisfaction. I definitely thank the government and the Party for that. (no. 12)

My experience is, the payment for scientists nowadays is far better. Like the decentralisation of the funding management, we enjoy more space to maximise the use of project funding. Our research also has nothing to do with politics or society, so why would I care about the change in the term limit, or Hong Kong issues? (no. 27)

The trifling but recurring benefits that individuals received from the current system somehow offset the risks they might incur from the inefficiency of society as a whole. These benefits also diverted people from serious reflection on the state–individual relationship. Personalised longitudinal comparison sometimes shoulders aside the horizontal and societal comparisons with other disadvantaged groups, especially when the information is asymmetric and controlled by the state.

If individuals felt personally unable to make a difference, or if personal interest was not affected, how did they imagine other people's attitudes? Would they have perceived potential discontent from their peers? As I explained in the theoretical discussion, social psychology scholars have identified a bias in group opinion whereby the group members mistakenly assume that the general group accepts a norm, even though most of the group members privately reject it. The idea of 'pluralistic ignorance' sums up a scenario in which few in the population believe, while the majority thinks that all the others believe. Kuran also argued that the fear inside individuals would lead to pluralistic ignorance, since the multitudes who objected to communism did not know how widely their resentment was shared (Kuran 1997):

Even if they could sense the repressed discontent of their conformist relatives and close friends or observe the hardships in the lives of their fellow citizen, they lacked reliable information on how many of their fellow citizens favoured radical political change. (Kuran 1997, p. 125)

The interview data verified part of the mechanism of 'unknowing' other's private opinions. Some of my interviewees personally realised the problems of the current system, but felt that the other people in the community would certainly support the regime at whatever cost. For instance:

> If you ask me, I really think most people, especially the ones who suffered a lot in former times, like farmers and rural residents, sincerely support the government. And it may also be true for people whose interests are not directly related to the social problems. They will surely support the party. I mean, if we really open up and get to the stage of a general election, like everyone has a right to vote, I believe most people, maybe 90%, will still vote for our current system. (no. 13)

> I feel like most people in the society don't really find 'big government' problematic. They think that there is nothing wrong with 'imperial power'; the only problem is 'there isn't a good empire yet'. In their mind, there's nothing fundamentally wrong in the system. (no. 10)

Pluralistic ignorance can actually interact with people's weak efficacy and political apathy and make them lose confidence and hope that they can change things through any kinds of participatory approach.

However, some respondents were more cautious in identifying other people's opinions, arguing that the whole population was too large to generalise about.

> Everyone has his or her own ideas, I mean, based on their experiences and their affiliation to certain social groups. I really have no idea of their true feelings. There are some popular opinions on the internet, but who knows? Many people are not keen to express their ideas. So many people live in our country, it's impossible to have a general idea regarding political issues, not even social issues. If any voice supports something, there must be some voices that disapprove of it. (no. 15)

5.5 Heterogeneity of social groups: education and generations

One important reason why people were unwilling to infer the nature of general public opinion was that the diversity of the subpopulations was so great. This diversity led to different reactions to the socio-economic changes, while their own experience and endowment varied the weights of the mechanisms that led to compliance falsification. As one interviewee argued,

> Falsification? I'm sure it exists in the population. However, I cannot really make a judgement on the society as a whole. It really depends, depends on the subgroups in the society. We have over 1.4 billion people, there are huge internal differences and variations, and there are many social classes. I can't really imagine it, to be honest. (no. 10)

In this section, I try to identify several important variations of the population that have marked implications for the diversity of falsified compliance. Education is one of the most important factors, in that it correlates with people's knowledge, cognitive capacity, and possible experiences. In a society such as China's where social, political, and economic capital are highly integrated, education-based social capital is also highly correlated with the distance to the core political power. Hence, more education may bring rights consciousness, independent thinking, and more resource for political participation. From the viewpoint of the authority, education is a crucial approach to socialising the governed, especially useful when no alternative explanations/stories are allowed or available. So, it may be the case that people who are doing well in the official education system are more likely to approve the notions and ideologies of the current system. I briefly unpack the complex ways in which education indicates people's political compliance, with evidence from formal interviews, informal conversations, and observations.

People who are more educated are generally more likely to be aware of the potential rewards brought by signalling loyalty to the incumbent authority. Hence, educated people are more likely to choose a specific public image that differs from their private image. An interviewee with a college degree addressed the notion of public/private faces as follows:

In current society you can enjoy a really good life if you have enough power. It's not like we never talk about the social or political issues, just it's only with people you are really familiar with ... There is no need to discuss political issues too much in public. Why do it? The upper level will never appreciate your sincerity, it just [needs] your loyalty. (no. 5)

If they were rational enough in reaching their decisions, would educated people show less compliance regarding nationalist requests from the state, such as helping with meeting the costs of the trade war? Not necessarily. My qualitative evidence shows that many highly educated people would identify the trade war as a good opportunity for China to establish itself, and therefore they were tolerant of the costs they might have needed to bear.

In addition, people who enjoy more social capital are more likely to acknowledge the potential punishment that could follow undesired actions. Enjoying more rewards, they are also more likely to react more strongly to the possibility of punishment compared to people ones who are relatively far from the system. For instance, one respondent working in a para-state body noted:

When you have seen or experienced more, you are more likely to understand the ruling tactics, whatever kind of authority is in power. Punishment will definitely come if you cross the line, so you will become more and more cautious in your choices ... Especially when you have too much to care about, your family, your career, all these [things] will hold you back when you are making choices. In making a decision, the more you have, the more concerned you are.

The pressure is also high for people who work in education, such as researchers and teachers, one of whom argued:

> The intellectuals are less likely to express their true opinions about the society and politics. If you conduct research in a mainland university and your topic entails sensitive issues, such as the constitution, modern or contemporary history, or civil society, you need to be very careful. There are cases in which a teacher in class was reported by the students because they found the teacher's speech not '[politically] correct'. (no. 23)

Informal conversations with social science scholars at top universities in mainland China verified the high pressure that they feel on their daily research and life. One of them complained in private that the landline in his office is monitored. Another mentioned that, because he came from Hong Kong, his mother-in-law (a government cadre in mainland China) had been investigated on tax issues, quite unjustifiably. A third case concerned a research topic, which had to be changed due to political pressure from political circles about the methodology to avoid potential disputes. These directly perceived pressures cause the people concerned to drastically disguise their public political attitudes, believing that it would not be a good idea to reveal their discontents in public.

Theoretically speaking, the social capital brought by education may increase individuals' confidence in political participation and raise their motivation to pursue their own interests. As Kuran argued, an individual's proficiency in pursuing their own interests may add to the inefficiency of society. Moreover, the falsified public preference of individuals could cause societal inefficiency to persist (Kuran 1997). In the interviews, many pragmatic opinions seemed to exaggerate the autonomy of individual-level choices in the current system and take a seemingly 'objective', 'neutral', or 'rational' stand on controversial social issues. Many people who have less sympathy for others' suffering would imagine that under the current system the space for the individual's personal choice is generous enough. So long as people do their best, it is possible to achieve social mobility and defend personal property. For instance, when they talked about the inequalities in education and the troubles for individuals brought by the inconsistency of educational policies, three respondents said:

> I don't feel the current system puts many restrictions on me. I mean, sure, there are some rules imposed by major structures, but the private space is quite enough for us to develop ... I don't deny that difficulties prevent some people from gaining access to educational resources, like some migrants from rural areas. I won't judge them on their actions or

choices, like, if they choose to defend their rights through exposure in the news or political appeals, that's totally fine. But every person in a society has a position that decides the [available] choices. I don't think I will end up in a similar [difficult] position … Of course, we need social responsibility and caring, but not [from] me. (no. 8)

The specific issues such as urban–rural inequalities, educational justice, resource distributions, all are crucial challenges for the government. But I feel like the main issue is still the limited resource in our country … the cake [of the economy] is not large enough for everyone to enjoy; some people must be left behind or sacrificed … Educational injustice is a problem of our time and it can be solved by creating more education resources … For individuals, there are many other solutions you can try. Like immigration, [attending] international or private schools [if you don't have a *hukou* in your area]. Do use your power to act. It won't help if you are too stubborn and just want to fight against the government. It's a waste of your time and energy to keep an eye on the institution. These are the facts, I would say; it's your problem if you remain disadvantaged. (no. 4)

As far as I know, the political opportunities are plenty. The key issue is still your own efforts. Society is already quite open. (no. 12)

There is nothing wrong with the 'perceived' potential space at the individual level. However, the illusion of 'free choices', whether social, economic, or political for different people, actually leads them to underestimate the disharmony between public and private faces. It also prevents them from sharing the pain of other disadvantaged groups and questioning systematic problems in society.

In addition to education, a person's age group is another factor that correlates with their social status, experience, cognitive capacity, and knowledge. It has been identified as a core factor that determines people's political attitudes and behaviours (Braungart and Braungart 1986). For instance, people who are born in a certain period are likely to experience similar social events, and therefore are quite likely to share a similar social memory (e.g. Schuman and Rieger 1992). Meanwhile, people in a different age group are in a life stage of their own and the issues and themes that they worry or care about are different. Thus, investigating heterogeneity in political compliance brought by generational variation is another main theme in this section.

Owing to the lack of statistical evidence, I give only a brief summary of the perceived generational difference from the interviews and the observational data. Existing studies suggest that the older generation was more cautious on political topics, while the younger generation was more liberal (e.g. Hahn and Logvinenko 2008; Rose and Carnaghan 1995). Qualitative data in my study suggested a generational difference as regards political compliance and the contradictions in whether or not to hide discontent. More importantly, the interaction between any two generations indicates the long shadow of falsified political attitudes in preserving a socially conservative ideology.

As I noted in the previous section, social knowledge can persist quite strongly in the shaping of people's political attitudes. The transmission of knowledge from one generation to another is one of the forces that helps social knowledge to persist (Glass, Bengtson, and Dunham 1986; Jennings 1996). The younger generation learns about what is 'thought' and 'unthought' from their society, family, and education. However, the existence of falsified public opinion has some long-term repercussions. If certain ideas are blocked due to social or political pressure, the younger generation cannot renew them and the older people will die with their ideas unspoken. The distribution of young people's public opinion will undoubtedly reflect the existing bias in social discourse. Imagine certain issues or topics that are unthinkable for one generation because of certain political or social constraints. The unexpressed ideas are less likely to be heard and incorporated into the ideas of the younger generation than the ones in public discourse. In this way, 'unthinkable' turns into 'unthought' as the generations succeed one another (Kuran 1997).

The interviews showed some cases where a son or daughter had certain ideas or thoughts about politics or historical events, while the parents refused to share their opinions:

> My education and my overseas experience have made me think a lot about politics and the history of Chinese politics ... But every time I plan to have a serious discussion with my parents about my ideas, they refuse to have a real conversation with me. They just dodge when I mention related topics. (no. 25)

Another interviewee described his interaction with his parents:

> My father worked abroad when he was young, it was something like a governmental delegation. I thought he might be quite open to different political attitudes ... There were times I expressed my disagreement with the government's behaviour – my Dad wasn't very happy and blamed me for being brainwashed by the foreign forces. (no. 14)

These cases of several interviewees with different political attitudes from their parents demonstrated the pressure, but also indicated the possibility of breaking apart the intergenerational heritage (Inglehart 2018; Svallfors 2010). As one respondent put it,

> as long as the state keep open and allows people to interact with the outside world in different ways, the younger generation will have some new ideas denied to their parents and will ultimately change the societal scenarios. (no. 26)

However, it might take a great effort from the younger generation to generate a counteracting bias against the existing bias in public opinion. People will not automatically reflect on existing theories or facts or become critical, even they when have received new information. Unless this information is powerful, their thoughts will tend to conform to the dominant ideas of their parents' generation and internalise the viewpoint that dominates public discourse, owing to inherently lazy thinking (Kuran 1997). In the last part, I want to consider further the potential breakthrough from the existing structural forces, social pressures, and the trap of generational knowledge transformation for individuals.

5.6 Heading (no)where: actions or agencies

One popular model that describes the interaction between the state and its subordinates is the 'exit, voice, and loyalty' (EVL) model originally proposed by Hirschman (1970). The state can be treated as an organisation and the population may choose to stay loyal, or voice their discontent through formal and informal political participation, or leave the state through emigration when they are unhappy with the authority's certain actions. Individuals' choice of reaction is evaluated on the basis of the benefits and costs of each option. The authority will also evaluate the possibilities of its population's choice in the policymaking process or subsequent amendments. If citizens can make a credible threat of leaving, the authority is less likely to impose controversial policies. Conversely, the option to exit will be reduced if loyalty is strong, or is not wholly appealing or feasible. At the other extreme, sincerely loyal members may be more likely to voice their opinion because they care more about the organisation succeeding in its aims.

How would falsified compliance affect these strategies? In other words, which of the EVL options would be chosen by people who falsify their loyalty to the authority? Theoretically speaking, preference falsification is often cheaper than escape or voice and it avoids the risks entailed in public protest. Yet, disguised public opinion may cause many to underestimate the extent of popular dissatisfaction and conceal the possibilities of change. In this section, I give some preliminary evidence of individuals' opinions regarding the political participation, and the degree of loyalty when controversial policies are imposed and some emigration choices are open. Further explorations such as formal models and statistical inferences can be made in future research.

Existing studies have argued that the Chinese government encourages many innovative 'voice' approaches to public participation, such as the mayor's mailbox, local government's comment boards, and so on (Distelhorst and Hou 2014; Su and Meng 2016). Does the general population find these approaches valid or helpful? How do they personally rate the effectiveness of individuals' voices in the policymaking process and politics in general? And what do they think of informal political participation (such as appeals, protests, or assembly) compared to formal approaches? The feedback from interviewees who had perceived more constraints in the previous several years was generally negative and passive regarding people's function in the current political system: it was both objectively not possible and subjectively not necessary. For instance:

> About the so-called 'deliberate decision making', like the ones you mentioned, the Mayor's mailbox, or Wenling's case of a collective meeting, I would say that only individuals who were desperate to solve their problems would participate. Normal people won't voice their opinions if they do not have to ... Several years ago, there were some cases of informal gatherings to protest against local government's misbehaviour or against some factory or something. [I] don't see many similar reports in recent years, maybe very occasionally ... Especially this year, these issues would definitely get blocked online. (no. 11)

> I don't think individual citizens have a say in policymaking. If some policies are claiming to encourage the public's opinion, we are mostly represented by some 'officials'. Even if votes are used to decide [something], I don't believe they are legitimate or transparent enough ... You don't know where those samples come from. I can definitely say, me and my friends have no idea or interest on these [political participation approaches ... they are] just for show. (no. 10)

How do people who are loyal to the authority explain the space for voice within the current system? Two interviewees gave their views:

> I understand that most people don't really want to publicly discuss issues of political reform, or controversial social issues. The key issue nowadays is still development. To achieve that, the state can't [afford to] be in a mess and no one really wants it become a battlefield (of opinions). (no. 2)

> I would say, seize the day. Any discussions about politics should be done under the umbrella of development and the stability of the whole society ... We should trust the judgement of our peers. The current authority is elected to power, so is Xi ... we should support whoever is in that position ... It's totally ok to express your own opinion, about the society or about politics, but it should be done in an appropriate way. It's better to engage in formal ways, like the Mayor's mailbox; things can be solved very quickly ... It's definitely unacceptable to ideologically oppose the state or the party ... The social problems we are encountering right now are accumulated problems from the past 40 years. We cannot rush, cannot solve the problems of certain social groups in a flash ... Some people will unavoidably be sacrificed during the process. (no. 4)

The importance of social stability was confirmed by many people, as in one summary from an informal conversation: 'stability suppresses all, this is the motive power of the current authority, higher than any other noble notions'. An interviewee said:

> Being [in] a[n ethnic] minority does have some inconveniences, such as applying for a visa, the process takes much longer than it does for my Han friends ... But I think so long as I don't commit any violation of the law, there is no need to worry. Cooperation with the police is everyone's obligation, it's especially necessary for security reasons ... Like, the security check on Shanghai's tube-trains is stricter than in any Japanese airport. People may complain but I don't really advocate abolishing it ... The anti-terrorism situation is serious for every country in the world. China just takes it more seriously than some other countries do. We value safety and security more ... Most of us citizens are willing to cooperate with the security checks at tube stations, as long as the process is efficient and the officers' attitudes are friendly ... We Chinese can really endure hardships and work really hard; we also have a high threshold of tolerance. (no. 3)

If using voice was not possible and if someone was not sincerely loyal, was there any preference for 'exit'? When I asked about or mentioned the option of emigration, many respondents were concerned about the cultural problem:

> I don't consider emigration as an option. Neither culturally nor in daily habits is it easy to change for people of our age. We also have jobs here, why ask for trouble? Besides, people in other countries won't really take you in as a fellow-citizen, I don't want to expend my energy and efforts in a foreign land. (no. 4)

Yet, if there was a chance, others would be happy to send their children abroad for a better view of the world:

> I'm not saying it's a bad idea to move to other countries if possible, just not for myself. The culture, habits, politics and even legal systems are so different. I don't think I can adjust to a new environment. Children might do, maybe when they were grown up and if they themselves wanted to go abroad. (no. 9)

Some interviewees who were more capable (or more self-confident) or more worried about the current system would more readily decide to choose 'exit':

> I am not sure who is going to take the leader's role and don't know what the society is going towards. So, I do consider moving abroad as an option, maybe once the child is a little older. (no. 5)

Yes, (for me) emigration is a possible choice, although I've not decided yet. Will (decide) on the basis of my further career plan. (no. 8)

However, for most people who do not possess the resources to leave, even if they are discontented and would wish to move elsewhere *if possible*, the possibilities are not on their side.

Many people who seem politically apathetic, or feel ignorant of political issues, are mostly heavily pre-occupied by social pressures, or everyday life: work, society and life. One example is the recent debate about the oppressive so-called '996' work schedule (from 9 am to 9 pm, six days a week), which is a common and even rampant phenomenon in high-tech and internet companies. In spite of the fact that the '996' work schedule already violates labour laws, many people actively supported the idea of 'hard work'. When the debate was at its peak, Jack Ma, founder of the Alibaba Group, stated in public that 'employees who get the "opportunity" to work according the "996" schedule are the lucky ones', because 'in many companies employees don't even get the chance to work long hours'.[12] The excessive workloads common in China leave people no time to think, read, or question the problems in their lives. As one interviewee put it, they felt like 'the capitalists and the politicians collude with each other, just to exploit people's labour, time and minds. Sometimes even our dignity' (no. 11).

There are some other 'tailored' social and political pressures for social subgroups in the population. For instance, women are more and more commonly encouraged to go back to the family and resume the traditional role of 'good wife'. In recent years, the official policy of encouraging families to have a 'second child', the official propaganda promoting traditional cultural values and the popularity of 'moral women'[13] modules have formed a political, cultural, and economic cage that prevents women from achieving their self-value and self-awareness.

Another example is the younger generation, whose members enjoy less and less possibility of upward social mobility. From the interview data, many young people complained of the pressure when they were asked about their ideas on the future of the state and themselves in the following five years. Even some who were positive about the state's development were concerned about the opportunities for younger people. All these pressures, initiated by the state or generated from the economic environment and traditional culture, left no space for many people to really think through the current political and societal conditions, to say nothing of deep reflection on the state–individual relationship.

Luckily, some voices among respondents still attested to the possibility of 'free will'. Unlike those who accepted the illusion of individual autonomy, there were some who wanted access to more knowledge and reflections on the state of society, arguing: 'I want to read more, books or news, to really understand what is going on with myself and the country. I truly want to be clear enough and see through the society' (no. 10). Another popular online post urged:

[I]n this time, ask yourself to never be lazy in thinking, never blindly follow the others. Try your best to understand the truth of all kinds of events, keep your sympathy for the disadvantaged, be aware of any kind of power. This is already a form of resistance. Even save an article that you find reasonable (and might disappear soon) and share it with others. This is resistance, too.

Conclusions

Ideological involution in current Chinese society follows from the totalising and individualising effects of the strong government. Confining the resources of social knowledge results in a diverged but limited increment. By assuming different faces in social life, individuals manage their cognitional counter-conduct. Yet, in many cases, the falsification of compliance or the change of faces is for many people unconscious. They tend to show more honesty on political issues in private without any distinguishable awareness. Many of them can recognise the obvious restrictions from the authority, such as censorship, the risk of punishment, lack of government accountability (and related weak political efficacy), but many people (and their contacts or friends) intentionally do not pay attention to or reflect on these issues.

The potential for 'falsification' in Chinese political compliance provides the 'people-side's story' to the overarching questions of my book – how state governmentality maintains an answering compliance in a rapidly transitioning Chinese society. Previous chapters showed how the state may intentionally use knowledge construction, policy experimentation, and interest allocation, among many other tactics, so as to effectively shape public opinion and maintain compliance from subordinates. However, individuals enjoy the possibility of hiding their true discontents or opinions when there are limited choices of voicing or exiting and falsified compliance can be dangerous for the authority regarding its long-term rule.

The qualitative insights given here cannot speak to the numerical distribution of viewpoints or attitudes across China's massive general population. But they do illuminate some of the pathways and details by which falsified political compliance can operate, and illuminate in an exploratory way the various potential factors that might lead to a change in people's public/private faces and heterogeneity across social groups. Such qualitative evidence can be useful in guiding areas or directions of future research. My analysis shows that people's compliance regarding different representatives of the state varied substantially with regard to specific issues and the atmosphere at the time. Although the central government, the party, and the top leader enjoyed more approval, and respondents demonstrated a sympathy for state or government's tasks, people in private conversations sometimes objected to bearing the political cost at an individual level. In addition to political trust, people's private political knowledge and public discourse sometimes ran along separate tracks. Although many people registered a disconnection between their private knowledge and public debate, as well as the discontinuity within official discourse, many chose to tolerate these gaps without further questioning. Why would many people still choose (intentionally or unconsciously) to arrange their public/private faces regarding certain political/societal issues? The reasons can be traced back to the existing cultural, historical, and educational factors that have socialised their ideas from the beginning. They can also be identified in the external force imposed by the state and society and the resulting fear, political apathy, and group ignorance in the population.

Does falsified compliance vary between the people in different social groups? Although my qualitative data cannot make any inferences about the distribution of attitudes in the population as a whole, the diverse people involved in interviews had different endowments, experiences, and human capital, and the detailed discussion sustained also illuminated many different preferences and nuances about political compliance. For instance, education can bring people more socio-economic capital, as well as a certain illusion of autonomy, but it also imposes a binding power when individuals face a threat from the state. Regarding generational differences, the past experience of the older generation may turn some of their 'unthinkable issues' into 'unthought issues' for the next generation. What, then, are the implications, for one's actions and for the possible breakthrough of individual subjectivity, of falsifying one's political attitudes? My evidence suggests that, although many people are pessimistic about any kind of political participation, some tend to preserve their awareness, consciousness, and rationality despite the pressure from the state and society.

Going one step further from the qualitative data of public opinion and individual private opinions, we can also identify some possibilities of subtle statecraft in the management of people's views. Drawing on the population's propensity to admire or sympathise with authority, the state may take a number of steps to direct popular opinion: it may allow public debate at a controllable level, sending opinion leaders to set the rhythm. Then, once the public debate reaches a certain level, the state can issue an 'official statement' in the name of 'neutrality' and 'justice'. If necessary, in dire cases, it may sacrifice some lower-ranking officials as scapegoats, and utter credible threats to society at critical moments. However, when the manipulation of popular opinion causes the state's credibility to backfire, leading to severe distrust or even considerable compliance falsification, it may produce a serious challenge to state rule in the long term. For individuals, it takes an effort to break out of the aggregated ideological and political power constraints, but it is not impossible.

Notes

[1] Xinhua Net, 'CPC proposes change on Chinese president's term in Constitution', See https://perma.cc/N38D-SLD6

[2] The 'CI SHI' system, or 'feudal prefectural governor' system, was originally established in the Qin and Han dynasties (around 202 BC) and continued to be used (with brief interruptions) until the Republic of China period in the early 1900s.

[3] Such as Yan'an, Jing Gangshan, etc., where the CCP originated, or where some historical event had taken place.

[4] BBC News, 2018-03-11, 'China's Xi allowed to remain "president for life" as term limits removed', https://perma.cc/3PDM-4UM6

[5] Swanson, Ana, 2018-07-05. 'Trump's trade war with China is officially underway'. *The New York Times.* https://perma.cc/TKZ6-EUL6

[6] A related theoretical article on the official website is Jing, Qi, Cui, Xiantao, 'Inheriting and promoting traditional culture', 2015-07-22, https://perma.cc /73ZA-TLFQ

[7] A related article and explanation is 'Xi Jinping becomes "core" leader of China', 2016-10-27, https://perma.cc/LD7G-SPE3

[8] 'Hong Kong democrats urge leader Carrie Lam to drop extradition law plans entirely and resign; Sunday protest to proceed'. *Hong Kong Free Press,* 2019-06-15. https://perma.cc/7SW8-M87L

[9] For more information on the Great Firewall in China's internet blocking, see Ensafi et al. (2015); Roberts (2018).

[10] The structural factors and the personal level factors are surely correlated in many ways. Here I make no causal inferences or comparisons between different mechanisms, but present a description of some observable factors.

[11] Current residence of the top leaders of the Party and central government (such as Central Politburo Standing Committee members).

[12] *China Daily,* '"996" schedule must not be imposed on workers', 2019-04-15, https://perma.cc/7QYP-NT28

[13] For further introduction, see: 'Some "moral women" promotions already touch the red line of the law' (in Chinese), 2017-05-22, https://perma.cc /TX83-YM3B

References

Asch, S. E.; and Guetzkow, H. (1951). 'Effects of group pressure upon the modification and distortion of judgments'. *Documents of Gestalt Psychology,* 222–236.

Blaydes, L. (2006). *Who Votes in Authoritarian Elections and Why? Vote Buying, Turnout, and Spoiled Ballots in Contemporary Egypt.* Paper presented at the APSA Annual Meeting, Philadelphia.

Braungart, R. G.; and Braungart, M. M. (1986). 'Life-course and generational politics'. *Annual Review of Sociology,* vol. 12, issue 1, 205–231. https://doi.org /10.1146/annurev.so.12.080186.001225

Bursztyn, L.; and Jensen, R. (2017). 'Social image and economic behavior in the field: Identifying, understanding, and shaping social pressure'. *Annual*

Review of Economics, vol. 9, 131–153. https://doi.org/10.1146/annurev
-economics-063016-103625. OA: http://www.nber.org/papers/w23013
.pdf

Cantoni, D.; Chen, Y.; Yang, D. Y.; Yuchtman, N.; and Zhang, Y. J. (2017). 'Curriculum and ideology'. *Journal of Political Economy*, vol. 125, issue 2, 338–392. https://
doi.org/10.1086/690951. OA: http://eprints.lse.ac.uk/91515/1/Yuchtman
_Curriculum-and-ideology.pdf

Centola, D.; Willer, R.; and Macy, M. (2005). 'The emperor's dilemma: A computational model of self-enforcing norms'. *American Journal of Sociology*,
vol. 110, issue 4, 1009–1040. https://doi.org/10.1086/427321. OA: https://
repository.upenn.edu/cgi/viewcontent.cgi?article=1604&context=asc
_papers

Chen, Y.; and Yang, D. Y. (2019). 'The Impact of Media Censorship: 1984 or Brave New World?' *American Economic Review*, vol. 109, issue 6, 2294–2332.
https://doi.org/10.1257/aer.20171765

Distelhorst, G.; and Hou, Y. (2014). 'Ingroup bias in official behavior: A national field experiment in China'. *Quarterly Journal of Political Science*, vol. 9, issue
2, 203–230. https://doi.org/10.1561/100.00013110

Duara, P. (1987). 'State involution: A study of local finances in north China,
1911–1935'. *Comparative Studies in Society and History*, vol. 29, issue 1,
132–161. https://doi.org/10.1017/s0010417500014389

Easton, D. (1965). *A Systems Analysis of Political Life*. John Wiley & Sons Ltd.

Easton, D. (1975). 'A re-assessment of the concept of political support'. *British Journal of Political Science*, vol. 5, issue 4, 435–457. https://doi.org/10.1017
/s0007123400008309

Edwards, A. L. (1957). *The Social Desirability Variable in Personality Assessment and Research*. USA: Dryden Press.

Ensafi, R.; Winter, P.; Mueen, A.; and Crandall, J. R. (2015). 'Analyzing the Great Firewall of China over space and time'. *Proceedings on Privacy Enhancing Technologies*, vol. 2015, issue 1, 61–76. https://doi.org/10.1515
/popets-2015-0005

Festinger, L. (1962). *A Theory of Cognitive Dissonance*, vol. 2. Stanford University Press.

Foucault, M. (2009). *Security, Territory, Population: Lectures at the Collège de France, 1977–78* (M. Senellart ed.). Palgrave Macmillan.

Frank, R. H. (1996). 'The political economy of preference falsification: Timur Kuran's Private Truths, Public Lies'. *Journal of Economic Literature*, vol. 34,
issue 1, 115. https://www.jstor.org/stable/2729412

Frye, T.; Gehlbach, S.; Marquardt, K. L.; and Reuter, O. J. (2017). 'Is Putin's popularity real?' *Post-Soviet Affairs*, vol. 33, issue 1, 1–15. https://doi.org/10
.1080/1060586x.2016.1144334

Fuchs, D. (2007). 'The political culture paradigm'. *The Oxford Handbook of Political Behavior*. https://doi.org/10.1093%2Foxfordhb%2F9780199270125.003
.0009

Geertz, C. (1963). *Agricultural Involution: The Process of Ecological Change in Indonesia*. University of California Press. https://doi.org/10.1525%2F9780520341821

Glass, J., Bengtson, V. L.; and Dunham, C. C. (1986). 'Attitude similarity in three-generation families: Socialization, status inheritance, or reciprocal influence?' *American Sociological Review*, 685–698. https://doi.org/10.2307/2095493

Goffman, E. (1978). *The Presentation of Self in Everyday Life*. UK: Harmondsworth.

Goffman, E. (2017). *Interaction Ritual: Essays in Face-to-Face Behavior*. Routledge.

Hahn, J. W.; and Logvinenko, I. (2008). 'Generational differences in Russian attitudes towards democracy and the economy'. *Europe-Asia Studies*, vol. 60, issue 8, 1345–1369. https://doi.org/10.1080/09668130802292168

Hirschman, A. O. (1970). *Exit, Voice, and Loyalty: Responses to Decline in Firms, Organizations, and States*, vol. 25. Harvard University Press.

Huang, H. (2017). 'A war of (mis) information: The political effects of rumors and rumor rebuttals in an authoritarian country'. *British Journal of Political Science*, vol. 47, issue 2, 283–311. https://doi.org/10.1017/s0007123415000253

Huang, P. C. (1990). *The Peasant Family and Rural Development in the Yangzi Delta, 1350-1988*. Stanford University Press.

Huang, P. C. (2012). 'Profit-making state firms and China's development experience: "State capitalism" or "socialist market economy"?' *Modern China*, vol. 38, issue 6, 591–629. https://doi.org/10.1177/0097700412455839

Inglehart, R. (2018). *Culture Shift in Advanced Industrial Society*. Princeton University Press. https://doi.org/10.2307%2Fj.ctv346rbz

Jennings, M. K. (1996). 'Political knowledge over time and across generations'. *Public Opinion Quarterly*, vol. 60, issue 2, 228–252. https://doi.org/10.1086/297749

Jiang, J.; and Yang, D. L. (2016). 'Lying or believing? Measuring preference falsification from a political purge in China'. *Comparative Political Studies*, vol. 49, issue 5, 600–634. https://doi.org/10.1177/0010414015626450

Kamenica, E.; and Gentzkow, M. (2011). 'Bayesian persuasion'. *American Economic Review*, vol. 101, issue 6, 2590–2615. https://doi.org/10.1257/aer.101.6.2590

Kelly, D. (2006). 'Citizen movements and China's public intellectuals in the Hu-Wen era'. *Pacific Affairs*, vol. 79, issue 2, 183–204. https://doi.org/10.5509/2006792183

Kuran, T. (1991). 'Now out of never: The element of surprise in the East European revolution of 1989'. *World Politics*, vol. 44, issue 1, 7–48. https://doi.org/10.2307/2010422

Kuran, T. (1997). *Private Truths, Public Lies: The Social Consequences of Preference Falsification*. Harvard University Press.

Lane, C. (1984). 'Legitimacy and power in the Soviet Union through socialist ritual'. *British Journal of Political Science*, vol. 14, issue 2, 207–217. https://doi.org/10.1017/s0007123400003537

Li, L. (2010). 'Rights consciousness and rules consciousness in contemporary China'. *The China Journal*, vol. 64, 47–68. https://doi.org/10.1086/tcj.64.20749246

Li, P.; and Zhang, Y. (1999). 'Social cost of state-owned enterprises: Investigation on 508 enterprises in 10 Chinese cities'. *Social Sciences in China*, vol. 5, issue 8.

Liu, T.; and Sun, L. (2016). 'Pension reform in China'. *Journal of Aging & Social Policy*, vol. 28, issue 1, 15–28. https://doi.org/10.1080/08959420.2016.1111725

Lust-Okar, E. (2006). 'Elections under authoritarianism: Preliminary lessons from Jordan'. *Democratization*, vol. 13, issue 3, 456–471. https://doi.org/10.1080/13510340600579359

Magaloni, B. (2006). *Voting for Autocracy: Hegemonic Party Survival and Its Demise in Mexico*, vol. 296. UK: Cambridge University Press. https://doi.org/10.1017/CBO9780511510274

Naughton, B.; and Tsai, K. S. (2015). *State Capitalism, Institutional Adaptation, and the Chinese Miracle*. Cambridge University Press. https://doi.org/10.1017%2Fcbo9781139962858

Nederhof, A. J. (1985). 'Methods of coping with social desirability bias: A review'. *European Journal of Social Psychology*, vol. 15, issue 3, 263–280. https://doi.org/10.1002/ejsp.2420150303

Ngok, K. (2013). 'Shaping social policy in the reform era in China'. *Handbook on East Asian Social Policy*, 105–128. https://doi.org/10.4337/9780857930293.00011

Noelle-Neumann, E. (1993). *The Spiral of Silence: Public Opinion, Our Social Skin*. University of Chicago Press.

O'Gorman, H. J. (1986). 'The discovery of pluralistic ignorance: An ironic lesson'. *Journal of the History of the Behavioral Sciences*, vol. 22, issue 4, 333–347.

Pepinsky, T. (2007). 'Autocracy, elections, and fiscal policy: evidence from Malaysia'. *Studies in Comparative International Development*, vol. 42, issue 1–2), 136–163. https://doi.org/10.1007/s12116-007-9006-4

Qiu, G.; and Wen, Z. (2007). 'Critical adjustment of rural migrant policy in China: towards new paradigm'. *Chinese Public Policy Review*, vol. 11.

Roberts, M. E. (2018). *Censored: Distraction and Diversion inside China's Great Firewall*. Princeton University Press. https://doi.org/10.23943%2F9781400890057

Rose, R. (2007). 'The democracy barometers (Part I): Learning to support new regimes in Europe'. *Journal of Democracy*, vol. 18, issue 3, 111–125. https://doi.org/10.1353/jod.2007.0054

Rose, R.; and Carnaghan, E. (1995). 'Generational effects on attitudes to communist regimes: A comparative analysis'. *Post-Soviet Affairs*, vol. 11, issue 1, 28–56. https://doi.org/10.1080/1060586X.1995.10641393

Rose, R.; Mishler, W.; and Munro, N. (2006). *Russia Transformed: Developing Popular Support for a New Regime*. Cambridge University Press. https://doi.org/10.1017%2Fcbo9780511492150

Schuman, H.; and Rieger, C. (1992). 'Historical analogies, generational effects, and attitudes toward war'. *American Sociological Review*, 315–326. https://doi.org/10.2307/2096238. OA: https://deepblue.lib.umich.edu/handle/2027.42/91764

Seidman, I. (2006). *Interviewing as Qualitative Research: A Guide for Researchers in Education and the Social Sciences*. Teachers College Press.

Shen, X.; and Truex, R. (2018). 'In search of preference falsification'. *Working Paper*.

Shi, T. (2001). 'Cultural values and political trust: A comparison of the People's Republic of China and Taiwan'. *Comparative Politics*, 401–419. https://doi.org/10.2307/422441

Stockmann, D. (2013). *Media Commercialization and Authoritarian Rule in China*. Cambridge University Press. https://doi.org/10.1017/CBO9781139087742

Su, Z.; and Meng, T. (2016). 'Selective responsiveness: Online public demands and government responsiveness in authoritarian China'. *Social Science Research*, vol. 59, 52–67. https://doi.org/10.1016/j.ssresearch.2016.04.017

Svallfors, S. (2010). 'Policy feedback, generational replacement, and attitudes to state intervention: Eastern and Western Germany, 1990–2006'. *European Political Science Review*, vol. 2, issue 1, 119–135. https://doi.org/10.1017/s1755773909990257

Tang, W. (2016). *Populist Authoritarianism: Chinese Political Culture and Regime Sustainability*. Oxford University Press. https://doi.org/10.1093/acprof:oso/9780190205782.001.0001

Tannenberg, M. (2017). 'The autocratic trust bias: Politically sensitive survey items and self-censorship'. *V-Dem Working Paper*, vol. 49. https://doi.org/10.2139/ssrn.2980727

Tong, Y.; and Lei, S. (2010). 'Large-scale mass incidents and government responses in China'. *International Journal of China Studies*, vol. 1, issue 2, 487–508. https://icsum.org.my/wp-content/uploads/2020/02/tonglei.pdf

Truex, R. (2016). 'Bias and trust in authoritarian media'. *Working Paper*. https://doi.org/10.2139/ssrn.2802841

Wedeen, L. (1999). *Ambiguities of Domination: Politics, Rhetoric, and Symbols in Contemporary Syria*. University of Chicago Press. https://doi.org/10.7208%2Fchicago%2F9780226345536.001.0001

Xiang, B. (2010). 'Ordinary people's state theory'. *Open Times*, vol. 10, 117–132.

Zhao, D. (2001). 'China's prolonged stability and political future: Same political system, different policies and methods'. *Journal of Contemporary China*, vol. 10, issue 28, 427–444. https://doi.org/10.1080/10670560120067126

CHAPTER 6

Pension issues, state governmentality, and falsified compliance in a comparative perspective

Armed with an extensive understanding of its subjects, the modern state is like a DJ on stage before a mass audience, wielding a mixture of tools and tones to affect people's emotions, interests, desires, and actions. These tones can be used both individually and simultaneously, and they can also be tailored for distinctive social groups. The analytical model I proposed of the state's strategic governance highlights the ruler's general design, which is constantly updated in light of its understanding of the current situation, the public, and its own objective, otherwise known as its 'governmentality'. This covers the many types of statecraft that can be used by a modern state to generate compliance: constructing social knowledge through propaganda and education, or manipulating information; building consensus through policy experimentation; or using interest exchange to buy off the population. The state may also use coercive approaches such as censorship and force to maintain a compliant surface.

Under the constraints of state capacity and information demand, tolerant and intolerant approaches are strategic substitutes for the ruler, limited by specific capacity at any given time; these approaches strategically complement one another to elicit information from the people. Individuals' objective is to optimise their personal situation, making choices in response to the statecraft that they encounter. In a situation where active counter-conduct such as rebellion, protest, and appeals are not possible, individuals may still use cognitional counter-conduct, such as falsifying their public compliance. Facing changing parameters – such as changing social and economic patterns of distribution and actors' strategies – their interactions adjust accordingly.

The relations between the hypotheses in Figure 1.1's 'thought map of compliance typology and respective statecraft' has thus been filled out empirically and

How to cite this book chapter:
Wang, Yan. 2022. *Pension Policy and Governmentality in China: Manufacturing Public Compliance*. London: LSE Press, pp. 181–199.
DOI: https://doi.org/10.31389/lsepress.ppc.g. License: CC BY

theoretically in intervening chapters. I begin this concluding chapters by giving a synoptic summary of these findings. The second section looks more widely (if necessarily briefly) at whether China's case is sui generis or whether it shares important features with other modern non-democratic regimes.

6.1 Government and legitimation issues in China

By investigating the trajectory of pension reforms in China, Chapters 2 and 3 showed how, when the government was promoting a retrenchment reform under economic pressure, it reallocated resources strategically in order to maintain reasonable compliance from the whole population. Looking in detail at the variations in the timing, direction, and content of the reform together created a holistic picture of the government's general design of welfare differentiation. By changing the practice of welfare provision and adjusting the definitions of 'privileged' and 'marginalised' among the recipients, the state lifted from its shoulders the heavy burden of funding the beneficiaries of the old welfare system, and also created new bases of support from social groups that required less in the way of financial investment. In step with the welfare reform, the government used official propaganda to promote the principles of 'contribution and rewards' and 'rights and obligations'. The knowledge of such concepts as the 'socialised self', 'fairness in social redistribution', 'contributing to the general good', and so on, was designed at different stages, tailored for different target groups, and aimed at different reform targets. During the process, the state evaluated various social groups on the basis of their membership, the value they could contribute to the state's legitimacy, and the resources they could bargain with. Individuals' personal lives were also gradually socialised and initiated into a broader system, one in which only self-motivated, self-regulated, and prudent citizens deserved respect from society.

The specific statecraft tools identified in Chapter 4 were policy experimentation and propaganda, combined in the reform of the social insurance scheme for elderly enterprise employees. To promote the reform and ease the anxieties of the target population, the state took a moderate approach and experimented with the new regulations in selected regions, allowing enough space for 'trial and error'. Meanwhile, official newspapers played the important role of buffering the negative effects that might have resulted from implementing new and unfamiliar policies. In addition to addressing the strategies that were used, Chapter 4 also asked whether these strategies were successful in changing the public's attitudes to the reform and the state. Using causal inference methods I showed that the government's strategies had mixed effects. A dynamic governmentality (using policy experimentation) was designed and adjusted by the state so that the boundary between 'public (state)' responsibility and 'private (individual)' responsibility was redrawn. Yet Chapter 4 also presented a crucial flaw in state governmentality: the complexity of its constitution and dependency on past tactics risked causing a mismatch between policy experimentation and local propaganda, and other simultaneously used tools, creating an important gap for people's cognitions to break through. People are capable of identifying potential inconsistencies in the state's governmentality, and their reflections on these flaws may result in a serious challenge on the state's legitimacy.

In the qualitative analysis in Chapter 5, I moved back up from considering pension reforms per se to investigate the broader issues of falsified compliance in China's population, exploring how it may be feasible identify its existence, variations, and implications for people's actions and for the long-term legitimacy of the state. Falsified compliance comes about in a coercive environment where people's common sense somehow does not match the external scenario constructed by the authority. It should be noted that the state may not necessarily be using observable threats at the time, because the prospect of pressure can effectively be inferred from historical events and reputation. The coexistence of 'the state as a moral icon' and 'the state as benefit provider' in Chinese political culture has presented a differentiated compliance falsification towards different representatives of the state. My exploratory account also pointed to a mismatch in people's political knowledge: although they may seem self-contradictory, private political knowledge and public political discourse sometimes run along different tracks. Many people choose to tolerate discrepancies without further questioning the persistent occurrence of disconnection and discontinuity. Individuals' tolerance regarding the inconsistencies in their knowledge and everyday lives acts as a buffer absorbing external shocks from the political apparatus and preserving some private space.

From the qualitative evidence, many Chinese people seem to be pessimistic regarding any kind of political participation. However, some people are still keen to preserve their awareness, consciousness, and rationality, in spite of the pressure from the state and society. These people's reflections on individual life choices, the state–individual relationship, and sometimes the subjectivity that they present every day can empower positive counter-conduct. It can turn into actions such as emigration (people voting with their feet) or active political participation at the level of local communities (local elections, public hearings, etc.). Moreover, when the manipulation of popular opinion reveals flaws and leads to severe distrust and falsified compliance, it may lead in the long run to a serious challenge to the legitimacy of the state. An active state, however, will register the changes, readjust its understanding of the current scenario, and improve its tactics before the flaws end in a 'cascade'.

In theoretical terms, governmentality is pictured here as an interactive relationship, involving diverse means directed to population compliance as the outcome. In regimes where liberal democratic processes for producing normative legitimacy are weak or imperfect, using governmentality to maximise various types of compliance from the public helps the regime to survive. Compliance as the objective of state governance here represents the condition of no public non-compliance, or, more specifically, no collective public non-compliance.

The umbrella concept of 'compliance' used here covers many possible sources of legitimacy built up through individuals' expectations and judgement based on experience and the information in existing studies. For instance, Weber distinguished between three ideal types of authority – traditional authority, charismatic authority, and legal-rational authority – as bases of the legitimation of power in modern states. Gramsci talks about 'consent' from the dominated population, which can be generated by civil society. Legitimacy can also be secured by the state's socio-economic performance.

These different sources of 'legitimacy' do not exclude each other but may coexist in a regime. Essentially, belief about the state's right to rule is a synthetic thing based on people's cognition and their perceived information, or, to borrow a Foucauldian term, based on a person's choice to '*disposer*' (or dovetail/organise/make dispositions about) the external factors. Individuals choose whether or not to offer compliance to the state authority according to their disposition of external information, personal experience, and aspirations. In this way, the individual story of 'belief' and 'consent' dovetails with the state story of 'compliance from the population' and 'legitimacy'.

With compliance as the state's aim, governmentality works as the means whereby the state – through information management, benefit distribution, and coercion, among many other approaches – maintains its rule over the population. Scholars have examined various tactics used by the state and emphasised the value of 'coercion' for generating passive compliance in non-democratic regimes. However, as clarified in Chapter 1, the state is an active actor that can take opportunities to enhance its rule by managing the trade-offs between opportunities and challenges when dramatic social change presents them. Moreover, its governmentality is not isolated but is part of a comprehensive design. I discuss the sophisticated tactics used by the Chinese government and its dynamic adjustments to cope with the challenges in its reform process. The skilled use of policy experimentation, in particular, exemplifies the idea that governmentality is a process with careful design and the authority has a strong consciousness of 'feed-forward' in its policymaking (Schneider and Sidney 2009).

Where does individuals' subjectivity fit within the grand structures of 'state theory'? Throughout the four empirical chapters, we have seen how the government manages to objectify the population with well-calculated welfare reform, political status-based reallocation of benefits, and strategic use of rationales from tradition, culture, communist rhetoric, and economics. Individuals struggle with the subjectivity imposed by the state and external society. Their counter-conduct can take shape passively, through falsified political attitudes when fear persists and information is controlled and manipulated by state power. However, reflections on the state–individual relationship can be seen in the population and collective reflection is sometimes possible. This recalls Foucault's words about the counter-conduct of people:

Probably the principal objective today is not to discover but to refuse what we are ... We have to promote new forms of subjectivity while refusing the type of individuality [more like 'collectivity' in China's case] that has been imposed on us for several centuries. (Foucault 1982, p. 785)

My analysis of China's pension reform has addressed the trajectory and rationale of the reforms with a methodological approach combining the holistic and the positive (Durkheim et al. 1938) with individualism and understanding (Weber 2017). The holistic and positive approach – in particular, comparative historical analysis, in the broad sense – focuses on the structure and involvement of the institution and interprets social facts in their historical context in order to understand the reasons for their emergence or change. This approach assumes that institutions or events unfold over time and in time. Therefore, features such as the length of the events and the timing of the appearance of the events affect the outcome or turnover of social facts. Studies following this tradition highlight processes over time, employing systematic and contextualised comparison (Mahoney and Rueschemeyer 2003). This analytical approach is commonly used in social policy studies (such as Esping-Andersen 1990; Flora 2017) to identify the reasons for, differences in, and outcomes of social policies/programmes. In this book I have traced the design of governmental programmes, sorted out the proposed timing of the reform and duration of the pension policy schemes for different social groups, and compared variations such as their generosity, coverage, and fairness. More importantly, I have set all these features in their own historical context and addressed their motivation as driven by other social and economic reforms at the time itself.

The other face of analysing governmentality is 'man' and the 'things' attached to 'man' (Foucault, 2009). A sophisticated design of statecraft draws from the state's understanding of individuals' possible choices and the possible formats of collective behaviour. In this sense, the approach of methodological individualism is useful for addressing the details in statecraft, such as why specific information is emphasised in a certain policy, or why certain types of public knowledge are blocked but not others. Individualistic analysis also confronts comparative historical analysis, by highlighting change in people's cognitional mode, people's expectations of others, and the way that these in the long term put pressure on institutional change in their turn. The individualistic approach that can address the connection between institutional reforms and individuals' cognitive reorientation is also important in investigating people's choice to report or conceal compliance/non-compliance in public or in private, as suggested in Chapter 5.

My work shows that methodological approaches are tools with which to investigate questions that are thrown up by social facts. With appropriate design and modification, different approaches can complement each other in answering the research question. Sociology has long debated the tension between 'understanding social action as a product of interest-motivated, conscious choices by actors [and] as a product of normatively-constrained, habitualized responses' (Hinings et al. 2008, p. 486). My approach of treating the range of actors' choices and behaviours (Tolbert and Zucker 1996) in reaction to different socio-economic/historical situations as a multidimensional space is helpful for shedding light on complexities so long as the researcher can specify the details of these situations.

The substantive puzzle that motivated this research is the Chinese government's active effort to grasp the opportunities presented by social change, while using governmentality to avoid fundamental challenges from the population. As my empirical evidence showed, the risks of leading a reform can largely be addressed by the state's constantly adjusting design of statecraft. What can also be figured out from the past 40 years of reform in China is that the Chinese government placed a considerable bet on rapid economic development as a way of maintaining its rule. Visibly enlarging the cake for all to share not only increased the state's ability to allocate social and economic benefits but also enhanced its capacity to issue propaganda and monitor information, imposing censorship and threats.

If economic growth declines, therefore, it can be dangerous for the state, pushing it to adjust and refine its governmentality again. Meanwhile, China's governance will also change as it suffers more from external pressures, such as the general trend against globalisation, the surging conservatism, increasing ideological polarisation, and more heated conflicts over resources across the world since the late 2010s – as seen in Trump's administration, Brexit, conservatism across Europe, the US–China trade war, and regional conflicts in the Middle East and Ukraine. This pressure may become heavier because of the tight economic connections with the rest of the world that China has built throughout its opening up and reform. The contemporary period could be a significant turning point comparable to 40 years ago, when the leaders of the Chinese government actively abandoned the socialist package and led the grand social and economic reform.

China's present situation could bring advantageous opportunities for it to reduce the risks to its governance implicit in any economic deterioration. For instance, as noted above, the modernisation process of Chinese society has been extremely fast-paced. Its transformation from an agricultural society to an industrial society and then to an information society, a process that took Western countries hundreds of years, was compressed into half a century. Such an intense process can be a risk for the incumbent authority, since the ideologies and thoughts of the population must change so fast. However, it can also be an opportunity for the government to manipulate public opinion with the appropriate guidance. As evidence from Chapter 5 shows, even after 30 years of opening up and reform, Chinese society still has no established consciousness or consensus regarding modern ideologies or values. Concepts such as freedom, justice, fairness, and so on are doubted by many people in such a highly divided society. Many Chinese people still interpret the world with concepts and logics drawn from a traditional or a socialist political culture. Once information and knowledge are controlled by the authority, it can easily lead to the aggravated 'involution' of the public's political ideology. If the government could take full advantage of the population's characteristics and information asymmetry, it could persuade the whole country to accept any slowdowns in economic growth and believe that the political system of 'democracy with Chinese characteristics' is legitimate, needing no fundamental political reform.

Some initial changes in China's governmentality have already been made. From 2015, there has been a tightening up of political power, an increase in the regulatory power of the party, and a trend towards 'delicacy social management' promoted by the government. Taking the 'delicacy social management' as an example, a case of city governance in Tianjin shows that the power of the social infrastructure infiltrates into the local community through the party system, mobilised community members, and technology:

Nowadays, Tianjin has expanded the party organisation into the buildings and blocks of the city ... the governance network is coordinated and all parts of the community are actively involved. 'Network governance' is not new, but in the past, each department had its own grid – they are all of different sizes. The governance responsibility lies mainly on the local community officials who don't really have enough energy or specific knowledge of social problems ... Therefore, Tianjin city divided the 16 districts into more than 170,000 grids and recruited specific officials as coordinators ... For instance, Beichen district has become 120 grids, each with one community police officer and three coordinators. Once they see a problem that they can't solve, they report it to a higher-ranking governance centre and the centre organises the proper department to solve the problem ... There are also communities and villages organising volunteers from the public in order to extend the power of this network governance ... such as the Chaoyangli community. Nowadays [in Chaoyangli] we have 1,382 registered volunteers, comprising 22% of the community population ... Technology is also helpful for Tianjin's social governance. In addition to the increased number of monitoring units, we have also designed Apps such as 'Hexi power', 'Beijing integrated governance', and so on, so users can upload pictures whenever possible.'[1]

In addition, further examples of change include official propaganda tending to play the nationalist card more often and more strongly when addressing the international situation; more technology-based monitors used by government, both online and offline; and more barriers imposed when individuals want more information than the state mouthpiece provides. As regards the economic stagnation, the Chinese state has accelerated the pace of its expanding overseas investment and influence in Africa, trying to help the state's capital to increase and the domestic industrial structure to make the transition. However, these tactics cannot completely remove the risks of economic deterioration or even collapse and social unrest. They themselves contain the possibility of collective non-compliance that may endanger the authority's rule. For instance, the state's strict preference for social monitoring and sustained social stability may lead to more conflicts when individuals or social groups seek to defend their personal interests. The expansion of state capital may usefully steady the current economy; however, it could also squeeze the space available to the private sector and damage the long-term economic environment. It is still very uncertain which direction the regime will follow and this is open to further academic investigation.

6.2 Welfare reforms and state rationales in a comparative lens

China's case is unique in many dimensions (not least the state's huge size), but it is also comparable in other respects to social welfare reforms in other countries. Despite the different political institutions and state capacities, the situations of other governments in rapidly developing countries facing considerable socio-economic transitions are largely comparable in the rationales and tactics considered here. They also try to manage their population and to manufacture compliance (within resource and information constraints). Here too, social welfare reforms (such as new pension models and expanding basic social protection schemes) commonly serve as policy patches mitigating the adverse aspects of key socio-economic transitions in the country – and may bring challenges for both the initiators and the policy receivers.

In spite of the commonly recognised Western belief that it is people's social right to receive social welfare, in practice the policy design of pensions is conventionally fragmented and scattered for various subpopulations. As with all other types of social policies, some levels of fragmentation are inevitable, considering the connection of pension benefits and elderly care with different age groups. Different models of pension policy design that are adapted and promoted by the governments signal varied rationales of governmentality. After 1945, there were two prominent types of pension models – World Bank models and International Labour Organization (ILO) models.

The World Bank models, especially the famed multi-pillars design, leant more towards a rationale of facilitating economic development and efficiency. In 1994 a key report was produced that subsequently shaped pension policies across the globe, *Averting the Old Age Crisis: Policies to Protect the Old and Promote Growth.*[2] This promoted creating pension arrangement based around three pillars:

1) a publicly managed system with mandatory participation and the limited goal of reducing poverty among the old, a targeted (not a universal) pay-as-you-go scheme;

2) a privately managed, defined contribution pension, with mandatory savings systems for workers/employees; and
3) voluntary savings.

The pay-as-you-go defined benefit (PAYG-DB) model advocated in the report has limitations – it will incur high social expenditure, will be unable to tackle the poverty issues of vast numbers of informal employees in developing countries, and will tend to be inefficient for economic development. Within the three-pillar system, the first pillar was designed to be redistributive and limited, while the second pillar would be the main 'heavy lifting' scheme for most people. The idea was that an accumulative scheme would be a better choice to cope with the ageing population crisis, while also reducing distortions of the labour market.

By contrast, the other pole of pension debates centred around ILO models, which promoted a universal basic pension plan as key, and leant more towards social justice in design. The ILO advocated a pension scheme that could maximise coverage and redistributive justice (Gillion 2000). It argued that all kinds of mandatory policies, whether in the form of pension or social insurance, will inevitably distort the labour market. Individual pension accounts, as proposed by the World Bank as the second pillar, will work to cause a deterioration in the pension return for low-income participants. Therefore, a wide, inclusive, and generous government-funded basic pension plan was a more desirable strategy, *especially* for developing countries.

Incumbent governments make various shifts on pension models to fit the general objectives and constraints of different stages of their regimes. In the 1990s, a large number of developing countries, including China, took the World Bank model and adapted partial privatisation of pension schemes. In East Europe, the former Soviet Union countries took a similar path of welfare retrenchment, moving away from the former socialist welfare models. The notional defined contribution (NDC) model is another alternative way of dealing with the old unsustainable PAYG-DB scheme, and it has been adopted by countries such as Russia, Poland, Latvia, and so on (Holzmann and Palmer 2006). The Chile model of the funded defined contribution pension scheme was among the most popular ones adopted in Latin America.

These pension reforms certainly helped in improving the fiscal sustainability of governments and adding more saving options for the population, yet they nevertheless failed in many ways. For instance, the reforms generally did not lead to higher coverage and more participants in pension schemes. Considerable transition costs were incurred, which landed on the current generation of workers, and the reforms proved a high administrative burden for developing countries. More importantly, they failed in the redistribution of social benefits because disadvantaged social groups – such as female workers, low-income groups, and people working in the informal sectors – suffered more after the reform. The return rate for the pensioners was also less satisfactory than expected. In response, in recent years there has been a tide of reversing pension privatisation in more than half of the former privatised countries (Ortiz et al. 2018).

The pension reforms in China from the 1990s extending to 2020 are among the good examples for showing the paradox and complexity of pension models and governmental designs. The Chinese government took the path of the Chile model and the World Bank approach in the 1990s when facing the sustainability issue of socialist pension plan brought by the economic reforms. The integration of individual accounts into the basic pension scheme, beginning in 1997 with the follow-up reforms of fully funding in the 2000s, was planned to increase individuals' responsibility and relieve the burden of pension contributions on the government. Yet, as Chapter 3 and 4 (and much other related research) have shown, the reforms did not achieve what was signed up for. Entering the 2010s, the government started to promote a more inclusive pension plan by expanding pension coverage, reducing contribution rates, encouraging participation, and integrating the urban and rural basic pension schemes. Despite the gestures of enriching the first pillar of the funded national pension scheme, the responsibility split between the state, enterprise, individual, family, and communities is still debatable, as well as the argument about the solutions for the administrative burden and transition cost.

The adjustments of pension models adapted by the governments are not simply about the pensions per se, however. They also relate closely to the more general arrangements of government public expenditure, workforce regulations, tax policies, and many others. Pension reforms cast profound shadows on many political-economic feature of welfare regimes as they appear to citizens, such as social stratification, the degree of decommodification, de-familiarisation, de-clientelisation, and many other criteria that have been commonly used as key configurations of welfare states since Esping-Andersen (Esping-Andersen 1990; Esping-Andersen 1999; Gough et al. 2004; Wood and Gough 2006). A comprehensive investigation of the welfare reforms could reveal not only the design rationales driving specific policies but also the changing welfare regime structure in countries that are constantly adjusting the directions of their social policies.

Decommodification is one key feature for modern social welfare policies and is among the main indexes for social rights measurement. The idea is that social welfare policies should provide the possibility for citizens to 'freely, and without potential loss of job, income, or general welfare, opt out of work when they themselves consider it necessary' (Esping-Andersen 1990, p. 23). In practice, social policy scholars measure decommodification following Esping-Andersen, using variables such as minimum income levels, requirements for pensions, maternity leave, parental leave, educational leave, and unemployment insurance. For instance, for sickness insurance this requirement would mean that individuals were guaranteed benefits equal to (or close to) their normal earnings, and the right to absence with minimal proof of medical impairment and for the duration that the individual deems necessary.

The decommodification index is largely shaped by the socio-economic scenarios of the country and so it might present in very distinctive directions in different sectors of welfare policies and with varied groups of subpopulations. Countries in Latin America and Eastern Europe, like China, experienced large-scale socio-economic reforms entering the 1980s and 1990s. Their radical 'neoliberal-style' economic reforms imposed considerable constraints on the universalised delivery of their social welfare policies. Decommodification decreased markedly for enterprise employees. Their social rights were tied to market conditions to a greater degree, tougher restrictions were applied on eligibility, and caps were put on entitlements. In many other cases, welfare scheme change occurred in the opposite direction, notably with the expansion of pensions into rural areas and informal sector workers in China and Latin America. These changes signalled an increase of decommodification for rural residents and urban non-employed residents, and the realisation of their social rights to a certain extent.

Stratification is another key measurement proposed in Anderson's model classifying the type of welfare states, and it takes in the social structure and the concern of redistribution. It describes the way in which social policy mediates and shapes societal inequalities. In different types and shapes, social policies could shape the social scenario in both designed and unintended ways. For instance, in traditional means-tested social assistance, recipients received confined benefits along with social stigmatisation. Similarly, parallel pension insurance systems in corporatist welfare regimes also promoted class politics, by consolidating labour divisions among different occupational groups and enhancing the privileges of segmented social status. Although universalistic policies are commonly regarded as pushes for equality among the population, they are fragile in the face of the changing demands of social groups, such as the rising middle class in developing nations (Esping-Andersen 1990).

A common lesson about welfare policy reforms (also constantly suggested in this book) is that the policies adopted by the governments are often far from pure ideal types. They do not operate on a single dimension, such as 'expansion versus retrenchment' or 'neoliberal versus solidaristic' (Haggard and Kaufman 2008), but instead use a more mixed set of tools that might feature different designs. For instance, the state may initiate new pension policies in the direction of 'status-distinctiveness', while in the meantime also promoting some expanded universalism in social assistance and also increasing funding for private welfare plans. Despite the difficulty of sorting out how to characterise these social policies in typological terms, we may find some useful clues by considering how social stratification has changed alongside the reforms and what this has meant for various subgroups.

Pension reforms in China have presented a changing scenario in the past 40 years but they have matched the social stratifications promoted by the state. Public sector employees were among the privileged groups as the government employees, yet they have been removed from the core elites camp entering the 2010s. The expanding coverage for informal sectors and rural residents has increased the egalitarian, inclusive notion in welfare arrangements. The welfare stratification effect demonstrates a mixture of market efficiency reinforcement and communal solidarity building. As explained in Chapter 2, these joint actions created special designs for the government to lead the socio-economic reforms while maintaining reasonable social legitimacy. Structurally speaking, China moved into a hybrid welfare state containing elements of all the three main welfare state models, even before we consider the many longitudinal and subnational differences across the country (Gao, Yang and Li 2013; Ratigan 2017).

Similarly, in other countries that are experiencing transformative welfare reforms, some key stratification corollaries of these policies have been observable – although we would need further justification for causal identifications. At a macro level it has been useful for policy researchers to better capture the structural changes in varied welfare states. Barrientos (2009) identified the changes in Latin America countries where labour market liberalisation and new forms of social assistance shifted the scenario of welfare segmentations. Some progressive universalism was also demonstrated in Brazil and Chile in the 2000s, both countries moved away from basic universalism in areas such as pensions and health care (Barrientos 2013; Dannreuther and Gideon 2008), and wider informal sector workers, female workers, and low-income groups were included.

It seems clear, therefore, that the twists and turns in social policy adjustments regularly involve redistribution of interests and shuffles in costs among different social groups. In transitional countries, the political-economic reforms have commonly meant a shift in stratifications and power relations inside society, creating the possibility of new class coalitions and subsequent policy changes. The implications for social policies of new class coalitions are much more profound in societies without transparent electoral politics processes, especially when the decision-making around the new system policies is not mature and does not incorporate enough checks and balances. In such cases, large paradigm changes in welfare policies, rather than small adjustments, are more likely to be observed.

Facing salient paradigm changes, different social groups have varied expectations and appeals, and the legacy of the past could nurture serious problems. In the Eastern European cases, the transition to the market required a fundamental shift of resources out of the state sector. In the previous socialist welfare structure, citizens were incorporated into a dense network of social entitlements where social rights were promised by the state. Reforms led to deterioration of the value of these protections and the quality of services, and scaling them back posed serious political risks (Haggard and Kaufman 2008).

In their work on post-communist reforms in Russia, Rose, Mishler, and Haerpfer (1997) found that the citizens did not embrace the ideology of a free market democracy and that their attitudes to politics and the state were still deeply shaped by the socialist legacy. Evidence from Eastern Europe also supports this observation, since 'literally over a single night, all the things that had been taken for granted were no longer valid' and many people suffered from a 'serious identity crisis' (Ekman and Linde 2005, p. 357). The socialist institutional settings not only equalised everyone's income and social risk but also cultivated a strong belief in an omnipotent government. Munro took the discussion a step further and argued that the persistent scenario of the socialist legacy also deeply shaped citizens' political behaviour (Munro 2006). Logvinenko's work suggests that the 2018 pension reform in Russia weakened the social contract between the authoritarian state and society regarding welfare benefits, posing increased chances of future political instability (Logvinenko 2020).

Similar situations can be found in Latin America, where the upswing of social rights in the mid-1980s reflected public preferences and expectations that favoured the government-supported social welfare. A 1995 poll of 10 countries by Latin Barometer suggested that 73% of respondents held the belief that pensions should be managed by the government (Madrid 2002). Formal and public sectors that were strengthened by the rapid industrialisation and institutional development imposed pressures on government through strong alliances (Haggard and Kaufman 2008).

For the incumbent authorities, the risks for the state–society relationship in promoting economic reforms are similar, potentially prompting a legitimacy crisis for the state. In Weber's three types of legitimacy – traditional, charismatic, and legal-rational (Weber 1978) – the third rests 'on a belief in the legality of enacted rules and the right of those elevated to authority under such rules to issue commands' (Weber 1978, p. 215). In the modern world this has tended to outmatch the other ideal types. In liberal democratic countries, competitive elections form the basis of legalised government. Provision for 'civilian security' through the welfare state is among three components of the modern state–citizen relationship (Offe 1987). In this relationship, the state turns to the 'people' for its ultimate source of authority, while the citizens, having lost both the feudal forms of paternalistic 'welfare' and individual economic autarchy, depend upon the state (Offe 1987).

In countries without representative institutions and the rule of law, governance by their ruling regimes has been widely seen as relying more on ideological legitimacy and performance-based legitimacy than is the case in their democratic counterparts. Among the key areas of performance, the economic and social fields are crucial for these regimes. Economic rights such as work, property, and economic security promise people access to the benefits of development and material resources. Some scholars have stated that economic rights are a 'basic need' of individuals and should be protected even before the issue of adequate political rights is resolved (e.g. Donnelly 1981; Howard 1983; Shue 1996; Streeten 1980). Benefits brought by social protection, assistance, and insurance are normally classified as individuals' social rights (Marshall 1964), whatever the regime. People have rights to health, education, and a dignified level of social and economic well-being, regardless of economic standing (Plant and Jones 1991). In regimes where the authorities are hesitating to issue political rights, social rights are more likely to be used as a political management tool.

Because of their direct importance for individuals in modern societies, the public is less likely to go easy with the paradigm changes in welfare systems. In some countries, the non-compliance of the public has been relatively obvious and strong, demonstrated by lobbying, union strikes, collective protests, and so on. In some other countries, public non-compliance with state policies is subtle but also persistent, and I have shown this by phenomena such as non-participation, refusal to pay pension fees, etc. Either way, the state needs to adjust its governmentality and make use of various tools to achieve the goals of the reforms. As Chapter 2 showed for China, population-based governance has been essential in managing the welfare distributions and fitted perfectly with the fragmented nature of social benefits.

More importantly than institutional design, it is essential for the state to manufacture consent among society and construct social legitimacy of its policies (and institutions) when reforming the distribution of social benefits:

> To acquire legitimacy, every kind of institution needs a formula that founds its rightness in reason and in nature … for a convention to turn into a legitimate social institution it needs a parallel cognitive convention to sustain it. (Douglas 1986, pp. 45–46).

A key state function in the modern period is educative and formative; it can train individuals to accept the existing production processes through influencing their 'common sense'. In this way, the state can diffuse its power through civil society. Unlike 'political society', which works through force, 'civil society' operates by constructing consent through schools, the media, and so on. As Gramsci said, 'they [civil society] operate without sanctions or compulsory obligations but still exert a collective pressure … and obtain objective results in the evolution of customs, ways of thinking, morality, etc.' (Gramsci, Hoare, and Nowell-Smith 1971, p. 242). In addition, when a state is experiencing 'transformation' and the 'redefinition' of a previous ideological and institutional hegemonic structure, it may help itself by re-articulating ideological factors and rebuilding a new world view for the governed (Gramsci, Hoare, and Nowell-Smith 1971).

In addition to civil society, the theory of 'social construction of target groups' proposes that the election elites would use certain portrayals to identify the target population of the policy they want to promote to maximise voters' support and minimise electoral costs (Schneider and Ingram 1993; Schneider, Ingram, and DeLeon 2014; Boushey 2016). These portrayals are constructed from social values, emotions, or stereotypes of the target population. They can not only influence the policy agenda, selection of policy tools, and the rationales for legitimate policy choices but also deliver messages that could be absorbed by citizens and affect their orientation and participation (Schneider and Ingram 1993). By so doing, the government can legitimise the proposed policy and alter the expectations, perceptions, and even behaviours of the citizens (Donovan 2001; Lawrence, Stoker, and Wolman 2013; Schneider and

Sidney 2009). Several additional theoretical developments stretch the package of social construction to a broader meaning of 'ideas' or 'discourse' (Béland 2005; Béland 2010; Hall 1993; Schmidt 2002). For instance, Cox (2001) examined the strategic rhetorical changes of core frames of welfare state in Europe when the policy initiators persuaded the public that the welfare reform was necessary. Eriksen and Molander (2019) further identified the 'justificatory narrative' used by Norwegian political actors in defending the law on work-oriented activities with a reframe of paternalistic concern for benefit recipients in communicating with the public.

The development of technology provides regimes with more tools for implementing 'meticulous governance'. For instance, in China as elsewhere, e-governance and big data have made it easier for the state to collect information about the population and conduct risk evaluations.[3] GPS technology has yielded more precise measurements of the territory. AI skills enable the police to identify and locate criminals (and others) via face recognition in a crowd. With better technology, the state could manage, model, share, and transfer data, turning the 'uncontrollable' into 'controllable'. For instance, with a smart supervision system, big data can analyse the correlations between events of small probability and improve the prediction of social risks, thereby reducing the unpredictability of public crises. This makes it easier for the state to manage a mobile and fragmented society. All these tools and skills extend the state's infrastructural power into every aspect of society and individual lives, improve the direction of the state's governmentality, and help implement the state's will.

Conclusions

The theoretical construction of state governmentality and public compliance attempted here demonstrates that a thorough investigation of governmentality can unpack not only the way that governmental activities unfold their effect but also how the individual's subjectification process is shaped by statecraft, and how the risks of resistance from the public affect statecraft in return. Analysing pension reform design and projection has helped unpack the complicated governmentality and dynamic tactics of the Chinese state, and its efforts in addressing the legitimation issue during the socio-economic transition. My discussion of public compliance, and the potential for consent falsification in society, illuminates the subtle problems of manufactured compliance and the possible choices and risks of modern states in the two-way story of governance.

Notes

[1] Li Kun, 'Tianjin: Enhancing the Party's leadership, construct a "three in one" new version of social governance system'. *Xinhua Net*, 2018-12-20 https://perma.cc/G4VW-NFYM. Author's translation.

[2] World Bank. (1994). *Averting the Old Age Crisis: Policies to Protect the Old and Promote Growth. Summary.* The World Bank. https://perma.cc/ZTN4 -GF55

[3] 'The project instruction on "Big data driven management and policy making" Project 2020' (in Chinese), https://perma.cc/5CDF-GXV9

References

Barrientos, A. (2009). 'Labour markets and the (hyphenated) welfare regime in Latin America'. *Economy and Society*, vol. 38, issue 1, 87–108. https://doi.org /10.1080/03085140802560553

Barrientos, A. (2013). *Social Assistance in Developing Countries.* Cambridge University Press.

Béland, D. (2005). 'Ideas and social policy: An institutionalist perspective'. *Social Policy & Administration*, vol. 39, issue 1, 1–18. https://doi.org/10.1111 /j.1467-9515.2005.00421.x

Béland, D. (2010). 'The idea of power and the role of ideas'. *Political Studies Review*, vol. 8, issue 2, 145–154.

Boushey, G. (2016). 'Targeted for diffusion? How the use and acceptance of stereotypes shape the diffusion of criminal justice policy innovations in the American states'. *American Political Science Review*, vol. 110, issue 1, 198–214. https://doi.org/10.1017/s0003055415000532

Cox, R. H. (2001). 'The social construction of an imperative: Why welfare reform happened in Denmark and the Netherlands but not in Germany'. *World Politics*, vol. 53, issue 3, 463–498. https://doi.org/10.1353/wp.2001.0008

Dannreuther, C.; and Gideon, J. (2008). 'Entitled to health? Social protection in Chile's plan AUGE'. *Development and Change*, vol. 39, issue 5, 845–864. https://doi.org/10.1111/j.1467-7660.2008.00508.x

Donnelly, J. (1981). 'Recent trends in UN human rights activity: Description and polemic'. *International Organization*, vol. 35, issue 4, 633–655. https:// doi.org/10.1017/s0020818300034263

Donovan, M. C. (2001). *Taking Aim: Target Populations and the Wars on AIDS and Drugs.* Georgetown University Press.

Douglas, M. (1986). *How Institutions Think.* Syracuse University Press.

Durkheim, E.; Catlin, G. E. G.; Mueller, J. H.; and Solovay, S. A. (1938). *The Rules of Sociological Method*, vol. 8. Free Press New York.

Ekman, J.; and Linde, J. (2005). 'Communist nostalgia and the consolidation of democracy in Central and Eastern Europe'. *Journal of Communist Studies and Transition Politics*, vol. 21, issue 3, 354–374. https://doi .org/10.1080/13523270500183512

Eriksen, A.; and Molander, A. (2019). 'Welfare reform and public justification'. *Policy Studies*, vol. 40, issue 6, 628–647.

Esping-Andersen, G. (1990). *The Three Worlds of Welfare Capitalism*. Princeton University Press.

Esping-Andersen, G. (1999). *Social Foundations of Postindustrial Economies*. UK: OUP. https://doi.org/10.1093%2F0198742002.001.0001

Flora, P. (2017). *Development of Welfare States in Europe and America*. Routledge. https://doi.org/10.4324%2F9781351304924

Foucault, M. (1982). 'The subject and power'. *Critical Inquiry*, vol. 8, issue 4, 777–795. https://doi.org/10.1086/448181

Foucault, M. (2009). *Security, Territory, Population: Lectures at the Collège de France, 1977–78* (M. Senellart ed.). Palgrave Macmillan.

Gao, Q. (2006). 'The social benefit system in urban China: Reforms and trends from 1988 to 2002'. *Journal of East Asian Studies*, vol. 6, issue 1, 31–67. https://doi.org/10.1017/s1598240800000035

Gillion, C. (2000). 'The development and reform of social security pensions: The approach of the International Labour Office'. *International Social Security Review*, vol. 53, issue 1, 35–63. https://doi.org/10.1111/1468-246x.00062

Gough, I.; Wood, G.; Barrientos, A.; Bevan, P.; Room, G.; and Davis, P. (2004). *Insecurity and Welfare Regimes in Asia, Africa and Latin America: Social Policy in Development Contexts*. Cambridge University Press. https://doi.org/10.1017%2Fcbo9780511720239

Gramsci, A.; Hoare, Q.; and Nowell-Smith, G. (1971). *Selections from the Prison Notebooks of Antonio Gramsci*. Lawrence and Wishart Limited.

Haggard, S.; and Kaufman, R. R. (2008). *Development, Democracy, and Welfare States: Latin America, East Asia, and Eastern Europe*. Princeton University Press.

Hall, P. A. (1993). 'Policy paradigms, social learning, and the state: the case of economic policymaking in Britain'. *Comparative Politics*, vol Vol. 25, No. 3, 275–296.

Hinings, C. R.; Tolbert, P. S.; Greenwood, R.; and Oliver, C. (2008). 'Emerging inequalities in central and Eastern Europe'. *The Sage Handbook of Organizational Institutionalism*, 473–492. UK: Sage. https://doi.org/10.4135%2F9781849200387.n20

Holzmann, R.; and Palmer, E. E. (eds) (2006). *Pension Reform: Issues and Prospects for Non-financial Defined Contribution (NDC) Schemes*. World Bank Publications. https://doi.org/10.1596%2F978-0-8213-6038-5

Howard, R. (1983). 'The full-belly thesis: Should economic rights take priority over civil and political rights-evidence from Sub-Saharan Africa'. *Human Rights Quarterly*, vol. 5, 467. https://doi.org/10.2307/762231

Lawrence, E.; Stoker, R.; and Wolman, H. (2013). 'The effects of beneficiary targeting on public support for social policies'. *Policy Studies Journal*, vol. 41, issue 2, 199–216. https://doi.org/10.1111/psj.12014

Logvinenko, I. (2020). 'Authoritarian welfare state, regime stability, and the 2018 pension reform in Russia'. *Communist and Post-Communist Studies*, vol. 53, issue 1, 100–116. https://doi.org/10.1525/cpcs.2020.53.1.100

Madrid, R. (2002). 'The politics and economics of pension privatization in Latin America'. *Latin American Research Review*, 159–182. https://www .jstor.org/stable/2692153

Mahoney, J.; and Rueschemeyer, D. (2003). *Comparative Historical Analysis in the Social Sciences*. Cambridge University Press. https://doi.org/10.1017 /CBO9780511803963

Marshall, T. H. (1964). 'Class, citizenship and social development'. *New York*, vol. 19642.

Munro, N. (2006). 'Russia's persistent communist legacy: Nostalgia, reaction, and reactionary expectations'. *Post-Soviet Affairs*, vol. 22, issue 4, 289–313. https://doi.org/10.2747/1060-586x.22.4.289

Offe, C. (1987). 'II. Democracy against the welfare state? Structural foundations of neoconservative political opportunities'. *Political Theory*, vol. 15, issue 4, 501–537. https://doi.org/10.1177/0090591787015004002

Ortiz, I.; Duran, F.; Urban, S.; Wodsak, V.; and Yu, Z. (2018). *Reversing Pension Privatization: Rebuilding Public Pension Systems in Eastern European and Latin American Countries* (2000-18). Available at SSRN 3275228.

Plant, R.; and Jones, D. (1991). *Modern Political Thought*. UK: Blackwell.

Ratigan, K. (2017). 'Disaggregating the developing welfare state: Provincial social policy regimes in China'. *World Development*, vol. 98, 467–484. https://doi.org/10.1016/j.worlddev.2017.05.010

Rose, R.; Mishler, W.; and Haerpfer, C. (1997). 'Social capital in civic and stressful societies'. *Studies in Comparative International Development*, vol. 32, issue 3, 85–111. https://doi.org/10.1007/bf02687332

Schmidt, V. A. (2002). Europeanization and the mechanics of economic policy adjustment. *Journal of European Public Policy*, vol. 9, issue 6, 894–912.

Schneider, A. L.; Ingram, H.; and DeLeon, P. (2014). 'Democratic policy design: Social construction of target populations'. In P. Sabatier and C. Weible (eds), *Theories of the Policy Process*, 3rd edn, 105–149.

Schneider, A.; and Ingram, H. (1993). 'Social construction of target populations: Implications for politics and policy'. *American Political Science Review*, vol. 87, issue 2, 334–347. https://doi.org/10.2307/2939044

Schneider, A.; and Sidney, M. (2009). 'What is next for policy design and social construction theory? 1'. *Policy Studies Journal*, vol. 37, issue 1, 103–119. https://doi.org/10.1111/j.1541-0072.2008.00298.x

Shue, H. (1996). *Basic Rights: Subsistence, Affluence, and US Foreign Policy*. Princeton University Press.

Streeten, P. (1980). 'Basic needs and human rights'. *World Development*, vol. 8, issue 2, 107–111. https://doi.org/10.1016/0305-750x(80)90019-4

Tolbert, P.; and Zucker, L. (1996). 'The institutionalization of institutional theory', *Handbook for Organization Studies*, 175–190. UK: Sage. https://doi.org /10.4135%2F9781446218556.n6

Weber, M. (2017). *Methodology of Social Sciences*. Routledge. https://doi
.org/10.4324%2F9781315124445

Wood, G.; and Gough, I. (2006). 'A comparative welfare regime approach to
global social policy'. *World Development*, vol. 34, issue 10, 1696–1712.
https://doi.org/10.1016/j.worlddev.2006.02.001. OA: http://eprints.lse.ac.uk
/36646

Appendix A. Data explanation and model validations

Appendix A presents explanations on additional data, variables, case lists, and so on for the main content of the empirical chapters and provides more statistical results for cross-validation.

A1. Additional data for Introduction

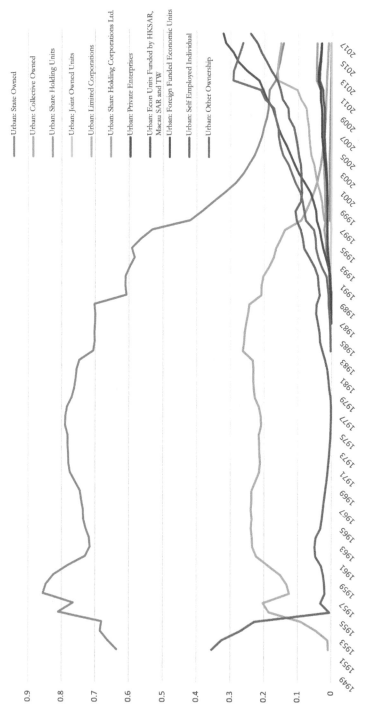

Figure A.1: Urban labour types: employment in different types of units.

Urban: State Owned
Urban: Collective Owned
Urban: Share Holding Units
Urban: Joint Owned Units
Urban: Limited Corporations
Urban: Share Holding Corporations Ltd.
Urban: Private Enterprises
Urban: Econ Units Funded by HKSAR, Macau SAR and TW
Urban: Foreign Funded Economic Units
Urban: Self Employed Individual
Urban: Other Ownership

Data source: CEIC data. (https://www.ceicdata.com/en)

A2. Statistical data in Chapter 2

The statistical data about pension schemes in Chapter 2 were collected from the China Labour Statistical Yearbooks, Local Fiscal Statistical Yearbooks, National Statistical Bureau Dataset and other datasets. The China Labour Statistical Yearbook is issued by the National Bureau of Statistics (Department of Population and Employment Statistics) and the Ministry of Human Resources and Social Security of the People's Republic of China (Department of Planning and Financial Affairs). The Local Fiscal Statistical Yearbook is issued by the Ministry of Finance of the People's Republic of China (Budget Department). The National Statistical Bureau Dataset is an online dataset provided by the National Bureau of Statistics through http://www.stats.gov.cn/tjsj. In Table A.1 I present a codebook for the variables used to picture the coverage, generosity, and funding sources of different pension schemes.

Table A.1: Codebook of pension schemes comparison and statistical data

Comparison category	Variable name	Variable label	Variable type	Data source (cross-validated)
Coverage	Total employees (eligible participants)	Number of eligible people (employee plus retiree)	continuous	Local Fiscal Statistical Yearbooks (manually calculated)
	Persons participated at the year end	Number of participants of pension scheme	continuous	China Labour Statistical Yearbooks
	Coverage rate	Participated/eligible participants	continuous	Manually calculated
	Residents number	Population of Residents (by pension scheme recipient's type)	continuous	National Statistical Bureau Dataset
	Revenue and expenses of pension fund	Revenue and expenses of pension fund	continuous	China Labour Statistical Yearbooks
Generosity	Benefit (per person)	Pension benefit per person (yuan)	continuous	China Labour Statistical Yearbooks (manually calculated)
	Increase rate	Increase rate each year of pension benefit (per person per year)	continuous	Manually calculated
	Salary	Employee salary (weighted by employee numbers)	continuous	China Labour Statistical Yearbooks (manually calculated)
	Replacement rate	Pension benefit/average salary	continuous	Manually calculated
Funding source	Government	Funding source including government	binary	Policy documents
	Enterprise	Funding source including enterprise	binary	Policy documents
	Individual	Funding source including individual	binary	Policy documents

A3. Textual data in Chapter 3

Corpus descriptive statistics

Figure A.2: Number of documents in the full corpus

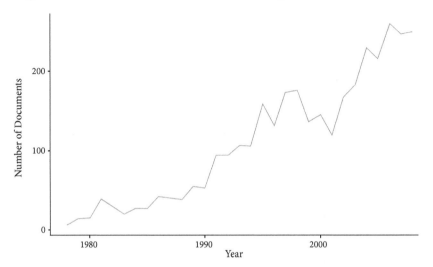

Validation of topics: optimal K

The text data include official news data from the *People's Daily* dataset supplemented by data from the China Knowledge Resource Integrated Database (CNKI database) and the Wisenews dataset. To find the optimal number of topics that can be drawn from the corpus using unsupervised models, I present the validations from *topicmodels* and *stm* respectively (with different pre-processings of the text), including a fivefold cross-validation of perplexity. The results from *topicmodels* indicate a K range around 100 to 140, while the results from perplexity and *stm* package indicate a K range from 30 to 60. In my main analysis in Chapter 3, I use the K number 30 since it is informative enough and relatively manageable.

Figure A.3: Optimal topic number with Topicmodels validation 1

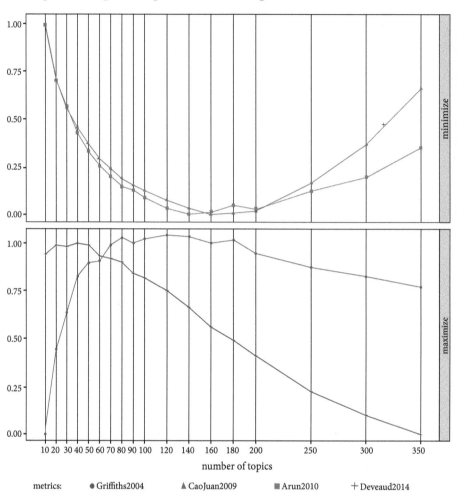

metrics: ● Griffiths2004   ▲ CaoJuan2009   ■ Arun2010   + Deveaud2014

Note: *FindTopicsNumber* in *topicmodels* package, segwords version 1.

Figure A.4: Optimal topic number with Topicmodels validation 2

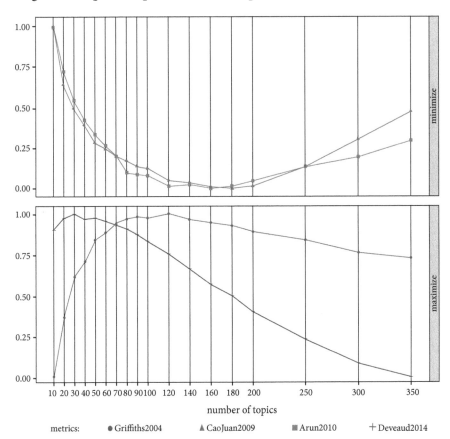

Note: *FindTopicsNumber* in *topicmodels* package, segwords version 2.

Figure A.5: Optimal topic number with perplexity

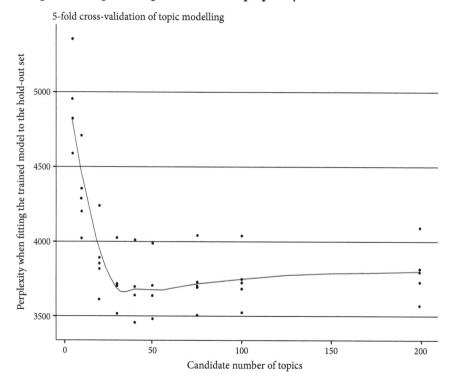

Note: fivefold cross-validation of topic modelling.

Figure A.6: Optimal topic number with STM validation 1

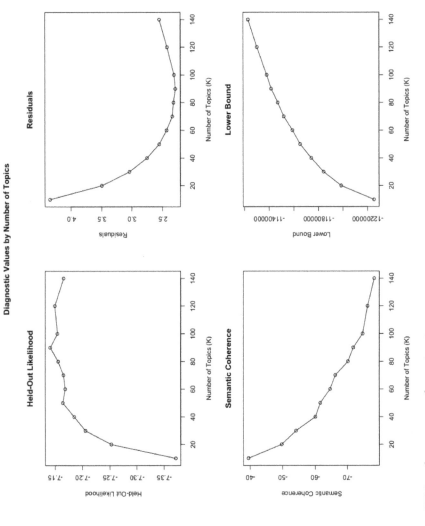

Note: *searchK* in *STM* package, segwords version 1.

Figure A.7: Optimal topic number with STM validation 2

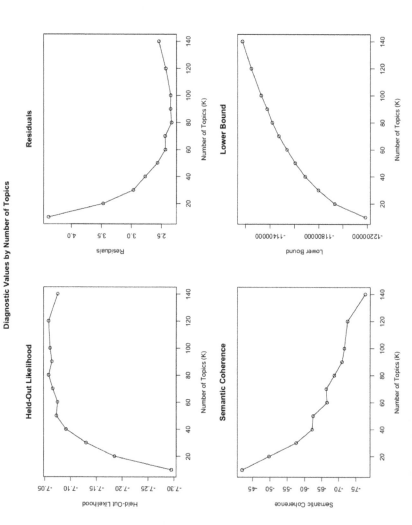

Validation of topics: topic content

In this section, I first show all the topics generated by the *STM* package with topic number K=30.

Table A.2: Topics with keywords with STM

Topic 1 'Global Issue' top words: Highest probability: day, month, meeting, hold, problem, government FREX: hold, Soviet Union, contact, Stan Lift: Judge, Baghdad, US Army, discharge, agreement, news Score: president, China-Portugal, parliament, date, Ukraine, Soviet Union	Topic 2 'Commercial Insurance' top words: Highest probability: insurance, company, invest, bank, market, China FREX: client, life, annuity, life insurance, company, business Lift: be clever, actuary, collusion Score: insurance, life insurance, company, life, annuity, client, bank
Topic 3 'HK-Macao' top words: Highest probability: Macao, administration, district, special, representative, law, Hong Kong FREX: Macao, legislation, motion, administrator, member of the standing committee, review, conference/meeting Lift: call out the votes, politician, offspring, blood line, roundabout Score: Hong Kong, Macao, administration, administrator, one country two system, motion, legislation	Topic 4 'SOE Reform' top words: Highest probability: enterprise, reform, state-owned, market, economy, operation, management FREX: state-owned, amalgamation, shares, transfer, bankrupt, enterprise, assets Lift: final fight, bad debt, strategy Score: enterprise, state-owned, reform, market, operation, assets, amalgamation
Topic 5 'Old-Age Care' top words: Highest probability: old, old people, society (social), disabled, elderly care, age, service FREX: old people, disabled, old age, care, recover Lift: few children Score: old people, old age, disabled, age, old, home-based, care	Topic 6 'Rural Development' top words: Highest probability: development, rural area, construction, enhance, promote, society, speed up FREX: promote, speed up, grain, enlarge, continue, strength Lift: function, law department, exaggerate, indigenous Score: rural area, promote, speed up, strength, construction, perfection, agriculture
Topic 7 'Community Care' top words: Highest probability: old people, life, family, difficulty, model worker, society FREX: model worker, visit, (Wen) Jiabao, supermarket, philanthropic, street level Lift: spare time, carefully care, filial daughter, depressed, filial Score: old people, work model, children, Wen Jiabao, street level, community	Topic 8 'Rural Officials' top words: Highest probability: village, officials, county, rural area, city, yuan, party FREX: party branch, party member, officials, village, town, committee -secretary, county Lift: shorts, Xichang, village commune Score: village, officials, rural area, county, party branch, party member, town

(Continued)

Table A.2: (Continued)

Topic 9 'Laid-Off Workers' top words: Highest probability: employment, employee, laid off, enterprise, labour, insurance, staff FREX: laid off, employment, unemployment, Liaoning, assure, positions, difficult Lift: apathetic, bureaus, bring Score: employment, laid off, employee, unemployment, state-owned, enterprise, insurance (protection)	Topic 10 'Europe/US/Russia' top words: Highest probability: employment, employee, laid off, enterprise, labour, insurance, staff FREX: laid off, employment, unemployment, Liaoning, assure, positions, difficult Lift: apathetic, bureaus, bring Score: employment, laid off, employee, unemployment, state-owned, enterprise, insurance (protection)
Topic 11 'Rural Residents' top words: Highest probability: village, yuan, 10,000, villager, home, town, district FREX: Nanling, whole village, Shaoxing, village Lift: loyal and filial, large and bright, orange tree, songs, green Score: village, villager, whole village, Nanling	Topic 12 'Overseas Chinese' top words: Highest probability: regulation, teacher, should, Chinese residing abroad, state, education, organisation FREX: crew, Chinese residing abroad, returned overseas national, family, teacher, ship Lift: academic group, family, short, bequeath, crew Score: crew, family, returned overseas national, Chinese residing abroad, teacher
Topic 13 'Auditing Supervision' top words: Highest probability: management, department, work, supervise, construction, audit, problem FREX: audit, migration, check, supervision Lift: officials and merchants collusion, take care, code, Wushan, Fengjie Score: audit, migration, supervision, law enforcement, management, examine	Topic 14 'Labour/Contracts' top words: Highest probability: labour, contract, work unit, employ, regulation, work, salary FREX: contract, employ, labour, issue (laws), trade union Lift: take advantage of others' misfortunes, doubtful (unsure), start (calculation), show permits, case, day-month-year Score: labour, contract, employ, set up, work unit
Topic 15 'State Budget' top words: Highest probability: finance, yuan, a hundred million, central (government), tax, budget, revenue FREX: budget, finance, expense, tax, central (government), tax revenue, national debt Lift: input VAT, pay, deduct, output VAT, break-even, wire transfer, stamp duty Score: finance, a hundred million, budget, yuan, tax, expense, central (government)	Topic 16 'Birth Control' top words: Highest probability: reproduction, plan, population, giving birth, work, women, development FREX: reproduction, women, plan, female, population, couple Lift: still, early marriage, boys, contraception, pregnancy, as low as Score: reproduction, population, women, plan, contraception, couple, giving birth

Table A.2: (Continued)

Topic 17 'Family' top words:	Topic 18 'China' top words:
Highest probability: one, in, old, money, month, two, no FREX: Yongshun, father Lift: one side, never die, Spruce, school students and teachers, ten bucks Score: son, child, daughter, elder, father	Highest probability: China, in, one, worker, culture, work, now FREX: sports games, performance, art, professor, giants Lift: serious and reserve, sampling, historical study, noisy, reputation, bullet Score: sports game, China, giants, workers, performance
Topic 19 'EE Pension Plan' top words:	**Topic 20 'Economic Reform' top words:**
Highest probability: insurance, elder-care (social security), social (society), enterprise, protection, employees, fees FREX: elder-care (social security), pay, insurance, trust, participate, social coordination, account Lift: rest of the life, transgression, account division, current, employed Score: insurance, elder-care (social security), pay, employee, society (social), protection, enterprise	Highest probability: economy, development, reform, market, society (social), job, state FREX: macro, control, current, price, rectify Lift: international market demand, victory, soft landing, signs, Keqiang, braveness, nothingness Score: economy, macro, reform, currency, finance, development, market
Topic 21 'Soldier/Social Service' top words:	**Topic 22 'Growth' top words:**
Highest probability: army, yuan, civil service, excel, 10,000, work, province FREX: soldier, support, military personnel, ex-serviceman, disaster (affected) area, Shantou, civil service Lift: new soldier, military district, storm, 25,000, patrol and defense, immediately, hide Score: police, soldier, civil service, off-service, support, army	Highest probability: a hundred million, growth, ten thousand, yuan, ten thousand people, whole country, point FREX: yearend, ton, whole year, compare, hectare, percent, output Lift: ten thousand boxes Score: growth, ton, a hundred million, yearend, whole year, yuan, ten thousand
Topic 23 'Institution Reform' top words:	**Topic 24 'Tech/Talents' top words:**
Highest probability: society (social), development, protection, institution(system), economy, reform, construction FREX: harmony, distribution, public, society (social), institution (system), ideology, fairness Lift: missing parts, variables, overstep, should Score: society (social), protection, institution (system), reform, economy, ideology, market, harmony	Highest probability: technology, talents, development, innovation, industry, enterprise, high FREX: talents, develop, technology, scientific research, skills, technology, industry Lift: new knowledge, ornaments, wood shavings, Shekou, dissolve, goods in stock, unique skill Score: talents, industry, skills, innovation, develop, technology, market

(Continued)

Table A.2: (Continued)

Topic 25 'Rural Migrants' top words:	Topic 26 'Develop/Party' top words:
Highest probability: peasant, rural area, worker, urban-rural, agriculture, city FREX: peasant, lose land, urban-rural, land, migrant, city Lift: Dujiangyan, deep water, whole scale, Pujiang, Xinyang Score: peasant, rural area, urban-rural, lose land, agriculture, worker, rural	Highest probability: development, construction, society, Party, economy, new, persist in FREX: view, persist in, characteristic, Hu Jintao, thoughts, ecology, comfortable (life) Lift: key knot, explore, not afraid of difficulties Score: development, construction, Party, ecology, innovation, principle, Hu Jintao
Topic 27 'Income/Production' top words:	**Topic 28 'Courts/Cases' top words:**
Highest probability: production, income, economy, ten thousand, development, equal, labour FREX: Kunshan, a thousand, two hundred, commune, one hundred, reclaim (wasteland) Lift: 1958, village, nine hundred, spice, dry land Score: Kunshan, commune member, commune, one hundred, output value, income	Highest probability: official, work, organisation, case, court, Hong Kong FREX: trial, court, judge, police, people's court, public service, case Lift: salary, innocent, sensitivity, fair judge, court, overseas business, embezzled funds Score: trail, judge, court, people's court, public affairs, Hong Kong, supervision
Topic 29 'Retired/Pension fee' top words:	**Topic 30 'Letter/Visits' Top Words**
Highest probability: retire, employee, yuan, fees, salary, enterprise FREX: factory director, factory, own, working years, surrender insurance, retire Lift: rumours Score: retirement, factory, employee, yuan, salary, fee, pension	Highest probability: people (general public), municipality (city), problem, appeal/visit, solve, government, work FREX: appeal/visit, Langfang, mayor, municipal communist party committee, letters, provincial communist party committee, municipal government Lift: notice in advance, flight, website, posts Score: Langfang, people (general public), municipal communist party committee, appeal/visit, municipality (city), provincial communist party committee, municipal government

Note: *STM* package, K=30.

To further validate the topics generated from the original text, I also present the topics generated with the package topicmodel, while these topics were generated using an estimated LDA model, for example the Gibbs sampling model. It is considered that the topics in Table A.3 roughly correspond with all the topics identified in Table A.2.

Table A.3: Topics with keywords with Topicmodels

Topic 1 'Social Service'
difficulty, life, disable, people, service, government, household, help, housing, family, district, difficult, poverty, social assistant, residents

Topic 2 'Development'
development, construction, enhance, service, promote, economy, rural area, -ism, speed up, society, improve, perfection, agriculture, enhance, policy

Topic 3 'Rural Area'
village, yuan, ten thousand, villager, household, township, village, town, factory, in, top, income, mountain, mu[unit of area, equal to 0.0667 hectare], plant

Topic 4 'Insurance'
insurance, company, industry, insur-, -rance, China, market, service, employee, in, business, insure, old-age, types, develop

Topic 5 'Labour'
law, labour, law, represent, supervision, whole country, People's Congress, problem, congress committee member, department, situation, in, audit, state, supervision/inspection

Topic 6 'Government/Governance'
work, day, meeting, month, central government, state council, whole country, problem/issue, point out, important, party, committee member, report, new, premier

Topic 7 'Health Care'
health care, hygiene, doctor/medicine, hospital, illness/sick, hospital, Shenzhen, fee, service, staff, Shanghai, medicine, room, month, protect

Topic 8 'Finance'
bank, invest, fund, management, finance, commune, loan, fee/charge, institution, funding/money, money, individual, amount, bank, saving

Topic 9 'Environment'
project/engineering, wood, district, construct, protect, eco system, ten thousand, region, water, tree, resource, environment, migrant, conduct, bureau

Topic 10 'China'
in/China, China, people, work model, one, group, one person, love, study, spirit, model, hope, one individual, learn, day

Topic 11 'Birth Control'
control, birth, talents, education, work, give birth, technology, population, teacher, school, high, state, career/public institution, staff, in/China

Topic 12 'Old-Age care'
old, elderly, elderly care, population, age, society, family, old people, old age, life, women, development, service, -ish, years

Topic 13 'Increase'
increase, billion, ten thousand, yuan, increase, point, country, percent, ten thousand people, year-round, ton, invest, price, production, yearend

(Continued)

Table A.3: (Continued)

Topic 14 'Social Protection'
society, social protection, institution, insurance, basic, health care, care, establish, system, elderly care, life, coverage, township/city, perfection/perfect, our country

Topic 15 'Pension'
insurance, old age care, employees, fee/pension, retirement, enterprise, fee/charge, society, pay, individual, staff, basic, fund, coordination, salary

Topic 16 'Old-Age'
money, old, in, one, old people, do, buy/purchase, nowadays, two, life, children, no, have not, car, home/family

Topic 17 'Rural/Countryside'
farmer, country side/rural area, industry, agriculture/rural, agriculture, urban-rural, land, city, city, township, -nisation (urbanisation), recruit, migrants, three

Topic 18 'Economic Reform'
reform, economy, market, institution, system, management/administration, establish, mechanism, development, society, -ish, government, deepen, perfect, system

Topic 19 'Economic Development'
development, economy, district/zone, -ify, new, industry, industry, city, market, high, municipality, explore, achieve, construction, technology

Topic 20 'Finance/Budget'
finance, yuan, a hundred million, center/central (government), tax, income/revenue, fund/capital, budget, expenditure, increase, local, policy, arrange, support, project

Topic 21 'Enterprise/SOE Reform'
enterprise, state-owned, employees, operation, system, production, factory, assets, company, middle/in, benefits/profits, collective, bankruptcy, business/industry, conglomerate

Topic 22 'HK-Macao'
district, Macao, administrative, special, Hong Kong, government, problem, staff, public service, committee member, law, basic, people, group, committee

Topic 23 'Labour/Employment'
labour, work unit, contract, regulation, employment, should, department, salary, line, work, according to the law, law, overseas Chinese, work

Topic 24 'Journalist'
Zhang, journalist, no/have not, one, business/things, month, Wang, Liu, money, in, vice, Chen

Topic 25 'Public/Society'
Society, development, principle, construction, party, people, China, economy, insist/persist, harmony, general public, new, political, ideology/thoughts, important

Topic 26 'Laid-Off workers'
employment, labour, employee, laid-off, staff, unemployment, work, service, enterprise, occupation, work/staff/worker, power, training, position

Topic 27 'Rural Officials'
cadre/official, village, general public, party, county, organisation, work, leader, party member, grassroot, secretary, city/municipality, level, rural area, committee

Table A.3: (Continued)

Topic 28 'Local Development' municipality, yuan, ten thousand, province, whole, county, this year, month, reach, whole city, last year, current, household, name, protection/insure
Topic 29 'International Issues' government, economy, month, US, country, day/Japan, president, dollar, pension, Russia, China, Russia
Topic 30 'Economy Issues' problem/issue, economy, our country, one, income, in/China, should, state, solve, need/necessary, level, development, no, cannot, -ish

Notes: *topicmodel* package, K=30, terms=15.

Hand coding: flowchart and second coder

To classify the documents into different key categories, I use both supervised models and human coder. In Figure A.8, I present the flowchart for coding category 'locus of responsibility' (the other classifications such as praise/denounce are quite intuitive). In addition to myself, I also asked a second coder (a trained PhD student) to code the 400 randomly selected documents in order to validate the stability, reproducibility, and accuracy of the labelled dataset. Table A.4 presents the Cohen's kappa for two coders. It can be seen that the coding of responsibility and praise is performed less satisfied compared to other categories.

Table A.4: Coding validation

	Mean_Coder 1	Mean_Coder 2	%-Agree	Cohen's K (unweighted)
Responsibility	0.6	0.52	86.8	0.675
Praise	0.17	0.16	91.2	0.684
Denounce	0.047	0.048	98.5	0.834
National situations	0.05	0.0675	97.2	0.752
Foreign experience	0.0675	0.05	97.8	0.757

Validation of classifiers

To select the best classifier, in this section I present the comparison of estimation performance with different classifiers (Naïve Bayes, Lasso regression, Support Vector Machines, random forest) using the full corpus. From the superficial number of precision, recall and F1, the models seem to perform

Figure A.8: Flowchart of hand coding

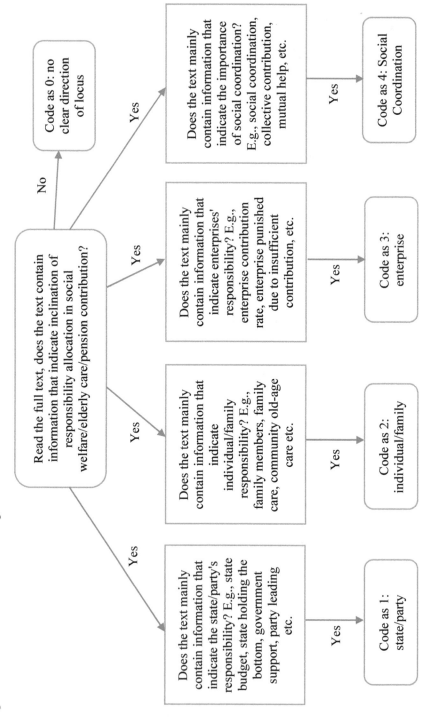

decently. However, as shown in the balanced accuracy, the models cannot provide predictions that are distinguishable from a random guess. The reason for the high precision and recall can be attributed to the large number of negative events, as shown in the two example confusion matrices below. Therefore, the supervised models perform less satisfactorily than expected. This can be an issue with the definitions of classifications since many of them are difficult to identify from the text, especially the responsibility allocation. Considering the normally rigid format of Chinese official news reports, it is the subtle tone and usage of phrases that distinguish the various categories. As explained in the main text, my analysis about the classified text is based on a combination of SVM classification and hand coding of the full corpus.

Responsibility classification (test set) using the Naïve Bayes model:

		Reference				
		0	1	2	3	4
	0	400	14	7	7	3
	1	66	25	2	4	0
Prediction	2	69	4	26	8	9
	3	33	0	0	4	1
	4	5	0	0	0	2

Foreign experience classification (test set) using the Naïve Bayes model:

		Reference	
		0	1
Prediction	0	623	3
	1	49	14

Table A.5: Performance of supervised models

Performance	Models[a]	Responsibility	Praise	Denounce	National situations	Foreign experience
Precision	Naïve Bayes	0.93	0.95	0.98	0.99	0.99
	Lasso regression	0.84	0.89	0.99	0.97	0.96
	Support Vector Machines	0.81	0.88	0.98	0.98	0.99
	Random forest	—	0.88	0.98	0.97	0.98
Recall	Naïve Bayes	0.7	0.69	0.95	0.91	0.93
	Lasso regression	0.99	0.99	0.99	0.99	0.99
	Support Vector Machines	0.97	0.89	0.99	0.99	0.99
	Random forest	—	0.99	0.98	0.99	0.99
Accuracy	Naïve Bayes	0.66	0.69	0.93	0.95	0.92
	Lasso regression	0.83	0.89	0.98	0.97	0.95
	Support Vector Machines	0.50~0.54[b] (balanced)	0.5[c] (balanced)	0.56 (balanced)	0.65 (balanced)	0.72 (balanced)
	Random forest	—[d]	0.5[e] (balanced)	0.5 (balanced)	0.5 (balanced)	0.5 (balanced)
F1	Naïve Bayes	0.8	0.8	0.97	0.95	0.96
	Lasso regression	0.91	0.94	0.99	0.99	0.98
	Support Vector Machines	0.88	0.88	0.99	0.98	0.99
	Random forest	—	0.94	0.99	0.98	0.99

Notes: *a*: The naïve Bayes and Lasso regression models are performed using *quanteda* package, Support Vector Machines and random forest models are performed using *caret* package; *b*: Using svmLinear with fivefold cross-validations and three repeats; range is for balanced accuracy for all the classes; *c*: Using *svmLinearWeights2*, as with other binary classifications; *d*: Not performed due to computing power constraints; *e*: Using ranger method (from *caTools*) for binary classifications.

Additional results: topic with covariates

In the following table, I present the statistical result including 'denounce' as the covariate in the topic proportion model.

Table A.6: Topic proportion by multiple covariates ('denounce')

Variables	Enterprise employees' pension reform	Laid-off workers	Rural migrants	Commercial insurance
Government/party	0.058** (0.014)	0.075*** (0.013)	0.022* (0.011)	−0.022* (0.009)
Individual/family	0.148*** (0.016)	−0.001 (0.011)	−0.012 (0.009)	0.106*** (0.014)
Enterprise	0.151*** (0.025)	0.021 (0.016)	−0.011 (0.016)	0.017 (0.019)
Social coordination	0.307*** (0.034)	0.032 (0.02)	−0.011 (0.016)	−0.017 (0.016)
Denounce	0.059 (0.045)	−0.019 (0.027)	0.019 (0.026)	−0.006 (0.026)
National condition	−0.016 (0.022)	−0.022 (0.015)	0.007 (0.014)	−0.029* (0.014)
Foreign experience	−0.013 (0.021)	−0.033* (0.014)	−0.025* (0.012)	−0.007 (0.014)
Government/party × Denounce	−0.143 (0.14)	−0.092 (0.099)	−0.074 (0.086)	−0.000 (0.093)
Individual/family × Denounce	−0.214 (0.195)	0.000 (0.137)	−0.084 (0.169)	−0.101 (0.13)
Enterprise × Denounce	−0.039 (0.073)	0.02 (0.049)	−0.038 (0.041)	−0.028 (0.047)
Social coordination × Denounce	−0.208 (0.242)	−0.023 (0.142)	−0.048 (0.12)	0.035 (0.132)

Note: *p<0.05; **p<0.01; ***p<0.001. In all the models, the mode of uncertainty is set as 'Global'.

A4. Additional statistics for Chapter 4

Selection of pilots

Individual balance

The legitimation of a counterfactual DID design relies on the parallel trend assumption, which assumes that the counterfactual 'natural' change in the outcome for the units in the treatment group between times 0 and 1 would have been the same as the change in the outcome for the units in the control group between periods 0 and 1. In this study, people's attitudes to the allocation of welfare responsibility or political attitude in the treatment provinces would have been the same as the ones in the control provinces if not for the policy experiment, or as shown in formula $E\left[Y_0\left(1\right)-Y_0\left(0\right)|D=1\right]=E\left[Y_0\left(1\right)-Y_0\left(0\right)|D=0\right]$ which was drawn from the derivation of the average treatment effect on the treated estimation under the DID design. Given that the parallel trend assumption is not directly testable, especially for two periods of data, we approached this assumption in several ways. First, we ran a simple t-test of our main outcome variable (LoR, a large value of the variable indicating considerable agreement on individual responsibility) of the 2004 survey samples (i.e. at period 0) by the treatment and control groups. $E\left[Y\left(0\right)|D=1\right]$ and $E\left[Y\left(0\right)|D=0\right]$ indicate no significant difference (p=0.51).

Second, being treated during the policy pilot programme is arguably exogenous to individual preferences and political attitudes. That is, ΔY_0 should be independent from the assignment of D. Most sites of policy experimentation in China are not randomly selected and potential bias with certain confounding factors may affect each province's likelihood of being selected as a pilot. Nevertheless, an in-depth case study on the development of the Chinese pension system implies that the urban pension insurance pilot scheme was designed by the central government, which carefully considered the issue of representativeness in selecting sites (Zhu and Zhao 2018). We conducted the following data description and balance check of key determinants in the selection of pilot regions to empirically address the identification challenge of DID. Third, we ran the baseline models depicted above with various control variables to minimise the bias brought by potential confounders. Finally, we leveraged the time effect conditional upon different groups (such as different propaganda intensities) with triple difference models.

Time trend

Although we cannot display the long-range development of individual perceptions owing to data constraints, we can present the variance of provincial-level covariates that may affect the outcome variables. We used the panel provincial data from 2000 to 2010 and compared the aggregated long-term trends of the treatment and control provinces on economic development, demographic features, and social conditions. As shown in Figure A.9, the trends of the two groups were nearly parallel to one another on most of the indices.

Regional balance

Scholars typically find it difficult to identify the selection of the pilot provinces. Several latent factors can cause potential self-selection bias in the process. For instance, provinces affected by the ageing problem in terms of demographic structure are more likely to be chosen as a pilot, but provinces with good fiscal and economic performance will probably be better at deploying the reform. Selection based on unobservable information, such as the motivations of provincial leaders, which vary across provinces, is also possible and the motivations may have changed as the stages of the leaders' tenure changed. Although we were constrained by the availability of insider stories, we could still rule out the endogenous problems through statistical analysis by using observable data (Gentzkow 2006).

Bearing in mind the nature of the selection of pilot provinces, we first constructed a provincial sample pool through sampling without replacement to address the potential selection bias. For each wave, denoted by year t, we used the social and economic data in year $t-1$ and then coded the province selected for the pilot pool as 1 and other provinces as 0. In the selection of the next wave of pilot provinces, the previously selected provinces were dropped from the selection pool. In other words, a province that had started to implement the pilot policy was not compared in the next round of pilot selection.

We then conducted an event history analysis (EHA) of the significant variables while satisfying the requirement of the variance inflation factor test to measure the imbalance between the selected and unselected provinces. The results are shown in Table A.7. Both the time discrete result and the time series result indicated that the difference between selected and unselected provinces was insignificant in terms of economic performance, fiscal condition, demographic situation, and the existing pension insurance system (column '*All samples*'). The three provinces in north-eastern China possessed some specific features not found in the other provinces: a larger proportion of SOEs, a longer history of industrialisation, a more severe problem of outflow emigration, and so on. Fortunately, these provinces were part of the first pilot wave and thus were not covered by the individual-level data in our study. Thus, we conducted an EHA test dropping on three provinces (columns '*2004–2009 samples*'). As shown by the result, the difference between the selected and unselected provinces in the second and third waves was greatly reduced. Thus, even if the provinces that participated in the pilot were not de facto in the random selection, they were still statistically representative.

Figure A.9: Time trend of provincial index

a

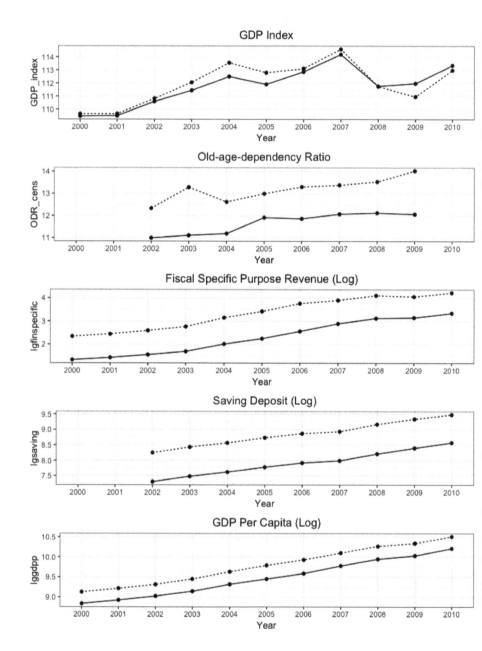

Figure A.9: Time trend of provincial index (continued)

b

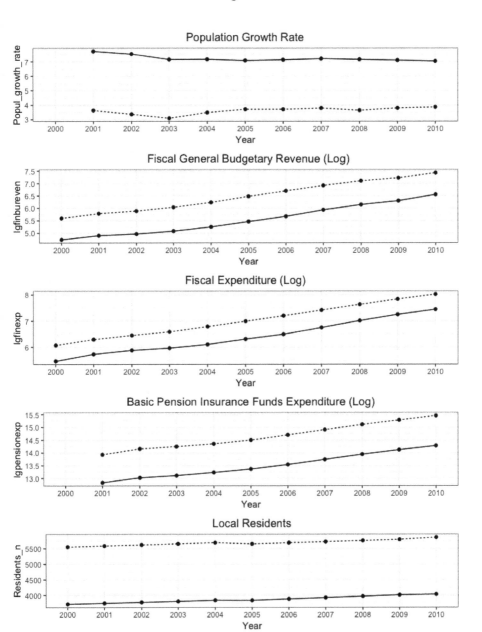

Dash line: Treatment Group; Solid line: Control Group

Table A.7: Balance check: event history analysis (EHA) of the provincial index

Probit regression	Treated			
	All samples		2004–9 samples (excluding first wave of pilots before 2004)	
	Time-discrete	Time-series	Time-discrete	Time-series
Population growth rate	−0.094	−0.043	−0.049	0.050
	(0.090)	(0.112)	(0.108)	(0.134)
Old-age dependency ratio (census data)	−0.225*	−0.199	−0.134	−0.067
	(0.127)	(0.126)	(0.138)	(0.138)
Urban retired employees' participation in pension insurance	−0.000	−0.000	−0.000	−0.001
	(0.001)	(0.001)	(0.001)	(0.001)
Urban retired employees' participation in pension insurance	0.009	0.010	0.009	0.008
	(0.006)	(0.007)	(0.007)	(0.007)
Log GDP per capita	0.609	0.900**	0.343	0.814*
	(0.440)	(0.400)	(0.477)	(0.452)
Log fiscal specific purpose revenue	0.479	0.780	0.151	0.562
	(0.465)	(0.536)	(0.505)	(0.590)
Log fiscal general budgetary revenue	−1.212	−1.508*	−0.489	−1.035
	(1.117)	(0.891)	(1.133)	(0.876)
Log basic pension insurance funds expenditure	0.636	0.729	0.216	0.649
	(1.156)	(1.118)	(1.183)	(1.300)
Year dummy		YES		YES
Observations	190	190	132	132

Note: $*p<0.1$, $**p<0.05$, $***p<0.01$.

Table A.8: Descriptive statistics of the main demographic variables

Variable	Years of survey	Obs	Mean	Std. dev.	Min	Max
Urban/rural	2004	2708	0.534	0.4998	0	1
	2009	2572	0.488	0.4999	0	1
Gender	2004	2708	0.476	0.4995	0	1
	2009	2572	0.522	0.4996	0	1
Age	2004	2708	41.486	13.112	18	70
	2009	2572	44.245	13.726	18	70
Minority	2004	2703	0.094	0.288	0	1
	2009	2543	0.087	0.282	0	1
CCP Member	2004	2708	0.075	0.263	0	1
	2009	2515	0.077	0.267	0	1
Education year	2004	2689	7.333	4.696	0	22
	2009	2431	7.323	4.692	0	22
Income	2004	2428	14630.26	40448.03	0	1500000
	2009	1832	23423.17	28633.99	250	250000
Income (log)	2004	2403	8.924	1.152	4.605	14.221
	2009	1832	9.453	1.240	5.521	12.429

Robustness test

Considering that all the models in the previous discussions are OLS regression estimations, we reran the empirical models with the ordered logit model for robustness testing. Table A.9 shows that the above results for the pilot policy effect were robust.

Table A.9: Robustness test with ordered logit model

	Locus of responsibility (ordered logit)		
Pilot effect (DID)	0.202		0.943***
	(0.126)		(0.218)
Duration effect (DID)		0.146***	
		(0.042)	
Policy propaganda			0.034***
			(0.011)
Policy propaganda × Pilot			−0.059**
			(0.026)
Policy propaganda × Post			0.156***
			(0.044)
Pilot effect × Policy propaganda (DDD)			−0.195***
			(0.054)
Demographic controls	Yes	Yes	Yes
Province dummies	Yes	Yes	Yes
Year dummies	Yes	Yes	Yes
Observations	3,790	3,790	3,790

Note: *p<0.1, **p<0.05, ***p<0.01.

In addition, we conducted tests by using multilevel models that allowed cross-province random intercepts, with results that were consistent with our main models. The model was constructed as follows:

$$LR_{itj} = \alpha_{0itj} + \beta_1 Treat_{ij} + \beta_2 Post_{tj} + \beta_3 Treat_{ij} Post_{tj} + \beta_4 X_{itj},$$

where $\alpha_{0itj} = \alpha_0 + \gamma_{0tj} + \varepsilon_{itj}$.

The multilevel model results are shown in Table A. 10: the direction and significance of main coefficients (such as the DID effect and DDD effect) did not change from those of our main models in Table 4.2 and Table 4.3.

Table A.10: Robustness test with multilevel model (random intercept at provincial level)

Locus of responsibility (multilevel logit)			
Pilot effect (DID)	0.089		0.466***
	(0.069)		(0.116)
Duration effect (DID)		0.072***	
		(0.024)	
Policy propaganda			0.010**
			(0.005)
Policy propaganda × Pilot			−0.018
			(0.013)
Policy propaganda × Post			0.056***
			(0.020)
Pilot effect × Policy propaganda (DDD)			−0.084***
			(0.026)
Demographic controls	Yes	Yes	Yes
Year dummies	Yes	Yes	Yes
Observations	3,790	3,790	3,790

Note: *p<0.1, **p<0.05, ***p<0.01.

We also conducted a test to identify intergenerational difference by adding retirement as a third dimension along with the cross-time and cross-province difference by using our data on the urban samples. As shown by the robustness test results in Table A.11, individuals who were retired at the time of the survey would have preferred the government to have taken more responsibility, but they did not show significantly different attitudinal change in terms of experiencing the pilot policy.

Table A.11: Robustness test with intergenerational difference

	Locus of responsibility			
	OLS	Ologit	OLS	Ologit
Retired	−0.672***	−1.304***	−0.726***	−1.425***
	(0.129)	(0.281)	(0.127)	(0.277)
Pilot effect (DID)	−0.071	−0.119		
	(0.117)	(0.243)		
Retired × Post	0.401**	0.764*	0.625***	1.215***
	(0.197)	(0.424)	(0.194)	(0.418)
Retired × Treat	0.432***	0.797**		
	(0.154)	(0.337)		
Retired × Pilot effect (DDD)	0.060	0.142		
	(0.236)	(0.501)		
Retired × Duration			0.183***	0.348***
			(0.051)	(0.113)
Duration effect			0.077**	0.162**
			(0.039)	(0.081)
Retired × Duration effect (DDD)			−0.106	−0.204
			(0.078)	(0.166)
Demographic controls	Yes	Yes	Yes	Yes
Province dummies	Yes	Yes	Yes	Yes
Year dummies	Yes	Yes	Yes	Yes
Observations	1,560	1,560	1,560	1,560
R-squared	0.163		0.165	
Pseudo R2		0.0636		0.0643

Note: *$p<0.1$, **$p<0.05$, ***$p<0.01$.

Finally, we tested the baseline models by adding other confounding variables, such as the expectation of upward mobility and whether the respondents were or were not receiving their pension insurance at the time of the survey. It may be argued that individuals with higher expectation of upward mobility are more aware of individual responsibility. However, after controlling or these variables in the models, the effect of the pilot policy and policy propaganda that we proposed and examined in the empirical section did not change, as shown in the following table, Table A.12.

Table A.12: Robustness test with other confounding variables

	Locus of responsibility					
Pilot effect (DID)	0.049 (0.069)		0.413*** (0.120)	0.101 (0.067)		0.504*** (0.117)
Duration effect (DID)		0.064*** (0.023)			0.079*** (0.023)	
Policy propaganda			0.017*** (0.006)			0.017*** (0.006)
Policy propaganda × Pilot			−0.027* (0.015)			−0.026* (0.014)
Policy propaganda × Pilot			0.077*** (0.024)			0.079*** (0.023)
Pilot effect × Policy propaganda (DDD)			−0.098*** (0.030)			−0.105*** (0.029)
Expectation of upward mobility	0.095*** (0.018)	0.096*** (0.018)	0.094*** (0.018)			
W/O pension insurance				−0.250*** (0.042)	−0.254*** (0.042)	−0.248*** (0.042)
Demographic controls	Yes	Yes	Yes	Yes	Yes	Yes
Province dummies	Yes	Yes	Yes	Yes	Yes	Yes
Year dummies	Yes	Yes	Yes	Yes	Yes	Yes
Observations	3,580	3,580	3,580	3,790	3,790	3,790
R-squared	0.157	0.158	0.163	0.156	0.158	0.163

Note: $^{*}p<0.1$, $^{**}p<0.05$, $^{***}p<0.01$.

A5. Interview data for Chapter 5

Table A.13: Case list

Case	Age range	Gender	Ethnicity	Education level	Occupation	Place	Non/local	Interview time
1	Post 1985	Female	Han	Postgraduate	Student	Shanghai	Non-local	2019.6
2	Post 1985	Female	Han	College	Government	Chengdu	Local	2019.6
3	Post 1980	Female	Minority	College	Public sector	Shanghai	Non-local	2019.6
4	Post 1980	Female	Han	College	Public sector	Nanjing	Non-local	2019.6
5	Post 1980	Male	Han	College	SOE; government	Beijing	Non-local	2019.6
6	Post 1990	Female	Minority	Postgraduate	Private enterprise	Beijing	Non-local	2018.11
7	Post 1995	Male	Han	High school	Private enterprise	Suzhou	Non-local	2019.6
8	Post 1995	Male	Han	Postgraduate	Private enterprise	Beijing	Non-local	2019.6
9	Post 1980	Male	Han	Postgraduate	SOE	Beijing	Non-local	2019.6
10	Post 1985	Female	Han	Postgraduate	New media	Beijing	Non-local	2019.6
11	Post 1985	Female	Han	Postgraduate	Foreign enterprise	Beijing	Non-local	2019.6
12	Post 1950	Male	Han	College	Retired (private sector)	Shanghai	Local	2019.6
13	Post 1980	Male	Han	College	Commercial media	Beijing	Non-local	2019.6
14	Post 1990	Male	Han	Postgraduate	Student	London	Non-local	2019.6

15	Post 2000	Female	Han	High school	Student	Xi'an	Local	2019.6
16	Post 1950	Male	Han	Junior high school	Retired (SOE)	Tianjin	Local	2018.11
17	Post 1950	Female	Han	High school	Retired (SOE)	Tianjin	Local	2018.11
18	Post 1950	Male	Han	College	Retired (public sector)	Jilin	Local	2018.11
19	Post 1970	Male	Han	PhD	Higher education	Beijing	Non-local	2018.12
20	Post 1970	Male	Han	PhD	Higher education	Beijing	Non-local	2018.12
21	Post 1960	Female	Han	High school	Public sector	Yuncheng	Local	2018.11
22	Post 1960	Male	Han	College	Government	Yuncheng	Local	2018.11
23	Post 1990	Female	Han	College	Finance sector	Beijing	Non-local	2018.12
24	Post 1990	Male	Han	College	Unemployed	Beijing	Non-local	2018.12
25	Post 1990	Female	Han	Postgraduate	SOE	Beijing	Non-local	Observation
26	Post 1960	Male	Han	PhD	Higher education	Overseas	Non-local	Observation
27	Post 1980	Female	Han	PhD	Higher education	Overseas	Non-local	2019.6

Note: The list is for both the interviews and some of the observation cases.

Appendix B. Data replication codebooks

Appendix B presents a brief explanation of the statistical methods used in the empirical chapters and instructions on the replication file for Chapters 3 and 4. All documents are available upon request.

B1. Text analysis (Chapter 3)

As explained in the main content, I use quantitative text analysis (QTA) to show the persuasive efforts of the government when intentionally producing truth and knowledge about pension benefits, social fairness, and the allocation of responsibility. The QTA part of my research included two subsections: an unsupervised structural topic model to identify the main topics in the text relating to pension reforms and supervised methods to label each document with categories that were of interest to my research. The main software used here was Rstudio (version 1.1.447) and the main QTA packages including Rwordseg, tmcn, stm, topicmodel (all available on https://cran.r-project.org). Helpful literature for further understanding the method can be found in work of Hopkins and King (2010), Grimmer and Stewart (2013), Lucas et al. (2015), and Roberts, Stewart, and Tingley (2014).

I provided code and data files necessary to replicate some of the main results reported in Chapter 3. Owing to the large amount of original data, I share the data-term-matrix and metadata. Since text segment and software simulation can be different each time, it may not be possible to replicate the exact results reported in the chapter, but, as long as the replication uses the same version of the packages, the results should be similar. It should be noted that the original data are in Chinese, and therefore the direct results (such as the generated topics) are also in Chinese.

Table B.1: Codebook for Chapter 3

Variable name	Variable label and measurement
X	Document number
Title	Title of the document
Author	Author of the document
Date	Date of the document
Year	Year
Month	Month
Day	Day
Year_Month	Year-month
Edition_name	Edition name of the document
Column	Column of the document
Text	Full text of the document
Responsibility	Identified welfare responsibility of the document (categorical variable), 'no clear direction of locus'=0, 'state/party'=1, 'individual/family'=2, 'enterprise'=3, 'social coordination'=4
National.condition	Whether the document emphasis national condition (Yes=1)
Foreign.experience	Whether the document emphasis foreign experience (Yes=1)
Praise	Whether the sentiment is positive (Yes=1)
Denounce	Whether the sentiment is negative (Yes=1)

B2. Causal inference (Chapter 4)

In Chapter 4, I used difference-in-differences when examining the causal relationship between the trajectory of welfare reform from state socialism to shared responsibility and individual changes of perception. The idea of causal inference here is that the causal effect of a treatment on some outcome can be assessed. The causal effect of the treatment on the outcome for unit i is the difference between its two potential outcomes: an observed outcome in a treated situation and an unobserved outcome in a control situation (i.e. something counterfactual). However, in practice, it is impossible to observe the values of Y_{1i} and Y_{0i} on the same unit i. Therefore, in empirical studies, scholars rely on statistical solutions to the fundamental problem of causal inference (Winship and Morgan 1999). Commonly used approaches include randomised experiments (e.g. Fisher 1960; Gerber and Green 2012), matching and weighting on covariates (e.g. Hainmueller 2012; Iacus, King, and Porro 2012; Morgan and Harding 2006), difference-in-differences (e.g. Ashenfelter 1978), a synthetic control method (Abadie and Gardeazabal 2003), instrumental variables (e.g. Angrist, Imbens, and Rubin 1996), causal mediation analysis (Imai, Keele, and Yamamoto 2010), and regression discontinuity design (Imbens and Lemieux 2008; Thistlethwaite and Campbell 1960).

The difference-in-differences method was developed from the 'simple difference estimator', which used the post-treatment outcome (Y_{11}) minus the pre-treatment outcome (Y_{01}) for the treatment group. However, owing to the existence of the time factor, the $Y_{11}-Y_{01}$ estimator is not actually the treatment effect. Therefore, the DID approach takes advantage of the control group, which did not receive any treatment of intervention, such as a policy/programme. If the assumption of a parallel trend holds, the estimator $(\bar{y}_{treat, after}-\bar{y}_{treat,before})-(\bar{y}_{control,after}-\bar{y}_{control,before})$ can be treated as the treatment effect of itervention.

We signed a confidentiality agreement to use the survey data (with Martin Whyte) and therefore cannot publish the original data used for Chapter 4. Instead, the code used to generate the results in the chapter is available upon request. The relevant codebook (individual level and provincial level) is presented in Table B.2.

Table B.2: Codebook for Chapter 4

Variable name	Variable label and measurement
Urban	Hukou registration (Urban=1)
Gender	Gender (Male=1)
Age	Age
Minority	Minority ethnic group (Minority=1)
CCP_member	Member of CCP (Member=1)
Edu_year	Years of education
Age_grp	Age group
Edu_grp	Education levels
Income_log	Annual income of the household (log value)
Unit_Enterprise	Occupational variation (Enterprise employees=1)
Unit_Governmental Employee	Occupational variation (Governmental employees=1)
Old-age dependency (oldcare_n)	Numbers of old-age person the family need to take care
Treated	Provinces being treated or controlled (treated=1)
Duration	Years each province being treated
Wave	Provinces in different waves of experiment
Post	Survey year (year 2009=1)
Province_n	Province code, 22 provinces in total
Respon_old	Locus of responsibility regarding old-age caring (attitudinal preference, individual responsibility=5)
Respon_med	Locus of responsibility regarding health caring (attitudinal preference, individual responsibility=5)
Respon_edu	Locus of responsibility regarding compulsory education (attitudinal preference, individual responsibility=5)
Respon_job	Locus of responsibility regarding employment (attitudinal preference, individual responsibility=5)
Trust_central	Political trust for central government (most trust=4)
Trust_province	Political trust for provincial government (most trust=4)
Trust_local	Political trust for prefectural/city government (most trust=4)
Province name	Province name
province_n	Province code
Year_Prov	Year-province panel
All news	All article number

Table B.2: (Continued)

Variable name	Variable label and measurement
Related_news	Identified article number relates to pension insurance/ old-age social insurance
Related_news_ratio	Ratio of Identified article number relates to pension insurance/old-age social insurance compare to all articles
Accumulated Related_ news_ratio (3 years)	Related News (2002+2003+2004)/ All News (2002+2003+2004) Related News (2007+2008+2009)/ All News (2007+2008+2009)
Accumulated Related_ news_ratio (5 years)	Related news (2000+2001+2002+2003+2004)/All News (2000+2001+2002+2003+2004) Related news (2005+2006+2007+2008+2009)/All News (2005+2006+2007+2008+2009)
Directly related news	Identified article number relates to fully funding the individual accounts pilot policy
Directly related news_ratio	Ratio of Identified article relates to fully funding the individual accounts pilot policy compare to all articles
Accumulated Directly Related_news_ratio (3 years)	Directly related news (2002+2003+2004)/ All news (2002+2003+2004) Directly related news (2007+2008+2009)/ All news (2007+2008+2009)
Accumulated Directly Related_news_ratio (5 years)	Directly related news (2000+2001+2002+2003+2004)/ All News (2000+2001+2002+2003+2004) Directly related news (2005+2006+2007+2008+2009)/ All News (2005+2006+2007+2008+2009)
Wave	Wave of pilot policy
Municipal_n	Number of municipalities of certain province
County_n	Number of counties of certain province
GDP_total	Province GDP (yuan)
GDP_per capita	Province GDP per capita (yuan)
GDP_index	Province GDP Index (previous year=100)
Residents_n	Yearend population of certain province (10,000)
Urban_residents	Urban population of certain province (10,000)
Rural_residents	Rural population of certain province (10,000)
Population growth rate	Population growth rate (‰)
Population	Population (census)
Old_population	Population of people above 65 (census)

(Continued)

Table B.2: (Continued)

Variable name	Variable label and measurement
ODR_cens	Old-age dependency rate (census)
Urban_employees	Urban employee population (10,000)
Fin_budgetary revenue	Local fiscal general budgetary revenue (hundred million)
Fin_revenue	Local fiscal revenue (hundred million)
Fin_specific purpose revenue	Local fiscal specific purpose revenue (hundred million)
Fin_non-tax revenue	Local non-tax revenue (hundred million)
Fin_general budgetary expenditure	Local fiscal general budgetary expenditure (hundred million)
Fin_general public service expenditure	Local fiscal general public service expenditure (hundred million)
Fin_social security and employment expenditure	Local fiscal social security and employment expenditure (hundred million)
Fin_health and medical expenditure	Local fiscal health and medical expenditure (hundred million)
Saving_deposit	Saving deposit (hundred million)
Ur_employee participants	Urban employee participants for old-age social insurance (10,000)
Ur_in service employee participants	Urban in service employee participants for old-age social insurance (10,000)
Ur_retired employee participants	Urban retired employee participants for Old-age social insurance (10,000)
Pension_revenue	Basic pension insurance funds revenue (10,000 yuan)
Pension_expen	Basic pension insurance funds expenditure (10,000 yuan)
Pension_balance	Basic pension insurance funds balance (10,000 yuan)

Bibliography

Acemoglu, D.; Ticchi, D.; and Vindigni, A. (2010). 'A theory of military dicta-torships'. *American Economic Journal: Macroeconomics*, vol. 2, issue 1, 1–42. https://doi.org/10.1257/mac.2.1.1. OA: https://dspace.mit.edu/bitstream /1721.1/61747/2/Acemoglu_A%20theory.pdf

Anderson, K.; and Ebbinghaus, B. (2011). *The Varieties of Pension Governance. Pension Privatization in Europe.*

Asch, S. E.; and Guetzkow, H. (1951). 'Effects of group pressure upon the modification and distortion of judgments'. *Documents of Gestalt Psychology*, 222–236.

Bank, C. M. (2017). *China Minsheng Bank Report.*

Barrientos, A. (2009). 'Labour markets and the (hyphenated) welfare regime in Latin America'. *Economy and Society*, vol. 38, issue 1, 87–108. https://doi.org /10.1080/03085140802560553

Barrientos, A. (2013). *Social Assistance in Developing Countries.* Cambridge University Press.

Beck, H. (1997). *The Origins of the Authoritarian Welfare State in Prussia: Con-servatives, Bureaucracy, and the Social Question, 1815–70.* University of Michigan Press. https://doi.org/10.3998%2Fmpub.13913

Beetham, D. (1991). 'Max Weber and the legitimacy of the modern state'. *Ana-lyse & Kritik*, vol. 13, issue 1, 34–45. https://doi.org/10.1515/auk-1991-0102

Beetham, D. (1995). 'What future for economic and social rights?' *Political Studies*, vol. 43, issue 1, 41–60. https://doi.org/10.1111/j.1467-9248.1995 .tb01735.x

Béland, D. (2005). 'Ideas and social policy: An institutionalist perspective'. *Social Policy & Administration*, vol. 39, issue 1, 1–18. https://doi.org/10.1111/j .1467-9515.2005.00421.x

Béland, D. (2010). 'The idea of power and the role of ideas'. *Political Studies Review*, vol. 8, issue 2, 145–154.

Benish, A.; Haber, H.; and Eliahou, R. (2017). 'The regulatory welfare state in pension markets: mitigating high charges for low-income savers in the United Kingdom and Israel'. *Journal of Social Policy*, vol. 46, issue 2, 313–330. https://doi.org/10.1017/S0047279416000593

Bennett, P.; and Naim, M. (2015). '21st century censorship: Governments around the world are using stealthy strategies to manipulate the media'. *Columbia Journalism Review*. https://archives.cjr.org/cover_story/21st_century _censorship.php

Bernstein, T. P. (2013). 'Resilience and collapse in China and the Soviet Union'. *Why Communism Did Not Collapse: Understanding Authoritarian Regime Resilience in Asia and Europe*, 40–63.

Bian, Y. (2002). 'Chinese social stratification and social mobility'. *Annual Review of Sociology*, vol. 28, issue 1, 91–116. https://doi.org/10.1146 /annurev.soc.28.110601.140823

Bian, Y.; and Logan, J. R. (1996). 'Market transition and the persistence of power: The changing stratification system in urban China'. *American Sociological Review*, 739–758. https://doi.org/10.2307/2096451

Blaydes, L. (2006). *Who Votes in Authoritarian Elections and Why? Vote Buying, Turnout, and Spoiled Ballots in Contemporary Egypt*. Paper presented at the APSA Annual Meeting, Philadelphia.

Boix, C.; and Svolik, M. W. (2013). 'The foundations of limited authoritarian government: Institutions, commitment, and power-sharing in dictatorships'. *The Journal of Politics*, vol. 75, issue 2, 300–316. https://doi.org/10.1017 /s0022381613000029

Boushey, G. (2016). 'Targeted for diffusion? How the use and acceptance of stereotypes shape the diffusion of criminal justice policy innovations in the American states'. *American Political Science Review*, vol. 110, issue 1, 198–214. https://doi.org/10.1017/s0003055415000532

Braungart, R. G.; and Braungart, M. M. (1986). 'Life-course and generational politics'. *Annual Review of Sociology*, vol. 12, issue 1, 205–231. https://doi.org /10.1146/annurev.so.12.080186.001225

Bray, D. (2005). *Social Space and Governance in Urban China: The Danwei System from Origins to Reform*. Stanford University Press.

Bursztyn, L.; and Jensen, R. (2017). 'Social image and economic behavior in the field: Identifying, understanding, and shaping social pressure'. *Annual Review of Economics*, vol. 9, 131–153. https://doi.org/10.1146/annurev -economics-063016-103625. OA: http://www.nber.org/papers/w23013.pdf

Cai, H.; and Treisman, D. (2006). 'Did government decentralization cause China's economic miracle?' *World Politics*, vol. 58, issue 4, 505–535. https://doi .org/10.1353/wp.2007.0005

Cai, Y. (2002). 'The resistance of Chinese laid-off workers in the reform period'. *The China Quarterly*, vol. 170, 327–344. https://doi.org/10.1017/s0009443902000219

Cai, Y.; Feng, W.; and Shen, K. (2018). 'Fiscal implications of population aging and social sector expenditure in China'. *Population and Development Review*, vol. 44, issue 4, 811–831. https://doi.org/10.1111/padr.12206

Cantoni, D.; Chen, Y.; Yang, D. Y.; Yuchtman, N.; and Zhang, Y. J. (2017). 'Curriculum and ideology'. *Journal of Political Economy*, vol. 125, issue 2, 338–392. https://doi.org/10.1086/690951. OA: http://eprints.lse.ac.uk/91515/1/Yuchtman_Curriculum-and-ideology.pdf

Centola, D.; Willer, R.; and Macy, M. (2005). 'The emperor's dilemma: A computational model of self-enforcing norms'. *American Journal of Sociology*, vol. 110, issue 4, 1009–1040. https://doi.org/10.1086/427321. OA: https://repository.upenn.edu/cgi/viewcontent.cgi?article=1604&context=asc_papers

Chan, K. W.; and Buckingham, W. (2008). 'Is China abolishing the hukou system?' *The China Quarterly*, vol. 195, 582–606. https://doi.org/10.1017/s0305741008000787

Chan, K. W.; and Zhang, L. (1999). 'The hukou system and rural-urban migration in China: Processes and changes'. *The China Quarterly*, vol. 160, 818–855. https://doi.org/10.1017/s0305741000001351

Chao, C.-m.; and Dickson, B. (2003). *Remaking the Chinese State: Strategies, Society, and Security*. Routledge.

Chen, J.; and Xu, Y. (2017). Why do authoritarian regimes allow citizens to voice opinions publicly? *The Journal of Politics*, vol. 79, issue 3, 792–803. https://doi.org/10.1086/690303. OA: https://ssrn.com/abstract=2318051

Chen, X.; and Shi, T. (2001). 'Media effects on political confidence and trust in the People's Republic of China in the post-Tiananmen period'. *East Asia*, vol. 19, issue 3, 84–118. https://doi.org/10.1007/s12140-001-0011-3

Chen, Y.; and Yang, D. Y. (2019). 'The Impact of Media Censorship: 1984 or Brave New World?' *American Economic Review*, vol. 109, issue 6, 2294–2332. https://doi.org/10.1257/aer.20171765

Cheng, T.; and Selden, M. (1994). 'The origins and social consequences of China's hukou system'. *The China Quarterly*, vol. 139, 644–668. https://doi.org/10.1017/s0305741000043083

Cook, L. J. (1993). *The Soviet Social Contract and Why It Failed: Welfare Policy and Workers' Politics from Brezhnev to Yeltsin*, vol. 86. Harvard University Press.

Cook, L. J. (2013). *Postcommunist Welfare States: Reform Politics in Russia and Eastern Europe*. Cornell University Press. https://doi.org/10.7591%2F9780801460098

Cox, R. H. (2001). 'The social construction of an imperative: Why welfare reform happened in Denmark and the Netherlands but not in Germany'. *World Politics*, vol. 53, issue 3, 463–498. https://doi.org/10.1353/wp.2001.0008

Dannreuther, C.; and Gideon, J. (2008). 'Entitled to health? Social protection in Chile's plan AUGE'. *Development and Change*, vol. 39, issue 5, 845–864. https://doi.org/10.1111/j.1467-7660.2008.00508.x

Dean, M. (2010). *Governmentality: Power and Rule in Modern Society*. Sage publications.

Denisova, I.; Eller, M.; Frye, T.; and Zhuravskaya, E. (2012). 'Everyone hates privatization, but why? Survey evidence from 28 post-communist countries'. *Journal of Comparative Economics*, vol. 40, issue 1, 44–61. https://doi.org/10.1016/j.jce.2011.11.001

Di Tella, R.; Galiani, S.; and Schargrodsky, E. (2012). 'Reality versus propaganda in the formation of beliefs about privatization'. *Journal of Public Economics*, vol. 96, issue 5–6, 553–567. https://doi.org/10.1016/j.jpubeco.2011.11.006

Dimitrov, M. K. (2013). 'Understanding communist collapse and resilience'. *Why Communism Did Not Collapse: Understanding Authoritarian Regime Resilience in Asia and Europe*, 3–39. https://doi.org/10.1017%2F cbo9781139565028.002

Distelhorst, G.; and Hou, Y. (2014). 'Ingroup bias in official behavior: A national field experiment in China'. *Quarterly Journal of Political Science*, vol. 9, issue 2, 203–230. https://doi.org/10.1561/100.00013110

Donnelly, J. (1981). 'Recent trends in UN human rights activity: Description and polemic'. *International Organization*, vol. 35, issue 4, 633–655. https://doi.org/10.1017/s0020818300034263

Donovan, M. C. (2001). *Taking Aim: Target Populations and the Wars on AIDS and Drugs*. Georgetown University Press.

Douglas, M. (1986). *How Institutions Think*. Syracuse University Press.

Duara, P. (1987). 'State involution: A study of local finances in north China, 1911–1935'. *Comparative Studies in Society and History*, vol. 29, issue 1, 132–161. https://doi.org/10.1017/s0010417500014389

Durkheim, E.; Catlin, G. E. G.; Mueller, J. H.; and Solovay, S. A. (1938). *The Rules of Sociological Method*, vol. 8. Free Press New York.

Easton, D. (1965). *A Systems Analysis of Political Life*. John Wiley & Sons Ltd.

Easton, D. (1975). 'A re-assessment of the concept of political support'. *British Journal of Political Science*, vol. 5, issue 4, 435–457. https://doi.org/10.1017/s0007123400008309

Edmond, C. (2013). 'Information manipulation, coordination, and regime change'. *Review of Economic Studies*, vol. 80, issue 4, 1422–1458. https://doi.org/10.1093/restud/rdt020

Edwards, A. L. (1957). *The Social Desirability Variable in Personality Assessment and Research*. USA: Dryden Press.

Egorov, G.; Guriev, S.; and Sonin, K. (2009). 'Why resource-poor dictators allow freer media: A theory and evidence from panel data'. *American Political Science Review*, vol. 103, issue 4, 645–668. https://doi.org/10.1017/s0003055409990219. OA: https://ssrn.com/abstract=898888

Egorov, G.; and Sonin, K. (2011). 'Dictators and their viziers: Endogenizing the loyalty–competence trade-off'. *Journal of the European Economic*

Association, vol. 9, issue 5, 903–930. https://doi.org/10.1111/j.1542-4774
.2011.01033.x

Ekman, J.; and Linde, J. (2005). 'Communist nostalgia and the consolidation of democracy in Central and Eastern Europe'. *Journal of Communist
Studies and Transition Politics*, vol. 21, issue 3, 354–374. https://doi.org
/10.1080/13523270500183512

Ensafi, R.; Winter, P.; Mueen, A.; and Crandall, J. R. (2015). 'Analyzing the
Great Firewall of China over space and time'. *Proceedings on Privacy
Enhancing Technologies*, vol. 2015, issue 1, 61–76. https://doi.org/10.1515
/popets-2015-0005

Eriksen, A.; and Molander, A. (2019). 'Welfare reform and public justification'.
Policy Studies, vol. 40, issue 6, 628-647.

Esping-Andersen, G. (1990). *The Three Worlds of Welfare Capitalism*. Princeton
University Press.

Esping-Andersen, G. (1999). *Social Foundations of Postindustrial Economies*.
UK: OUP. https://doi.org/10.1093%2F0198742002.001.0001

Fan, X.; and Fu, W. (2009). 'The new scheme of rural compulsory education:
Effectiveness, problem, and solution'. *Journal of Huazhong Normal University*, vol. 4.

Festinger, L. (1962). *A Theory of Cognitive Dissonance*, vol. 2. Stanford University Press.

Fisher, R. A. (1960). 'The design of experiments'. *The Design of Experiments*,
7th ed.

Flora, P. (2017). *Development of Welfare States in Europe and America*. Routledge. https://doi.org/10.4324%2F9781351304924

Foucault, M. (1982). 'The subject and power'. *Critical Inquiry*, vol. 8, issue 4,
777–795. https://doi.org/10.1086/448181

Foucault, M. (2009). *Security, Territory, Population: Lectures at the Collège de
France, 1977-78* (M. Senellart ed.). Palgrave Macmillan.

Foucault, M.; Davidson, A. I.; and Burchell, G. (2008). *The Birth of Biopolitics:
Lectures at the Collège de France, 1978-1979*: Springer.

Frank, R. H. (1996). 'The political economy of preference falsification: Timur
Kuran's Private Truths, Public Lies'. *Journal of Economic Literature*, vol. 34,
issue 1, 115. https://www.jstor.org/stable/2729412

Frazier, M. W. (2010). *Socialist Insecurity: Pensions and the Politics of Uneven
Development in China*. USA: Cornell University Press.

Frye, T.; Gehlbach, S.; Marquardt, K. L.; and Reuter, O. J. (2017). 'Is Putin's
popularity real?' *Post-Soviet Affairs*, vol. 33, issue 1, 1–15. https://doi.org/10
.1080/1060586x.2016.1144334

Fuchs, D. (2007). 'The political culture paradigm'. *The Oxford Handbook of
Political Behavior*. https://doi.org/10.1093%2Foxfordhb%2F9780199270125
.003.0009

Gallagher, M.; and Hanson, J. K. (2009). 'Coalitions, carrots, and sticks: economic inequality and authoritarian states'. *PS: Political Science & Politics*,
vol. 42, issue 4, 667–672. https://doi.org/10.1017/s1049096509990096

Gallagher, M. E. (2011). *Contagious Capitalism: Globalization and the Politics of Labor in China*. Princeton University Press.

Gao, Q. (2006). 'The social benefit system in urban China: Reforms and trends from 1988 to 2002'. *Journal of East Asian Studies*, vol. 6, issue 1, 31–67. https://doi.org/10.1017/s1598240800000035

Gao, Q.; Yang, S.; and Li, S. (2013). 'The Chinese welfare state in transition: 1988–2007'. *Journal of Social Policy*, vol. 42, issue 4, 743–762. https://doi.org /10.1017/s0047279413000329

Garnaut, R.; Song, L.; and Fang, C. (2018). *China's 40 Years of Reform and Development: 1978–2018*. ANU Press.

Geertz, C. (1963). *Agricultural Involution: The Process of Ecological Change in Indonesia*. University of California Press. https://doi.org/10.1525% 2F9780520341821

Gehlbach, S.; and Keefer, P. (2011). 'Investment without democracy: Ruling-party institutionalization and credible commitment in autocracies'. *Journal of Comparative Economics*, vol. 39, issue 2, 123–139. https://doi.org/10.1016 /j.jce.2011.04.002

Gentzkow, M. (2006). 'Television and voter turnout'. *The Quarterly Journal of Economics*, vol. 121, issue 3, 931–972. https://doi.org/10.1162/qjec.121.3.931

Gerber, A. S.; and Green, D. P. (2012). *Field Experiments: Design, Analysis, and Interpretation*. W. W. Norton.

Giddens, A. (1981). *A Contemporary Critique of Historical Materialism: The Nation-State and Violence*. University of California Press.

Gillion, C. (2000). 'The development and reform of social security pensions: The approach of the International Labour Office'. *International Social Security Review*, vol. 53, issue 1, 35–63. https://doi.org/10.1111/1468-246x.00062

Glasberg, D. S.; and Shannon, D. (2010). *Political Sociology: Oppression, Resistance, and the State*. SAGE Publications.

Glass, J., Bengtson, V. L.; and Dunham, C. C. (1986). 'Attitude similarity in three-generation families: Socialization, status inheritance, or reciprocal influence?' *American Sociological Review*, 685–698. https://doi.org /10.2307/2095493

Goffman, E. (1978). *The Presentation of Self in Everyday Life*. UK: Harmondsworth.

Goffman, E. (2017). *Interaction Ritual: Essays in Face-to-Face Behavior*. Routledge.

Goode, E.; and Ben-Yehuda, N. (1994). 'Moral panics: Culture, politics, and social construction'. *Annual Review of Sociology*, vol. 20, issue 1, 149–171. https://doi.org/10.1146/annurev.so.20.080194.001053

Gough, I. (2001). 'Globalization and regional welfare regimes: The East Asian case'. *Global Social Policy*, vol. 1, issue 2, 163–189. https://doi .org/10.1177/146801810100100202. OA: https://eprints.lse.ac.uk/43959

Gough, I.; Wood, G.; Barrientos, A.; Bevan, P.; Room, G.; and Davis, P. (2004). *Insecurity and Welfare Regimes in Asia, Africa and Latin America: Social*

Policy in Development Contexts. Cambridge University Press. https://doi.org
/10.1017%2Fcbo9780511720239

Gramsci, A.; Hoare, Q.; and Nowell-Smith, G. (1971). *Selections from the Prison Notebooks of Antonio Gramsci*. Lawrence and Wishart Limited.

Gregory, P. R.; Schröder, P. J.; and Sonin, K. (2006). 'Dictators, repression and the median citizen: An "eliminations model" of Stalin's Terror' (Data from the NKVD Archives). https://doi.org/10.2139/ssrn.948667

Gries, P. H. (2004). *China's New Nationalism: Pride, Politics, and Diplomacy*. University of California Press.

Grimes, M. (2008). 'Consent, political trust and compliance: Rejoinder to Kaina's remarks on "Organizing consent"'. *European Journal of Political Research*, vol. 47, issue 4, 522–535. https://doi.org/10.1111/j.1475-6765.2008.00774.x

Grimmer, J.; and Stewart, B. M. (2013). 'Text as data: The promise and pitfalls of automatic content analysis methods for political texts'. *Political Analysis*, vol. 21, issue 3, 267–297. https://doi.org/10.1093/pan/mps028

Grün, B.; Hornik, K.; and Grün, M. B. (2018). Package 'topicmodels'.

Gu, E. X. (1999). 'From permanent employment to massive lay-offs: the political economy of "transitional unemployment" in urban China (1993–8)'. *Economy and Society*, vol. 28, issue 2, 281–299. https://doi.org /10.1080/03085149900000006

Gu, E. X. (2001). 'Dismantling the Chinese mini-welfare state?: Marketization and the politics of institutional transformation, 1979–1999'. *Communist and Post-Communist Studies*, vol. 34, issue 1, 91–111. https://doi.org/10.1016 /s0967-067x(00)00025-8

Guriev, S.; and Treisman, D. (2015). *How Modern Dictators Survive: An Informational Theory of the New Authoritarianism*. Retrieved from https://doi .org/10.3386%2Fw21136

Guthrie, D. (2012). *China and Globalization: The Social, Economic and Political Transformation of Chinese Society*. Routledge.

Hacker, J. S. (2002). *The Divided Welfare State: The Battle over Public and Private Social Benefits in the United States*. Cambridge University Press. https:// doi.org/10.1017%2Fcbo9780511817298

Haggard, S.; and Kaufman, R. R. (2008). *Development, Democracy, and Welfare States: Latin America, East Asia, and Eastern Europe*. Princeton University Press.

Hahn, J. W.; and Logvinenko, I. (2008). 'Generational differences in Russian attitudes towards democracy and the economy'. *Europe-Asia Studies*, vol. 60, issue 8, 1345–1369. https://doi.org/10.1080/09668130802292168

Hainmueller, J. (2012). 'Entropy balancing for causal effects: A multivariate reweighting method to produce balanced samples in observational studies'. *Political Analysis*, vol. 20, issue 1, 25–46. https://doi.org /10.1080/09668130802292168

Hall, P. A. (1993). 'Policy paradigms, social learning, and the state: the case of economic policymaking in Britain'. *Comparative Politics*, vol Vol. 25, No. 3, 275–296.

Hall, P. A. (2001). 'The evolution of economic policy'. *Developments in French Politics*, vol. 2, 172–191.

Han, R. (2015). 'Defending the authoritarian regime online: China's "voluntary fifty-cent army"'. *The China Quarterly*, vol. 224, 1006–1025. https://doi .org/10.1017/s0305741015001216

Heilmann, S. (2008a). 'From local experiments to national policy: The origins of China's distinctive policy process'. *The China Journal*, vol. 59, 1–30. https://doi.org/10.1086/tcj.59.20066378

Heilmann, S. (2008b). 'Policy experimentation in China's economic rise'. *Studies in Comparative International Development*, vol. 43, issue 1, 1–26. https:// doi.org/10.1007/s12116-007-9014-4

Hinings, C. R.; Tolbert, P. S.; Greenwood, R.; and Oliver, C. (2008). 'Emerging inequalities in central and Eastern Europe'. *The Sage Handbook of Organizational Institutionalism*, 473–492. UK: Sage. https://doi.org /10.4135%2F9781849200387.n20

Hirschman, A. O. (1970). *Exit, Voice, and Loyalty: Responses to Decline in Firms, Organizations, and States*, vol. 25. Harvard University Press.

Holzmann, R.; and Palmer, E. E. (eds) (2006). *Pension Reform: Issues and Prospects for Non-financial Defined Contribution (NDC) Schemes*. World Bank Publications. https://doi.org/10.1596%2F978-0-8213-6038-5

Hopkins, D. J.; and King, G. (2010). 'A method of automated nonparametric content analysis for social science'. *American Journal of Political Science*, vol. 54, issue 1, 229–247. https://doi.org/10.1111/j.1540-5907.2009.00428.x. OA: http://nrs.harvard.edu/urn-3:HUL.InstRepos:5125261

Howard, R. (1983). 'The full-belly thesis: Should economic rights take priority over civil and political rights-evidence from Sub-Saharan Africa'. *Human Rights Quarterly*, vol. 5, 467. https://doi.org/10.2307/762231

Huang, H. (2013). 'Signal left, turn right: Central rhetoric and local reform in China'. *Political Research Quarterly*, vol. 66, issue 2, 292–305. https://doi.org /10.1177/1065912912443874

Huang, H. (2015). 'Propaganda as signaling'. *Comparative Politics*, vol. 47, issue 4, 419–444. https://doi.org/10.5129/001041515816103220

Huang, H. (2017). 'A war of (mis) information: The political effects of rumors and rumor rebuttals in an authoritarian country'. *British Journal of Political Science*, vol. 47, issue 2, 283–311. https://doi.org/10.1017/s0007123 415000253

Huang, H. (2018). 'The pathology of hard propaganda'. *The Journal of Politics*, vol. 80, issue 3, 1034–1038. https://doi.org/10.1086/696863

Huang, P. C. (1990). *The Peasant Family and Rural Development in the Yangzi Delta, 1350-1988*. Stanford University Press.

Huang, P. C. (2012). 'Profit-making state firms and China's development experience: "State capitalism" or "socialist market economy"?' *Modern China*, vol. 38, issue 6, 591–629. https://doi.org/10.1177/0097700412455839

Huang, X. (2014). *Social Protection under Authoritarianism: Politics and Policy of Social Health Insurance in China*. Columbia University.

Huang, X. (2020). *Social Protection under Authoritarianism: Health Politics and Policy in China*. Oxford University Press. https://doi.org/10.1093%2Foso %2F9780190073640.001.0001

Huntington, S. P. (2006). *Political Order in Changing Societies*. Yale University Press.

Hynes, B. O. D.; and Hayes, N. (2011). 'Who benefits from early childcare subsidy design in Ireland?' *Journal of Poverty and Social Justice*, vol. 19, issue 3, 277–288. https://doi.org/10.1332/175982711x597017. OA: https://arrow .tudublin.ie/cgi/viewcontent.cgi?article=1034&context=cserart

Iacus, S. M.; King, G.; and Porro, G. (2012). 'Causal inference without balance checking: Coarsened exact matching'. *Political Analysis*, vol. 20, issue 1, 1–24. https://doi.org/10.1093/pan/mpr013

Im, D.-K.; and Meng, T. (2015). 'The policy–opinion nexus: The impact of social protection programs on welfare policy preferences in China'. *International Journal of Public Opinion Research*, vol. 28, issue 2, 241–268. https:// doi.org/10.1093/ijpor/edv013

Imai, K.; Keele, L.; Tingley, D.; and Yamamoto, T. (2011). 'Unpacking the black box of causality: Learning about causal mechanisms from experimental and observational studies'. *American Political Science Review*, vol. 105, issue 4, 765–789. https://doi.org/10.1017/s0003055411000414. OA: http://hdl.handle .net/1721.1/84065

Imai, K.; Keele, L.; and Yamamoto, T. (2010). 'Identification, inference and sensitivity analysis for causal mediation effects'. *Statistical Science*, 51–71. https://doi.org/10.1214/10-sts321

Imbens, G. W.; and Lemieux, T. (2008). 'Regression discontinuity designs: A guide to practice'. *Journal of Econometrics*, vol. 142, issue 2, 615–635. https:// doi.org/10.1016/j.jeconom.2007.05.001

Inglehart, R. (2018). *Culture Shift in Advanced Industrial Society*. Princeton University Press. https://doi.org/10.2307%2Fj.ctv346rbz

Jefferson, G. H.; and Rawski, T. G. (1994). 'Enterprise reform in Chinese industry'. *Journal of Economic Perspectives*, vol. 8, issue 2, 47–70. https://doi.org /10.1257/jep.8.2.47

Jennings, M. K. (1996). 'Political knowledge over time and across generations'. *Public Opinion Quarterly*, vol. 60, issue 2, 228–252. https://doi.org /10.1086/297749

Jiang, J.; and Yang, D. L. (2016). 'Lying or believing? Measuring preference falsification from a political purge in China'. *Comparative Political Studies*, vol. 49, issue 5, 600–634. https://doi.org/10.1177/0010414015626450

Kamenica, E.; and Gentzkow, M. (2011). 'Bayesian persuasion'. *American Economic Review*, vol. 101, issue 6, 2590–2615. https://doi.org/10.1257/aer .101.6.2590

Karshenas, M.; and Moghadam, V. M. (2006). *Social Policy in the Middle East: Economic, Political and Gender Dynamics*. UK: Palgrave Macmillan.

Keefer, P.; and Khemani, S. (2011). *Mass Media and Public Services: The Effects of Radio Access on Public Education in Benin*. The World Bank. https://doi .org/10.1596%2F1813-9450-5559

Kelly, D. (2006). 'Citizen movements and China's public intellectuals in the Hu-Wen era'. *Pacific Affairs*, vol. 79, issue 2, 183–204. https://doi.org /10.5509/2006792183

Kennedy, J. J. (2009). 'Maintaining popular support for the Chinese Communist Party: The influence of education and the state-controlled media'. *Political Studies*, vol. 57, issue 3, 517–536. https://doi.org/10.1111/j.1467-9248 .2008.00740.x

Kohli, A.; Shue, V.; and Migdal, J. S. (1994). *State Power and Social Forces: Domination and Transformation in the Third World*. UK: Cambridge University Press.

Kornai, J. (1992). *The Socialist System: The Political Economy of Communism*. Oxford University Press. https://doi.org/10.1515%2F9780691228020

Kricheli, R.; Livne, Y.; and Magaloni, B. (2011). *Taking to the Streets: Theory and Evidence on Protests under Authoritarianism*. Paper presented at the APSA 2010 Annual Meeting Paper.

Kuran, T. (1991). 'Now out of never: The element of surprise in the East European revolution of 1989'. *World Politics*, vol. 44, issue 1, 7–48. https://doi.org /10.2307/2010422

Kuran, T. (1997). *Private Truths, Public Lies: The Social Consequences of Preference Falsification*. Harvard University Press.

Lane, C. (1984). 'Legitimacy and power in the Soviet Union through socialist ritual'. *British Journal of Political Science*, vol. 14, issue 2, 207–217. https://doi .org/10.1017/s0007123400003537

Lane, D. (2007). 'Post-state socialism: A diversity of capitalisms?' *Varieties of Capitalism in Post-communist Countries*, 13–39. Springer. https://doi .org/10.1057%2F9780230627574_2

Lawrence, E.; Stoker, R.; and Wolman, H. (2013). 'The effects of beneficiary targeting on public support for social policies'. *Policy Studies Journal*, vol. 41, issue 2, 199–216. https://doi.org/10.1111/psj.12014

Le Bon, G. (1897). *The Crowd: A Study of the Popular Mind*. Fischer.

Lee, M.-k. (2000). *Chinese Occupational Welfare in Market Transition*. Springer. https://doi.org/10.1057/9780333982549

Lessenich, S. (2010). 'Constructing the socialized self: Mobilization and control in the "active society"'. *Governmentality*, 312–328. Routledge.

Leung, J. C.; and Nann, R. C. (1995). *Authority and Benevolence: Social Welfare in China*. Chinese University Press.

Leung, J. C.; and Wong, H. S. (1999). 'The emergence of a community-based social assistance programme in urban China'. *Social Policy & Administration*, vol. 33, issue 1, 39–54. https://doi.org/10.1111/1467-9515.00130

Leung, J. C.; and Xu, Y. (2015). *China's Social Welfare: The Third Turning Point*. John Wiley & Sons.

Levi, M. (1997). *Consent, Dissent, and Patriotism*. Cambridge University Press.

Li, B.; and Zhong, Y. (2009). 'How did China's transitions impact people's welfare benefits in the reform era?' *Journal of Contemporary China*, vol. 18, issue 62, 813–829. https://doi.org/10.1080/10670560903174606

Li, J. (2019). Package 'tmcn'.

Li, J.; and Ge, K. (2010). 'Review of pension insurance individual account studies'. *Social Security Studies*, vol. 2, 21–26.

Li, L. (2010). 'Rights consciousness and rules consciousness in contemporary China'. *The China Journal*, vol. 64, 47–68. https://doi.org/10.1086/tcj.64.20749246

Li, Z.; and Wang, H. (2009). 'Return rate and replacement rate of individual account in basic pension insurance'. *Journal of Public Management*, vol. 6, issue 4, 45–51.

Lin, D.; and Ding, Y. (2007). 'New pension policy: Replacement rate comparison of new-old pension insurance policies'. *Population and Economy*, vol. 1, 69–74.

Lipset, S. M. (1959). 'Some social requisites of democracy: Economic development and political legitimacy'. *American Political Science Review*, vol. 53, issue 1, 69–105. https://doi.org/10.2307/1951731

Lipset, S. M.; and Man, P. (1960). *The Social Bases of Politics*. USA: Johns Hopkins University Press.

Liu, T.; and Sun, L. (2016). 'Pension reform in China'. *Journal of Aging & Social Policy*, vol. 28, issue 1, 15–28. https://doi.org/10.1080/08959420.2016.1111725

Logvinenko, I. (2020). 'Authoritarian welfare state, regime stability, and the 2018 pension reform in Russia'. *Communist and Post-Communist Studies*, vol. 53, issue 1, 100–116. https://doi.org/10.1525/cpcs.2020.53.1.100

Lohmann, S. (1993). 'A signaling model of informative and manipulative political action'. *American Political Science Review*, vol. 87, issue 2, 319–333. https://doi.org/10.2307/2939043

Lohmann, S. (1994). 'The dynamics of informational cascades: The Monday demonstrations in Leipzig, East Germany, 1989–91'. *World Politics*, vol. 47, issue 1, 42–101. https://doi.org/10.2307/2950679

Lord, C.; and Beetham, D. (2001). 'Legitimizing the EU: Is there a post-parliamentary basis for its legitimation?' *JCMS: Journal of Common Market Studies*, vol. 39, issue 3, 443–462. https://doi.org/10.1111/1468-5965.00298

Lorentzen, P. (2014). 'China's strategic censorship'. *American Journal of Political Science*, vol. 58, issue 2, 402–414. https://doi.org/10.1111/ajps.12065

Lü, X. (2014). 'Social policy and regime legitimacy: The effects of education reform in China'. *American Political Science Review*, vol. 108, issue 2, 423–437. https://doi.org/10.1017/s0003055414000124

Lu, X.; and Perry, E. J. (1997). *Danwei: The Changing Chinese Workplace in Historical and Comparative Perspective*. Me Sharpe.

Lucas, C.; Nielsen, R. A.; Roberts, M. E.; Stewart, B. M.; Storer, A.; and Tingley, D. (2015). 'Computer-assisted text analysis for comparative politics'. *Political Analysis*, vol. 23, issue 2, 254–277. https://doi.org/10.1093/pan/mpu019. OA: https://dash.harvard.edu/handle/1/38057808

Lust-Okar, E. (2006). 'Elections under authoritarianism: Preliminary lessons from Jordan'. *Democratization*, vol. 13, issue 3, 456–471. https://doi.org/10.1080/13510340600579359

Madrid, R. (2002). The politics and economics of pension privatization in Latin America. *Latin American Research Review*, 159–182. https://www.jstor.org/stable/2692153

Magaloni, B. (2006). *Voting for Autocracy: Hegemonic Party Survival and Its Demise in Mexico*, vol. 296. UK: Cambridge University Press. https://doi.org/10.1017/CBO9780511510274

Mahoney, J.; and Rueschemeyer, D. (2003). *Comparative Historical Analysis in the Social Sciences*. Cambridge University Press. https://doi.org/10.1017/CBO9780511803963

Mares, I.; and Carnes, M. E. (2009). 'Social policy in developing countries'. *Annual Review of Political Science*, vol. 12, 93–113. https://doi.org/10.1146/annurev.polisci.12.071207.093504

Marshall, T. H. (1964). 'Class, citizenship and social development'. *New York*, vol. 19642.

Mashaw, J. L. (2006). 'Accountability and institutional design: Some thoughts on the grammar of governance'. *Public Law Working Paper*, vol. 116, 115–156. https://ssrn.com/abstract=924879

Mattingly, Daniel C. (2019). *The Art of Political Control in China*. Cambridge University Press.

Maynard-Moody, S. W.; Musheno, M.; and Musheno, M. C. (2003). *Cops, Teachers, Counselors: Stories from the Front Lines of Public Service*. University of Michigan Press. https://doi.org/10.3998%2Fmpub.11924

McCarthy, J. D.; and Zald, M. N. (1977). 'Resource mobilization and social movements: A partial theory'. *American Journal of Sociology*, vol. 82, issue 6, 1212–1241. https://doi.org/10.1086/226464

McMillan, J.; and Zoido, P. (2004). 'How to subvert democracy: Montesinos in Peru'. *Journal of Economic Perspectives*, vol. 18, issue 4, 69–92. https://doi.org/10.1257/0895330042632690

McQuail, D. (1987). *Mass Communication Theory: An Introduction*. Sage Publications.

Mei, C.; and Liu, Z. (2014). 'Experiment-based policy making or conscious policy design? The case of urban housing reform in China'. *Policy Sciences*, vol. 47, issue 3, 321–337. https://doi.org/10.1007/s11077-013-9185-y

Meng, K. (2018). *China's Pension Reforms: Political Institutions, Skill Formation and Pension Policy in China*. Routledge. https://doi.org/10.4324%2F9781351061667

Meyer, D. S.; and Staggenborg, S. (1996). 'Movements, countermovements, and the structure of political opportunity'. *American Journal of Sociology*, vol. 101, issue 6, 1628–1660. https://doi.org/10.1086/230869

Montinola, G.; Qian, Y.; and Weingast, B. R. (1995). 'Federalism, Chinese style: The political basis for economic success in China'. *World Politics*, vol. 48, issue 1, 50–81. https://doi.org/10.1353/wp.1995.0003

Moore, B. (1966). *Social Origins of Democracy and Dictatorship*. USA: Beacon.

Morgan, S. L.; and Harding, D. J. (2006). 'Matching estimators of causal effects: Prospects and pitfalls in theory and practice'. *Sociological Methods & Research*, vol. 35, issue 1, 3–60. https://doi.org/10.1177/0049124106289164

Munro, N. (2006). 'Russia's persistent communist legacy: Nostalgia, reaction, and reactionary expectations'. *Post-Soviet Affairs*, vol. 22, issue 4, 289–313. https://doi.org/10.2747/1060-586x.22.4.289

Myerson, R. B. (2008). 'The autocrat's credibility problem and foundations of the constitutional state'. *American Political Science Review*, vol. 102, issue 1, 125–139. https://doi.org/10.1017/s0003055408080076

Nathan, A. (2003). 'China's changing of the guard: Authoritarian resilience'. *Journal of Democracy*, vol. 14, issue 1, 6–17. https://doi.org/10.1353/jod.2003.0019

Naughton, B.; and Tsai, K. S. (2015). *State Capitalism, Institutional Adaptation, and the Chinese Miracle*. Cambridge University Press. https://doi.org/10.1017%2Fcbo9781139962858

Nederhof, A. J. (1985). 'Methods of coping with social desirability bias: A review'. *European Journal of Social Psychology*, vol. 15, issue 3, 263–280. https://doi.org/10.1002/ejsp.2420150303

Nee, V. (1996). 'The emergence of a market society: Changing mechanisms of stratification in China'. *American Journal of Sociology*, vol. 101, issue 4, 908–949. https://doi.org/10.1086/230784

Ngok, K. (2013). 'Shaping social policy in the reform era in China'. *Handbook on East Asian Social Policy*, 105–128. https://doi.org/10.4337/9780857930293.00011

Noelle-Neumann, E. (1993). *The Spiral of Silence: Public Opinion, Our Social Skin*. University of Chicago Press.

OECD. (2005). *Organization for Economic Cooperation and Development (OECD) Annual Report*. Retrieved from https://www.oecd.org/about/34711139.pdf

Offe, C. (1987). 'II. Democracy against the welfare state? Structural foundations of neoconservative political opportunities'. *Political Theory*, vol. 15, issue 4, 501–537. https://doi.org/10.1177/0090591787015004002

O'Gorman, H. J. (1986). 'The discovery of pluralistic ignorance: An ironic lesson'. *Journal of the History of the Behavioral Sciences*, vol. 22, issue 4, 333–347.

Ortiz, I.; Duran, F.; Urban, S.; Wodsak, V.; and Yu, Z. (2018). *Reversing Pension Privatization: Rebuilding Public Pension Systems in Eastern European and Latin American Countries* (2000-18). Available at SSRN 3275228.

Pan, J. (2020). *Welfare for Autocrats: How Social Assistance in China Cares for Its Rulers*. USA: Oxford University Press. https://doi.org/10.1093%2Foso%2F9780190087425.001.0001

Pepinsky, T. (2007). 'Autocracy, elections, and fiscal policy: evidence from Malaysia'. *Studies in Comparative International Development*, vol. 42, issue 1–2), 136–163. https://doi.org/10.1007/s12116-007-9006-4

Perry, E. J. (2007). 'Studying Chinese politics: Farewell to revolution?' *The China Journal*, vol. 57, 1–22. https://doi.org/10.1086/tcj.57.20066239. OA: https://dash.harvard.edu/bitstream/1/11595641/1/farewell.pdf

Perry, E. J. (2017). 'Higher education and authoritarian resilience: The case of China, past and present'. Harvard-Yenching Institute Working Paper Series. OA: https://dash.harvard.edu/handle/1/30822717

Perry, E. J.; and Heilmann, S. (2011). 'Embracing uncertainty: Guerrilla policy style and adaptive governance in China'. *Mao's Invisible Hand: The Political Foundations of Adaptive Governance in China*.

Pierson, P. (1994). *Dismantling the Welfare State?: Reagan, Thatcher and the Politics of Retrenchment*. Cambridge University Press. https://doi.org/10.1017%2Fcbo9780511805288

Pierson, P. (2001). 'Post-industrial pressures on the mature welfare states'. *The New Politics of the Welfare State*, vol. 1, 80–105. https://doi.org/10.1093%2F0198297564.003.0004

Plant, R.; and Jones, D. (1991). *Modern Political Thought*. UK: Blackwell.

Polanyi, K.; and MacIver, R. M. (1944). *The Great Transformation*. USA: Beacon.

Pozen, R. C. (2013). *Tackling the Chinese Pension System*. USA: Paulson Institute.

Qiu, G.; and Wen, Z. (2007). 'Critical adjustment of rural migrant policy in China: towards new paradigm'. *Chinese Public Policy Review*, vol. 11.

Ratigan, K. (2017). 'Disaggregating the developing welfare state: Provincial social policy regimes in China'. *World Development*, vol. 98, 467–484. https://doi.org/10.1016/j.worlddev.2017.05.010

Riedmüller, B. (2008). *Private Pensions Versus Social Inclusion?: Non-state Provision for Citizens at Risk in Europe*. Edward Elgar Publishing.

Rimlinger, G. V. (1971). *Welfare Policy and Industrialization in Europe, America and Russia*. USA: Wiley.

Ringen, S.; and Ngok, K. (2017). 'What kind of welfare state is emerging in China?' *Towards Universal Health Care in Emerging Economies*, 213–237. Springer. https://doi.org/10.1057%2F978-1-137-53377-7_8

Roberts, M. E. (2018). *Censored: Distraction and Diversion inside China's Great Firewall*. Princeton University Press. https://doi.org/10.23943%2F9781400890057

Roberts, M. E.; Stewart, B. M.; and Tingley, D. (2014). stm: R package for structural topic models. *Journal of Statistical Software*, vol. 10, issue 2, 1–40. https://doi.org/10.18637/jss.v091.i02

Roberts, M. E.; Stewart, B. M.; and Tingley, D. (2016). Navigating the local modes of big data. *Computational Social Science*, vol. 51. https://doi.org/10.1017%2Fcbo9781316257340.004

Rose, R. (2007). 'The democracy barometers (Part I): Learning to support new regimes in Europe'. *Journal of Democracy*, vol. 18, issue 3, 111–125. https://doi.org/10.1353/jod.2007.0054

Rose, R.; and Carnaghan, E. (1995). 'Generational effects on attitudes to communist regimes: A comparative analysis'. *Post-Soviet Affairs*, vol. 11, issue 1, 28–56. https://doi.org/10.1080/1060586X.1995.10641393

Rose, R.; Mishler, W.; and Haerpfer, C. (1997). 'Social capital in civic and stressful societies'. *Studies in Comparative International Development*, vol. 32, issue 3, 85–111. https://doi.org/10.1007/bf02687332

Rose, R.; Mishler, W.; and Munro, N. (2006). *Russia Transformed: Developing Popular Support for a New Regime*. Cambridge University Press. https://doi.org/10.1017%2Fcbo9780511492150

Scharping, T. (2013). *Birth Control in China 1949-2000: Population Policy and Demographic Development*. Routledge. https://doi.org/10.4324%2F9781315027777

Schmidt, V. A. (2002). Europeanization and the mechanics of economic policy adjustment. *Journal of European Public Policy*, vol. 9, issue 6, 894–912.

Schneider, A.; and Ingram, H. (1993). 'Social construction of target populations: Implications for politics and policy'. *American Political Science Review*, vol. 87, issue 2, 334–347. https://doi.org/10.2307/2939044

Schneider, A.; and Sidney, M. (2009). 'What is next for policy design and social construction theory? 1'. *Policy Studies Journal*, vol. 37, issue 1, 103–119. https://doi.org/10.1111/j.1541-0072.2008.00298.x

Schneider, A. L.; Ingram, H.; and DeLeon, P. (2014). 'Democratic policy design: Social construction of target populations'. In P. Sabatier and C. Weible (eds), *Theories of the Policy Process*, 3rd edn, 105–149.

Schneider, A. L.; and Ingram, H. M. (2019). 'Social constructions, anticipatory feedback strategies, and deceptive public policy'. *Policy Studies Journal*, vol. 47, issue 2, 206–236. https://doi.org/10.1111/psj.12281

Schuman, H.; and Rieger, C. (1992). 'Historical analogies, generational effects, and attitudes toward war'. *American Sociological Review*, 315–326. https://doi.org/10.2307/2096238. OA: https://deepblue.lib.umich.edu/handle/2027.42/91764

Seidman, I. (2006). *Interviewing as Qualitative Research: A Guide for Researchers in Education and the Social Sciences*. Teachers College Press.

Selden, M.; and You, L. (1997). 'The reform of social welfare in China'. *World Development*, vol. 25, issue 10, 1657–1668. https://doi.org/10.1016/s0305-750x(97)00055-7

Shen, X.; and Truex, R. (2018). 'In search of preference falsification'. *Working Paper*.

Shi, S. J.; and Mok, K. H. (2012). 'Pension privatisation in Greater China: Institutional patterns and policy outcomes'. *International Journal of Social Welfare*, vol. 21, S30–S45. https://doi.org/10.1111/j.1468-2397.2012.00875.x https://doi.org/10.1111/j.1468-2397.2012.00875.x

Shi, T. (2001). 'Cultural values and political trust: A comparison of the People's Republic of China and Taiwan'. *Comparative Politics*, 401–419. https://doi.org/10.2307/422441

Shi, T. (2014). *The Cultural Logic of Politics in Mainland China and Taiwan*. Cambridge University Press. https://doi.org/10.1017/CBO9780511996474

Shirk, S. L. (2011). *Changing Media, Changing China*. Oxford University Press.

Shue, H. (1996). *Basic Rights: Subsistence, Affluence, and US Foreign Policy*. Princeton University Press.

Siebert, F. S.; Peterson, T.; and Schramm, W. (1956). *Four Theories of the Press: The Authoritarian, Libertarian, Social Responsibility, and Soviet Communist Concepts of What the Press Should Be and Do*. University of Illinois Press.

Simon, J. (2014). *The New Censorship: Inside the Global Battle for Media Freedom*. Columbia University Press. https://doi.org/10.7312%2Fcolumbia%2F9780231160643.001.0001

Smoke, R. (1994). 'On the importance of policy legitimacy'. *Political Psychology*, 97–110. https://doi.org/10.2307/3791441

Song, S.; and Chu, G. S. F. (1997). 'Social security reform in China: The case of old-age insurance'. *Contemporary Economic Policy*, vol. 15, issue 2, 85–93. https://doi.org/10.1111/j.1465-7287.1997.tb00468.x

Song, Y. (2014). 'What should economists know about the current Chinese hukou system?' *China Economic Review*, vol. 29, 200–212. https://doi.org/10.1016/j.chieco.2014.04.012

State Council. (1997). *Decision on Establishing a Unified System of Basic Pension Insurance for Enterprise Employees (State Council [1997] No.26)*. Retrieved from http://www.gov.cn/ztzl/nmg/content_412509.htm.

State Council. (2000a). *Opinions on Accelerating the Process of Social Welfare Socialization*. Retrieved from http://shfl.mca.gov.cn/article/zcfg/200809/20080900019761.shtml.

State Council. (2000b). *The Notice of Issuing the Pilot Program of Urban Social Security System (State Council [2000] No.42)*. Retrieved from http://www.gov.cn/xxgk/pub/govpublic/mrlm/201011/t20101112_62507.html.

State Council. (2002). *New Rural Collaborative Health Insurance Scheme*.

State Council. (2005). *Decision on Perfecting Basic System of Pension Insurance for Enterprise Employees (State Council [2005] No.38)*. Retrieved from http://www.gov.cn/zwgk/2005-12/14/content_127311.htm.

State Council. (2009). *New Rural Old-age Social Insurance Plan (State Council [2009] No. 32)* Retrieved from http://www.gov.cn/zwgk/2009-09/04/content_1409216.htm.

State Council. (2014). *Urban-Rural Residents Basic Old-age Social Insurance Scheme (State Council [2014] No. 8)*. Retrieved from http://www.gov.cn /zwgk/2014-02/26/content_2621907.htm.

Stockmann, D. (2013). *Media Commercialization and Authoritarian Rule in China*. Cambridge University Press. https://doi.org/10.1017/CBO9781139087742

Streeten, P. (1980). 'Basic needs and human rights'. *World Development*, vol. 8, issue 2, 107–111. https://doi.org/10.1016/0305-750x(80)90019-4

Su, Z.; and Meng, T. (2016). 'Selective responsiveness: Online public demands and government responsiveness in authoritarian China'. *Social Science Research*, vol. 59, 52–67. https://doi.org/10.1016/j.ssresearch.2016.04.017

Svallfors, S. (2007). *The Political Sociology of the Welfare State: Institutions, Social Cleavages, and Orientations*. USA: Stanford University Press. https:// doi.org/10.11126%2Fstanford%2F9780804754354.001.0001

Svallfors, S. (2010). 'Policy feedback, generational replacement, and attitudes to state intervention: Eastern and Western Germany, 1990–2006'. *European Political Science Review*, vol. 2, issue 1, 119–135. https://doi.org/10.1017 /s1755773909990257

Svolik, M. W. (2012). *The Politics of Authoritarian Rule*. Cambridge University Press. https://doi.org/10.1017/CBO9781139176040

Szelenyi, I. (1978). 'Social inequalities in state socialist redistributive economies'. *International Journal of Comparative Sociology*, vol. 19, issue 1–2, 63–87. https://doi.org/10.1177/002071527801900105

Szelenyi, I.; and Kostello, E. (1996). 'The market transition debate: Toward a synthesis?' *American Journal of Sociology*, vol. 101, issue 4, 1082–1096. https://doi.org/10.1086/230791

Szelenyi, I.; and Szelenyi, B. (1994). 'Why socialism failed: Toward a theory of system breakdown—Causes of disintegration of East European state socialism'. *Theory and Society*, vol. 23, issue 2, 211–231. https://doi.org/10.1007 /bf00993815

Tang, W. (2016). *Populist Authoritarianism: Chinese Political Culture and Regime Sustainability*. Oxford University Press. https://doi.org/10.1093/acp rof:oso/9780190205782.001.0001

Tannenberg, M. (2017). 'The autocratic trust bias: Politically sensitive survey items and self-censorship'. *V-Dem Working Paper*, vol. 49. https://doi .org/10.2139/ssrn.2980727

Thistlethwaite, D. L.; and Campbell, D. T. (1960). 'Regression-discontinuity analysis: An alternative to the ex post facto experiment'. *Journal of Educational Psychology*, vol. 51, issue 6, 309. https://doi.org/10.1037/h0044319

Tilly, C. (2017). 'Coercion, capital, and European states, AD 990–1990'. *Collective Violence, Contentious Politics, and Social Change*, 140–154. Routledge. https://doi.org/10.1080/714005469

Tolbert, P.; and Zucker, L. (1996). 'The institutionalization of institutional theory', *Handbook for Organization Studies*, 175–190. UK: Sage. https://doi.org /10.4135%2F9781446218556.n6

Tong, Y.; and Lei, S. (2010). 'Large-scale mass incidents and government responses in China'. *International Journal of China Studies*, vol. 1, issue 2, 487–508. https://icsum.org.my/wp-content/uploads/2020/02/tonglei.pdf

Truex, R. (2016). 'Bias and trust in authoritarian media'. *Working Paper*. https://doi.org/10.2139/ssrn.2802841

Wang, D.; and Chai, Y. (2009). 'The jobs–housing relationship and commuting in Beijing, China: the legacy of danwei'. *Journal of Transport Geography*, vol. 17, issue 1, 30–38. https://doi.org/10.1016/j.jtrangeo.2008.04.005

Wang, L.; Béland, D.; and Zhang, S. (2014). 'Pension fairness in China'. *China Economic Review*, vol. 28, 25–36. https://doi.org/10.1016/j.chieco.2013.11.003

Weber, M. (1978). *Economy and Society: An Outline of Interpretive Sociology*, vol. 1. University of California Press.

Weber, M. (2017). *Methodology of Social Sciences*. Routledge. https://doi.org/10.4324%2F9781315124445

Wedeen, L. (1999). *Ambiguities of Domination: Politics, Rhetoric, and Symbols in Contemporary Syria*. University of Chicago Press. https://doi.org/10.7208%2Fchicago%2F9780226345536.001.0001

Weingast, B. R. (1995). 'The economic role of political institutions: Market-preserving federalism and economic development'. *Journal of Law, Economics, & Organization*, 1–31. https://doi.org/10.1093/oxfordjournals.jleo.a036861

Whyte, M. K. (2012). 'China's post-socialist inequality'. *Current History*, vol. 111, issue 746, 229–234. https://doi.org/10.1525/curh.2012.111.746.229. OA: https://online.ucpress.edu/currenthistory/article-pdf/111/746/229/392449/curh_111_746_229.pdf

Winship, C.; and Morgan, S. L. (1999). 'The estimation of causal effects from observational data'. *Annual Review Of sociology*, vol. 25, issue 1, 659–706. https://doi.org/10.1146/annurev.soc.25.1.659. OA: https://dash.harvard.edu/bitstream/1/3200609/1/Winship_EstimationCausal.pdf

Wintrobe, R. (1990). 'The tinpot and the totalitarian: An economic theory of dictatorship'. *American Political Science Review*, vol. 84, issue 3, 849–872. https://doi.org/10.2307/1962769

Wintrobe, R. (2007). 'Dictatorship: analytical approaches', *The Oxford Handbook of Comparative Politics*. UK: Oxford University Press. https://doi.org/10.1093%2Foxfordhb%2F9780199566020.003.0016

Wong, L. (2005). *Marginalization and Social Welfare in China*. Routledge. https://doi.org/10.4324%2F9780203982990

Wong, L.; and Ngok, K. (2006). 'Social policy between plan and market: Xiagang (off-duty employment) and the policy of the re-employment service centres in China'. *Social Policy & Administration*, vol. 40, issue 2, 158–173. https://doi.org/10.1111/j.1467-9515.2006.00482.x

Wood, G.; and Gough, I. (2006). 'A comparative welfare regime approach to global social policy'. *World Development*, vol. 34, issue 10, 1696–1712.

https://doi.org/10.1016/j.worlddev.2006.02.001. OA: http://eprints.lse.ac.uk
/36646

Xiang, B. (2010). 'Ordinary people's state theory'. *Open Times*, vol. 10, 117–132.

Xie, Y. (2016). 'Understanding inequality in China'. *Chinese Journal of Sociology*, vol. 2, issue 3, 327–347. https://doi.org/10.1177/2057150x16654059.
OA: https://europepmc.org/article/MED/29854420

Xie, Y.; Lai, Q.; and Wu, X. (2009). 'Danwei and social inequality in contemporary urban China'. *Research in the Sociology of Work*, vol. 19, 283. https://
dx.doi.org/10.1108%2FS0277-2833(2009)0000019013. OA: https://www
.ncbi.nlm.nih.gov/pmc/articles/PMC2828673

Yan, X. (2017). *How Is China Maintain Stable? Observation and Thoughts from Fieldwork [Zhongguo Heyi Wending: Laizi Tianye de Guancha yu Sikao]*.
Hong Kong: Joint Publishing.

Yang, Y.; Wang, W.; and Zhang, M. (2010). 'Operational safety of social insurance fund: Experience from fully funding the individual accounts'. *Chinese Public Administration*, vol. 5, 61–66.

Zhao, D. (2001). 'China's prolonged stability and political future: Same political system, different policies and methods'. *Journal of Contemporary China*, vol. 10, issue 28, 427–444. https://doi.org/10.1080/10670560120067126

Zheng, G. (2016). *Evaluation of China's Social Protection Policies*. Retrieved from https://www.euchinasprp.eu/images/documents/Component1Cn/2017
-assessment-eport/EvalSSCn.pdf

Zheng, Q. (2015). *Identity Acceptance and Production Politics: Research on Labour Relations in Changes of State-Owned Enterprises*. China: Beijing Book Co.

Zhu, X.; and Zhao, H. (2018a). 'Experimentalist governance with interactive central–local relations: Making new pension policies in China'. *Policy Studies Journal*. https://doi.org/10.1111/psj.12254

Zhu, X.; and Zhao, H. (2018b). 'Recognition of innovation and diffusion of welfare policy: Alleviating urban poverty in Chinese cities during fiscal recentralization'. *Governance*, vol. 31, issue 4, 721–739. https://doi.org/10.1111
/gove.12332

Lightning Source UK Ltd.
Milton Keynes UK
UKHW021000111122
411997UK00010B/103